THE COMPLETE GUIDE TO
TRIM & FINISH CARPENTRY

Installing Moldings, Wainscoting & Decorative Trim

Creative Publishing
International

Contents

TRIMWORK PLANNING & PREPARATION

Creative Publishing international

Copyright © 2006
Creative Publishing international, Inc.
18705 Lake Drive East
Chanhassen, Minnesota 55317
1-800-328-3895
www.creativepub.com
All rights reserved

Printed in China

10 9 8 7 6 5 4 3

President/CEO: Ken Fund

Publisher: Bryan Trandem
Assistant Managing Editor: Tracy Stanley
Senior Editor: Mark Johanson
Senior Art Directors: Dave Schelitzche, Jon Simpson
Photo Editor: Julie Caruso
Creative Director, Photography: Tim Himsel
Lead Photographer: Steve Galvin
Scene Shop Carpenter: Randy Austin
Editors: Tom Lemmer, Andrew Karrre
Contributing Writers: Paul Gorton, Sid Korpi
Proofreader: Alison Baker
Technical Reviewer: John Langan
Additional Photography: Andrea Rugg, Joel Schnell
Production Manager: Laura Hokkanen

THE COMPLETE GUIDE TO TRIM & FINISH CARPENTRY
Created by: The Editors of Creative Publishing international, Inc., in cooperation with Black & Decker. Black & Decker® is a trademark of The Black & Decker Corporation and is used under license.

Library of Congress
Cataloging-in-Publication Data

The complete guide to trim & finish carpentry: installing moldings,
wainscoting & decorative trim.
   p. cm.
Summary: "Teaches readers how to effectively choose, finish, and
install all manner of trim moldings, from ornate baseboards to
decorative crown moldings and ceiling medallions. It also includes
an update on how to select and work with the new materials now
gaining popularity, including rigid fiberglass moldings and metal
ceiling panels"--Provided by publisher.
  Includes bibliographical references and index.
  ISBN-13: 978-1-58923-248-8 (soft cover)
  ISBN-10: 1-58923-248-8 (soft cover)
  1. Finish carpentry--Handbooks, manuals, etc. 2. Trim
carpentry--Handbooks, manuals, etc.
  TH5640.C66 2006
  694'.6--dc22
                  2006000670

Other Complete Guides from Creative Publishing international include:

*The Complete Guide to Home Wiring, The Complete Guide to Home
Plumbing, The Complete Guide to Decks, The Complete Guide to
Painting & Decorating, The Complete Guide to Home Carpentry, The
Complete Guide to Home Masonry, The Complete Guide to Creative
Landscapes, The Complete Guide to Wood Storage Projects, The
Complete Guide to Windows & Doors, The Complete Guide to Bath-
rooms, The Complete Guide to Kitchens, The Complete Guide to Ce-
ramic & Stone Tile, The Complete Guide to Roofing & Siding, The
Complete Guide to Outdoor Wood Projects, The Complete Guide to
Easy Woodworking Projects, The Complete Guide to Choosing Land-
scape Plants, The Complete Guide to Yard & Garden Features, The
Complete Photo Guide to Home Repair, The Complete Photo Guide
to Home Improvement, The Complete Photo Guide to Outdoor Home
Improvement.*

Introduction

Unlike any other element of a home, trimwork defines the spaces we live in. Trimwork adds warmth, architectural detail, and depth to any space regardless of the wall color or furnishings. Many homebuyers decide to purchase a house initially because they like its style. Trimwork is a core component of that style.

Homeowners have a unique ability to recreate the style of their home through trim remodeling. Even subtle changes like adding decorative bead moldings to window and door casings can overwhelmingly improve the feel of a room. Trim also offers the homeowner an opportunity to add personal style to any space with options ranging from elaborate Victorian-style casings to bare-bones Modern.

In newer construction, trimwork has sadly been left behind. Openings are often made with basic wallboard corners, and baseboard and window casings are plain and lacking in detail. Other elements such as wainscoting, chair rail, or crown molding are completely absent. These components add character and hospitality to living spaces, making them more inviting.

With an infinite number of trim arrangements, styles, and finishes, *The Complete Guide to Trim & Finish Carpentry* will steer you through the options, helping you choose and install the type of trim components that best suit your needs.

The first section of this book features historical styles of trimwork. This section covers four very general architectural styles of the past and present, helping you define an existing style that's complementary to your home—or even to create a brand-new style that's uniquely yours. You may find some exciting ideas that you haven't considered before.

Before beginning your trim project, do plenty of planning and familiarize yourself with the tools, materials, and techniques of trim carpentry. "Preparing For a Trim Project" and "Basic Techniques" sections cover these areas, with helpful hints from estimating costs to fitting joints.

"Installing Trimwork" covers the installation of wall moldings from the floor up. You'll learn to deal with obstructions like heat registers and go beyond the basics with decorative installations of built-up moldings.

"Finishing Door & Window Openings" will explain how to trim out an egress window and hang doors, while also covering the basics of desiging and installing casing for common doors and windows.

You will find "Installing Decorative Wall & Ceiling Elements" indispensable if you are embarking on an elaborate project, such as installing tin ceiling tiles or building beautiful Arts & Crafts wainscoting. You'll also see how to transform a weathered porch ceiling by installing beaded board.

The last section, "Creating Custom Moldings" is an advanced section on creating your own trim moldings in your workshop. When you can't find a stock molding to suit your needs, creating your own is a viable option (and the DIY approach can be a great cost-saver, too).

Whether you only need to learn the basics of installing baseboard or you want to mill and install your own crown molding, *The Complete Guide to Trim & Finish Carpentry* gives you the information and insight to get the job done right.

Trim Styles
Victorian Style

Victorian style began in the mid-nineteenth century and lasted approximately sixty years. Trimwork of this style is generally very ornate with large elaborate casings that emphasize curves and decoration rather than material. Moldings were built by stacking layers multiple times, rather than using a single piece.

Victorian style is generally seen in houses with higher ceilings. Due to the sheer size and nature of these moldings, they may tend to crowd a standard 8-ft.-tall room, especially if all types of trim elements are included from the floor up. However, the term "Victorian" encompasses many different variations and can be successfully installed in smaller homes by sizing down the scale of the trimwork.

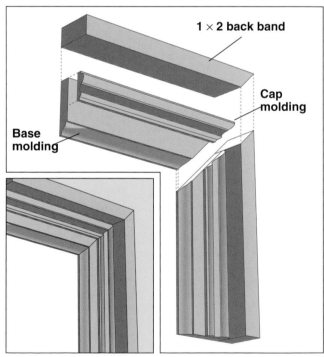

This Victorian door casing is not made up of casing at all, but actually a combination of baseboard and cap molding with 1 × 2 as a back band. The overall width of the casing is 4", creating a strong statement when compared to a single-piece stock molding.

Victorian frame and panel walls were often so elaborate that they were constructed outside the home and brought in to be installed.

Baseboards were commonly 7" tall or greater, with plinth blocks at door openings rather than a straight casing to the floor.

Victorian style cornice moldings were often very large and elaborate. Made up of multiple pieces of material, the decoration can sometimes be seen as out of proportion with current construction standards.

Trim Styles
Arts & Crafts Style

Arts & Crafts style originated near the turn if the twentieth century. Trim components of this style generally emphasize wood grain, function, and simplicity in design. Typical Arts & Crafts furnishings and trim are made from quartersawn white oak, but painted trim work is a less expensive alternative that still maintains the style.

There are many variations of Arts & Crafts style. The projects provided in this book illustrate only a few common trim techniques. Research the movement if you like the idea of wider, straight-line casings, but don't see exactly what you want. The installation techniques are the same, with variations in joinery and style elements.

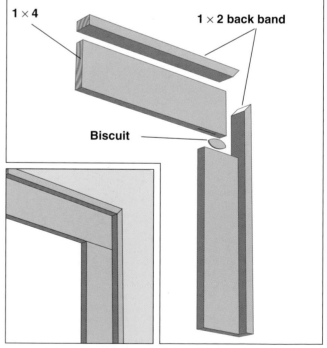

Use biscuits to join butted joints of an Arts & Crafts window or door treatment. Mitered corner molding wraps around the perimeter of the solid stock, to add depth to the casing.

White oak is the preferred Arts & Crafts wood type. The window apron above is from quartersawn white oak, the preferred cut. The wainscot panels are plainsawn white oak veneer plywood.

Arts & Crafts plate rail doubles as wainscot cap, which is usually higher than wainscot in other decorating vernaculars. In a typical Arts & Crafts installation, the wainscot is between 48" and 54" high. Corbels located above frame-and-panel stiles are a common motif.

Fancy Arts & Crafts embellishments, like the newel post (above) and the wraparound window header (left), still feature relatively plain wood treatments with a very linear appearance.

Trim Styles

Neoclassical Style

The term "Neoclassical" refers to any style derived from classic Roman or Greek architecture. Specific Neoclassical styles include Federal and Georgian styles. Traditional Greek buildings had structural components such as columns and pedestals, which, in modern time, have been replaced with interior trim elements such as door casings and baseboard. An example of a Neoclassical door trim would be a fluted casing with plinth blocks at the floor. This style is a direct, but flatter version, of classic Greek architecture.

Neoclassical style is also represented in many of the buildings of the U.S. Federal Government. Many national monuments have Neoclassical elements in their window and door treatments as well as the obvious exterior trim components such as columns.

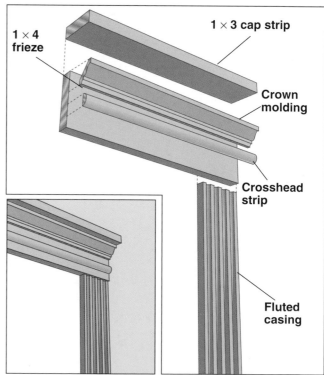

This illustrated Neoclassical fluted casing is capped off with a 4-piece decorative head including: half-round crosshead strip, 1 × 4 frieze board, crown molding, and 1 × 3 cap strip.

In this Neoclassical doorway, decorative "keystones" highlight the archway over the door and are repeated in the cornice molding as well.

Not all Neoclassical trim is extremely ornate. The clean lines of this door casing and plinth blocks are crisp and graceful, an effect that is enhanced by the white painted finish.

Neoclassical moldings often are very ornate, like this Federal-style exterior door head molding.

Dentil moldings are also common in crown moldings, mantels, and frieze boards.

Trim Styles

Modern Style

Modern style can be characterized by its complete lack of decorative carving or molding. Where Victorian trim pieces are elaborate multiple-piece moldings high on decoration, Modern trim consists of plywood cut to a uniform width with clean lines and butted joints. Hardware on modern cabinetry, doors, and windows is generally sleek, with chrome or black oxide coating. Six-panel doors are replaced with slab doors and industrial materials are incorporated into the design whenever possible, including revealing the internal systems of a home such as heating ducts and electrical lines.

More so than the styles of the past, Modern style represents a complete change in how we view trim and architecture. Traditional ideas about what materials should be used and where and how they are installed are challenged. The focus of modern style is function, never purely decoration.

Birch plywood, commonly known as Baltic Birch, is frequently used to make Modern style trim. The plywood is ripped to strips of desired width and installed with an exposed plywood edge.

Less is more often is the primary design guideline in Modern homes. The areas around the window openings above are a case in point. Note the absence of trim on the sides and top of the opening. A simple sill is installed to create a durable surface.

Plain Colonial or ranch casings are mitered at the header of the door in the typical Modern home. Matching base moldings are butted against the door casings without a plinth block.

Glass block is a Modern style material that allows light into a room without sacrificing safety. The window trim shown is made of ceramic tile rather than wood.

Dinning Room Trim

36 lin. ft. -3" door Casing — oak.
18 lin. ft. -2 ¼" window Casing — o—
6 - 3×3" Plinth blocks
50 lin. ft. -4" base — Oak
50 lin. ft. -3/4" cap — oak
50 lin. ft. ___

Preparing for a Trim Project

Choosing a style

When you begin to design your new trim project you will want to make choices about the style and the types of moldings that are most appropriate for your home. Balance and scale, existing furnishings, and the applied finish will all change the effect your project has on the room as well as the overall house.

Choosing a specific style for your trim project can be as difficult as the actual installation. Architectural styles evoke different feelings from each individual. To help you choose a style, start with the feeling that you are trying to achieve in the room. The simplistic nature of Arts & Crafts may be relaxing to you, or maybe you find it boorish and unappealing. Neoclassical style may create a formal appearance for a dining

room or den. It is possible that maintaining the existing style of your home is important to you. Or perhaps you would prefer to change the style in an individual room to make it more relaxed than the rest of your home. Whatever the case is, keep in mind there are no rules written in stone that state what you can and cannot do.

Most homes are a combination of several different styles. Successful mixing of trim components can be difficult. Try to install trim with similar dimensions to avoid large visible drops in trim height. Keep style changes subtle with elements of different rooms that are visible from a single location. Doing so may prevent a clash in style that is glaringly out of place.

Balance & Scale

Scale can be defined as the size of a particular object in relation to its surroundings. When considering a trim style, scale is very important because moldings that are too large or small might not impact a room the way you had planned.

Moldings that are well balanced create a sense of comfort and stability in a room and are well proportioned to each other—that is, they are scaled proportionally. For example, if you originally wanted to install very tall base molding, the crown or cornice treatment should be similar in scale or the room may be thrown out of balance.

When choosing trim elements for your project, keep in mind the existing moldings of the room so that the new trim will have the effect you desire. It is a good idea to maintain balance and scale.

While our eye, in general, does not like surprises when it comes to scale, it is possible to create effective illusions by violating the normal rules of proportional scale. For example, by trimming a small room with an elaborate built-up crown you can make the room appear taller. But use caution—if not handled graciously the trick can backfire and simply make your room look small and cluttered.

Scale can be used to your advantage—with an elaborate, built-up crown detail, this standard-height room looks like it has a taller ceiling than it actually does.

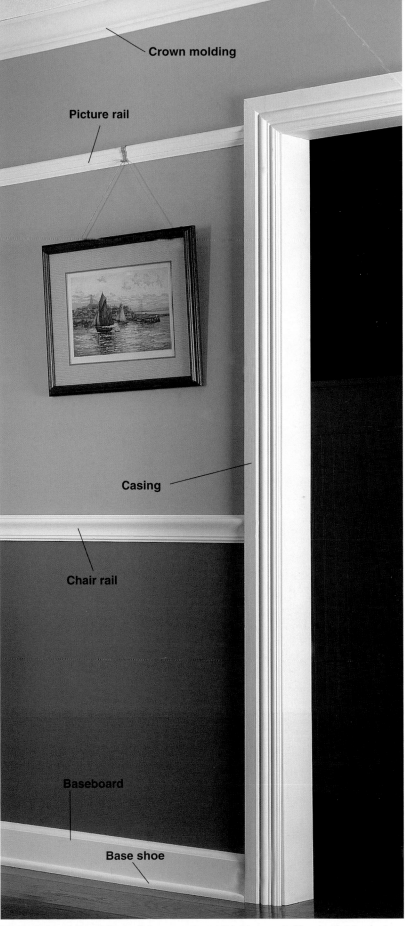

Crown molding

Picture rail

Casing

Chair rail

Baseboard

Base shoe

The style of the trim in this room is well balanced. The individual elements are similar in color and molding profile and do not overpower each other with strong differences in size.

These Mission-style furnishings match nicely with the Arts & Crafts trim elements of the room.

Working with Furnishings

Existing furnishings can sometimes lead you in the right direction for choosing the style of a room. This often-overlooked element of your home adds a considerable amount of style, and says a lot about how you want the room to feel. If you have invested in high-quality furnishings, why not add trim elements that complement them? There may be a particular set of table and chairs you have always wanted for your dining room. Even if you plan on purchasing it in the future, take that into account when choosing trimwork.

Antique furniture and family heirlooms are other types of furnishings worthy of consideration. Many are one-of-a-kind by nature and are not items that fit into your home decor seamlessly. Changing the trim to complement these items may be a wise decision.

Regardless of what types of furnishings you own, they should not be ignored when choosing a style for trim. If you complement your furnishings with good trim choices, the end result will be a space with better design and greater depth, emphasizing the feel you are striving for.

Choosing a Finish

Finish type plays a vital role in the overall appearance of your trimwork and affects the cost and installation of your project. Choosing between the two can be difficult. Clear-coated trim adds a warm and natural appearance by highlighting the wood rather than covering it up. However, there are a few drawbacks to staining. Installation techniques require a higher level of precision because blemishes and gaps are not easy to hide. Fitting stain-grade joints just requires greater time and attention to detail. Stain-grade moldings also cost more than paint grade because they require long lengths of high-quality hardwood.

Paint-grade moldings blend into their surroundings better and aren't as busy. Paint-grade moldings are commonly made of a variety of materials such as polymers, medium-density fiberboard, finger-jointed soft-woods, and fine-grained hard-woods. These materials vary in cost as well as durability, so check with a home center representative to find out which type will work best in your situation.

No matter what type of finish you choose, remember that a poor finishing job can make even the best installation look bad. If you don't skip any steps of proper finishing (page 46) either option will enhance the look of your project.

Arts & Crafts Style trimwork is normally stained rather than painted to show off the grain detail of quartersawn white oak.

This identical baseboard has a very different appearance when it is painted rather than stained. The finish you choose alters the cost of your project as well.

Tools & Materials
Hand Tools

Installing finish trim and casings is a challenging job that requires patience, attention to detail, and the right tool for each task. Without these requirements, the end result will suffer. Start off right by using high-quality tools. Good tools last longer and are generally more accurate than cheaper versions.

Many people buy tools only as they are needed to avoid purchases they will not use. This rationale should only apply to power tools and higher-priced specialty items. A high-quality basic tool set is important for every do-it-yourselfer to have on hand and ready when you need to use it. Doing so avoids improper tool usage and makes your job easier, with improved results.

The hand tools you will need for most finish carpentry jobs can be broken down into two types: layout tools and construction tools. It is common for most people to own construction tools, but lack necessary layout tools for basic trim jobs. Purchase the highest-quality layout tools you can afford. They are crucial for accurate measuring and marking of trim, and help you avoid costly mistakes with expensive stock.

Layout Tools

Layout tools help you measure, mark, and cut materials and surfaces with accuracy. Many layout tools are inexpensive and simply provide a means of measuring for level, square, and plumb lines. However, recent technologies have incorporated lasers into levels, stud finders, and tape measures, making them more accurate than ever before, at a slightly higher price. Although these new tools are handy in specific applications, their higher price is not always warranted and the average do-it-yourselfer can produce quality results.

- **A tape measure** is one of the most common tools around. The odds are good that you already own a few. Trim projects require a sturdy tape measure with a length greater than your longest trim piece. A 25-ft. tape measure has a wider and thicker reading surface than a 16-ft. variety, but either is adequate for most trim jobs. If you can't tell the difference between the smaller lines on a standard tape, consider purchasing an "Easy Read" variety. It is important to read the tape accurately.

- **A framing square,** also known as a carpenter's square, is commonly used to mark sheet goods and check recently installed pieces for position. Framing squares are also used as an initial check for wall squareness and plumb in relation to a floor or ceiling.

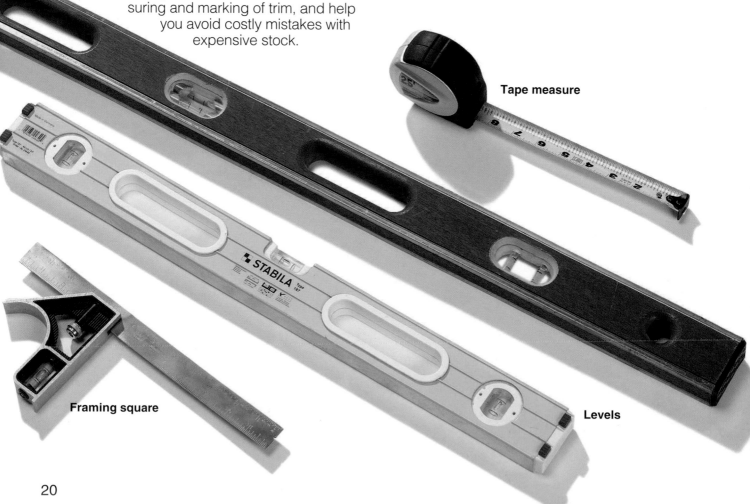

Tape measure

Framing square

Levels

- **Chalk lines** are used to make temporary straight lines anywhere one is needed. The case of a chalk line, or the "box," is tear shaped so that the tool doubles as a plumb bob. Use a chalk line to mark sheet goods for cutting or to establish a level line in a room. Keep in mind that chalk can be difficult to remove from porous surfaces.

- **A stud finder** is used to locate the framing members in a wall or ceiling. Higher-priced versions also find plumbing, electrical, or other mechanicals in the wall. Although a stud finder is not completely necessary, they are convenient when installing a larger job.

- **Levels** are available in a variety of lengths and price ranges. The longer and more accurate the level, the higher the price. The two most commonly used sizes are 2-ft. and 4-ft. lengths. 2-ft. levels are handy for tighter spaces, while the 4-ft. variety serves as a better all-purpose level. Laser levels are handy for creating a level line around the perimeter of a room or for level lines along longer lengths. They provide a wide range of line or spot placement, depending on the model.

- **A T-bevel** is a specialized tool for finding and transferring precise angles. T-bevels are generally used in conjunction with a power miter saw to gauge angled miters of nonsquare corners. This tool is especially handy in older homes where the concepts of square, plumb, and level do not necessarily apply.

- **A profile gauge** uses a series of pins to recreate the profile of any object so that you may transfer it to a work piece. Profile gauges are especially useful when dealing with irregular obstructions.

- **A combination square** is a multi-function square that provides an easy reference for 45- and 90-degree angles, as well as marking reveal lines or a constant specific distance from the edge of a work piece.

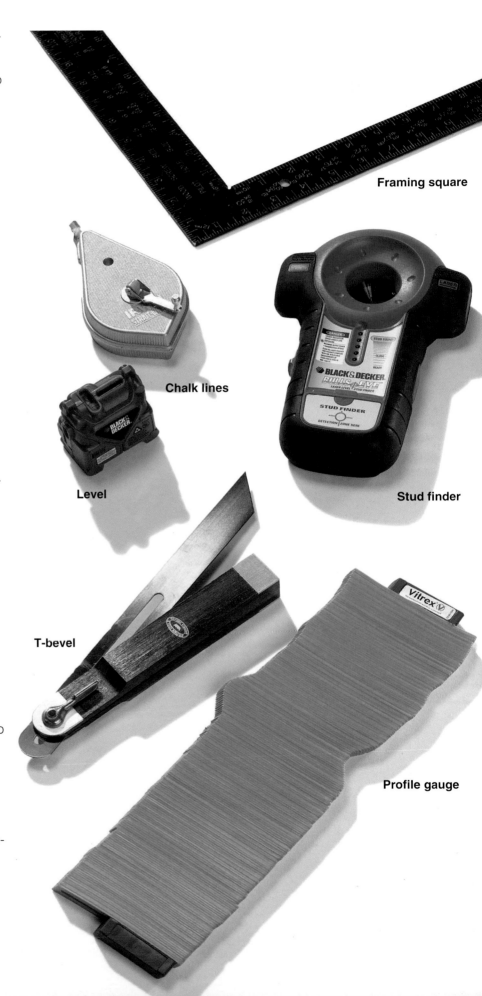

Framing square

Chalk lines

Level

Stud finder

T-bevel

Profile gauge

Construction Tools

- **A good quality hammer** is a must for every trim carpentry project. A 16-oz. curved claw hammer, otherwise known as a finish hammer, is a good all-purpose choice. Some people prefer a larger straight claw hammer for heavy teardown projects and rough framing, but these hammers are too clumsy and heavy for driving smaller casing and finish nails, and tend to mar the surface of trim.

- **Utility knives** are available in fixed, retracting, and retractable blades. This tool is used for a wide variety of cutting tasks from pencil sharpening to back-beveling miter joints. Always have additional blades readily available. Folding fixed-blade utility knives offer the durability and strength of a fixed blade with the protection of a folding handle.

- **A set of chisels** is necessary for installing door hardware as well as notching trim around obstacles and final fitting of difficult pieces. Keep a set only for use with wood, and try not to substitute them for screwdrivers.

- **Block planes** are used to fit doors into openings and remove fine amounts of material from trim. A finely tuned block plane can even be used to clean up a sloppy miter joint.

- **A coping saw** has a thin, flexible blade designed to cut curves and is essential for making professional trim joints on inside corners. Coping saw blades should be fine toothed, between 16 and 24 teeth per inch for most hardwoods, and set to cut on the pull stroke of the saw to offer you more blade control.

- **A sharp handsaw** is convenient for quick cut offs and in some instances where power saws are difficult to control. Purchase a crosscut saw for general-purpose cutting.

- **Protective wear,** including safety glasses and ear protection, is required any time you are working with tools. Dust masks are necessary when sanding.

- **Pry bars** come in a variety of sizes and shapes. A quality forged high-carbon steel flat bar is the most common choice for trim projects. Wrecking bars make lighter work of trim and door removal due to their added weight. No matter what type of pry bar you use, protect finished surfaces from scratches with a block of wood when removing trim.

- **Side cutters and end nippers** are useful for cutting off and pulling out bent nails. The added handle length and curved head of an end nippers makes them ideal for larger casing nails. Pneumatic brad nails and smaller pins will pull out easier with side cutters. Purchase a nail set for countersinking nail heads. Three-piece sets are available for different nail sizes.

- **A rasp and metal file set** are important for fitting coped joints precisely. The variety of shapes, sizes, and mills allow for faster rougher removal of material, or smoother slower removal, depending on the file.

- **Use a putty knife** to fill nail holes with putty and for light scraping tasks.

Pry bars

Protecti

Handsaws

Putty knife

IRWIN.

Nail set

Utility knives

Coping saw

Hammer

Rasp and metal file set

Side cutters and end nippers

Chisels

Block plane

Compound power
miter saw

Circular saw

Jig saw

Reciprocating
saw

Cordless drill

Power Tools

Despite the higher price as compared to hand tools, power tools are a great value. They allow you to do work more quickly and accurately than with hand tools and make repetitive tasks like sanding, drilling, and sawing more enjoyable. Basic trim jobs do not require every power tool shown here, but some tools, such as a power miter box, are crucial for professional results. Purchase power tools on an as-needed basis, keeping in mind that while the cheapest tool is not always your best option, the most expensive and powerful is probably not necessary, either. Cheaper tools generally sacrifice precision, while the most expensive tools are made for people who use them every day, not occasional use. Power tools that are midrange in price are a good choice for the do-it-yourselfer.

- **A cordless drill** is one of the handiest tools available. Although drills are not normally used to install trim, they make quick work of installing wood backing for wainscoting and other trim features. Occasionally, trim head screws are used to install trim rather than nails. This situation is most common with steel-stud walls, and necessitates a drill.

- **A circular saw** is ideal for straight cuts in plywood and quick cut offs of solid material. Purchase a plywood blade to make smooth cuts in plywood, and a general-purpose blade for other cuts.

- **A jig saw** is the perfect tool for cutting curves, or notching out trim around obstructions. Jig saw blades come in an array of designs for different styles of cuts and different types and thicknesses of materials. Always use the right type of blade and do not force the saw during the cut or it may bend or break.

Router

Random orbit sander

Biscuit joiner

Power planer

Finish sander

Belt sander

Table saw

- **A biscuit joiner** is a specialty tool used to make strong joints between two square pieces of stock.

- **A reciprocating saw** is used for removal and tear-down applications for trim projects. This tool is especially handy to remove door jambs.

- **A power miter saw, or chop saw,** will yield professional trim results. Most have a 10" or 12" diameter blade. A compound power miter saw has a head that pivots to cut bevels and miters at the same time. Sliding miter saws have more cutting capacity but are less portable. A fine-tooth carbide-tipped blade is best for trim projects.

- **A belt sander** is not essential but is a handy tool for quick removal of material.

- **Random-orbit sanders** are a good choice for smoothing flat areas, such as plywood, quickly.

Random-orbit sanders leave no circular markings, like a disc sander, and can sand in any direction regardless of wood grain.

- **Finish sanders** are available in a variety of sizes and shapes for different light sanding applications.

- **A power planer** is used to trim doors to fit openings and flatten or straighten out materials. Power planes are faster to use than manual hand planes, but results are more difficult to control.

- **A table saw** is the best tool for ripping stock to width and larger models can be fitted with a molding head for cutting profiles.

- **A router** (plunge router is shown here) has many uses in trim carpentry, especially for cutting edge profiles to make your own custom wood trim.

Pneumatic Tools

Along with a good power miter saw, pneumatic tools are the key to timely, professional trim results. Pneumatic tools save time and energy over traditional hammer-and-nail installation. Not only do they drive fasteners quickly, but they countersink at the same time, avoiding multiple strikes to the trim, which could throw joints out of alignment. Predrilled holes are not necessary with pneumatic tools. Splitting occurs infrequently if the work piece is held firmly in place and the nails are positioned at least 1" from trim ends. Nail guns also allow you to concentrate on the placement of the work piece with one hand and fasten it with the other. You needn't fumble around with single fasteners because they are already loaded in the gun.

Cost of pneumatic tools, compressors, and fasteners has decreased over the years, making them not only the professional's choice, but a great option for the do-it-yourselfer as well. Pneumatic kits are available at home centers with two different guns and a compressor at a value price. For smaller trim jobs, consider renting pneumatics.

Portable compressors are available in different styles, including pancake and tumbler styles. Any compressor with air pressure of 90 psi or greater will work for a finish gun or brad nailer. Consider options like tank size, weight of the unit, and noise levels while the compressor is running. Talk to a home center specialist about what your specific compressor needs are and keep in mind any future pneumatic tools you might want.

The two basic pneumatic tools used in trim carpentry are a finish nailer, and a brad nailer. A finish nailer drives 15-gauge nails ranging from 1" to 2½". These nails work for a variety of moldings, door and window trim, and general-purpose fastening. Angled finish nailers are easier to maneuver in tight corners than straight guns, but either option will work. Brad nailers drive smaller 18-gauge fasteners ranging in length from ½" to 2". Some brad nailers' maximum length is 1¼". Because the fasteners are smaller, it is no surprise that the gun is lighter and smaller that a finish gun. Brad nailers are used to attach thinner stock, with less tendency of splitting the trim. Headless pinners drive fasteners similar to brad nailers without the head. These nails have less holding power, but are normally used to hold small moldings in place until the glue dries. Be sure to load headless pins with the points down, taking note of the label on the magazine. ⅜" crown staplers are used to attach backing to trim pieces and in situations where maximum holding power is needed, but the fastener head will not be visible. Because staples have two legs and a crown that connects them, their holding power is excellent. However, the hole left by the staple's crown is large and can be difficult to fill.

Brad nailer

Stapler

Pin nailer

Angled finish nailer

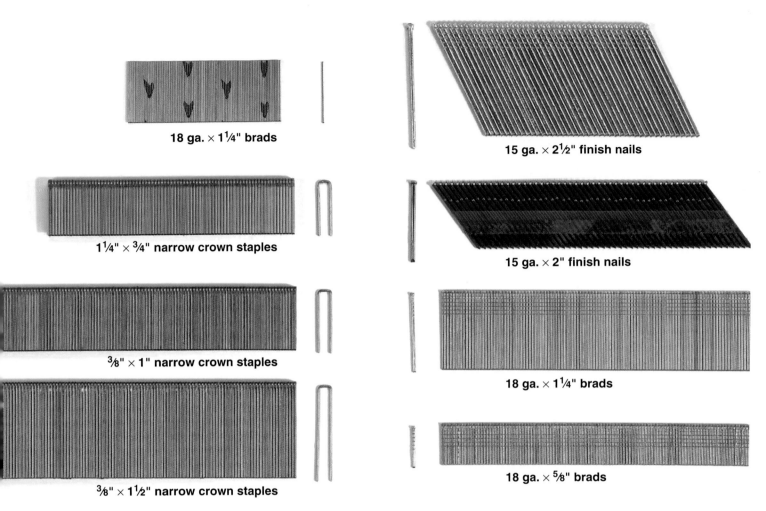

18 ga. × 1¼" brads

15 ga. × 2½" finish nails

1¼" × ¾" narrow crown staples

15 ga. × 2" finish nails

⅜" × 1" narrow crown staples

18 ga. × 1¼" brads

⅜" × 1½" narrow crown staples

18 ga. × ⅝" brads

Pneumatic Fasteners

15-gauge angled finish nails and finish nails range in length up to 2½". The angled variety are exactly the same as the straight nails, but come in angled clips. These nails are also available galvanized for exterior applications. Use finish nails to attach larger moldings and trim casings. Drive fasteners at regular intervals along the moldings and keep the position of the nails at least 1" from the molding ends. Fastener length is dependent upon the size of molding installed and what the backing is. Typical stock moldings are approximately ¾" thick. The fastener must pass through the molding and wallboard and into the stud behind. Generally, half the fastener should be embedded in the backing or stud, so in standard trim applications, 2"

fasteners should suffice. 18-gauge brad nails range in length up to 2" for some guns and leave smaller holes to fill than finish guns. Brad nails are commonly used for thinner casings that are nailed directly to a solid backer. A specific example of this is along the inner edge of a door or window casing. The outer edge of the trim is nailed with a finish gun through the wallboard, while the inside edge rests against the door jamb, so it can be fastened with a brad nailer. Headless pins leave almost no nail hole to fill but are limited in length to 1". Their holding power is greatly diminished due to the lack of head, but they are generally used in conjunction with wood glue. ⅜" crown staples are used only when the fastener head will not be visible.

AC fir plywood

Maple plywood

Cherry MDF

Baltic birch

Lumber core maple

MDO

MDF

Walnut panel

Sheet Goods

There are many different types of plywood for a wide array of uses. For trim projects, finish-grade or paint-grade plywood is commonly used. Each type is made up of thinly sliced layers called plies. These layers are made of solid hardwood, softwood, or wood products. The more plies a sheet good has, the more structurally stable it will be. This is only true for veneer-based plies. Medium density fiberboard, or MDF, is made of wood fibers that have been glued and pressed together. These panels are extremely stable and rarely shrink, expand, or warp. Plywood thicknesses range from $\frac{1}{8}$" to 1". Many species of wood are available for the outer plywood veneers. Therefore, the core, or inner plies, give the panel its distinguishable characteristics.

$\frac{3}{4}$" or $^{23}/_{32}$" AC plywood has a finish-grade face on one side and a utility grade on the other. Standard AC plywood is made of seven plies of softwood, such as spruce or pine. This plywood is a good choice for paint-grade moldings. $\frac{3}{4}$" hardwood veneer plywood is available in red oak, maple, and birch at most home centers. Its inner core is basically the same as AC plywood, but it has a hardwood outer face. $\frac{3}{4}$" MDF oak veneer plywood is made up of three layers: two outer oak veneers and a solid core made of MDF. This plywood tends to be less expensive than a veneer core product and has a smoother face, but is heavy, less durable, and does not hold fasteners as well.

MDF is available with or without an outer veneer. $\frac{3}{4}$" Baltic birch plywood is made up of thirteen plies, making it more dimensionally stable than regular veneer core plywood. This panel is commonly used in Modern style trim and can be painted or stained. $\frac{3}{4}$" Classic Core© plywood has seven plies with a hardwood outer face, but the two plies below the face veneers are MDF rather than solid wood. This gives the panel the improved flatness and stability of an MDF core panel with the fastener holding power of a veneer sheet. Classic Core© plywood is available only at lumber distributors. Medium density overlay, or MDO, plywood has a solid wood veneer core with an MDF face. This panel eliminates the weight of a MDF panel and has the fastening strength of a solid veneer core. The MDF face is perfect for paint-grade applications. Wainscoting paneling is available in several thicknesses from $\frac{3}{16}$" to $\frac{5}{8}$".

Solid Material

Solid hardwood is available at most home centers in varying widths. Species vary, depending on your location. These boards make good solid stock material to combine with or mill into new trim moldings because they are already planed to a uniform thickness. If you can't find the type of lumber you need at a home center, look for a lumberyard or a small cabinet shop in your area. For larger runs with a uniform thickness, many cabinet shops will charge a nominal flat fee to thickness the boards for you. They may even be willing to order the material for you through a local distributor.

Whenever possible, do a quick inspection of each board before you purchase it. Because hardwood lumber is often stained, carefully take note of cosmetic flaws such as splits, knots, checks, and wanes. These issues can sometimes be cut around, but once the finish is applied, the imperfection will show through. Lumber that is twisted, cupped, or crooked should not be used at full length. If a board is slightly bowed, you can probably flatten it out as you nail it. In any case, always choose the straightest, flattest lumber you can find.

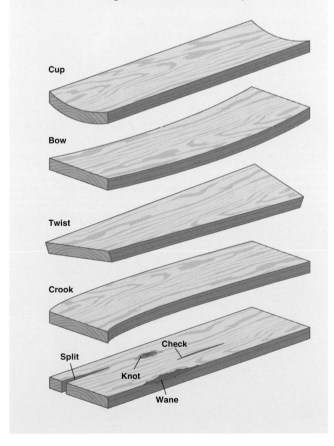

Molding Profiles

Trim moldings in stock profiles are available off the shelf at most home centers. Most molding manufacturers assign codes such as "WM166," or "HWM127" to every profile and size. However, you will find that the codes are not applied uniformly, making them virtually worthless if you're trying to track down specific molding profiles. The best way to order molding is to obtain a catalog from your molding supplier and use their labeling conventions.

There are a few conventions that are fairly consistently applied. In general, moldings labeled with a code starting with "WM" are paint-grade or softwood moldings. "HWM" designates the trim piece as a hardwood molding. If you like the style of a softwood molding, but would prefer to buy the piece in a hardwood species, ask for the equivalent in hardwood from the lumber yard sales associate.

Even though moldings are commonly found under categories such as "baseboard" or "cove," these categories relate to the style of the trim piece, not necessarily where it should be used. In fact, even among seasoned trim carpenters you'll frequently encounter arguments over which type a particular size or profile belongs to. The similarities are especially apparent when comparing base molding to case molding, as the following photos will confirm.

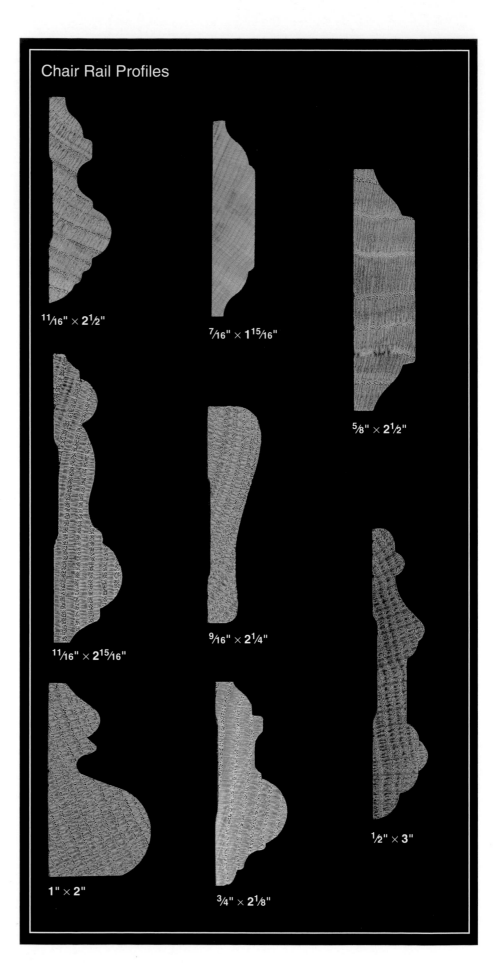

Chair Rail Profiles

$^{11}/_{16}" \times 2^{1}/_{2}"$

$^{7}/_{16}" \times 1^{15}/_{16}"$

$^{5}/_{8}" \times 2^{1}/_{2}"$

$^{11}/_{16}" \times 2^{15}/_{16}"$

$^{9}/_{16}" \times 2^{1}/_{4}"$

$^{1}/_{2}" \times 3"$

$1" \times 2"$

$^{3}/_{4}" \times 2^{1}/_{8}"$

Case Molding Profiles

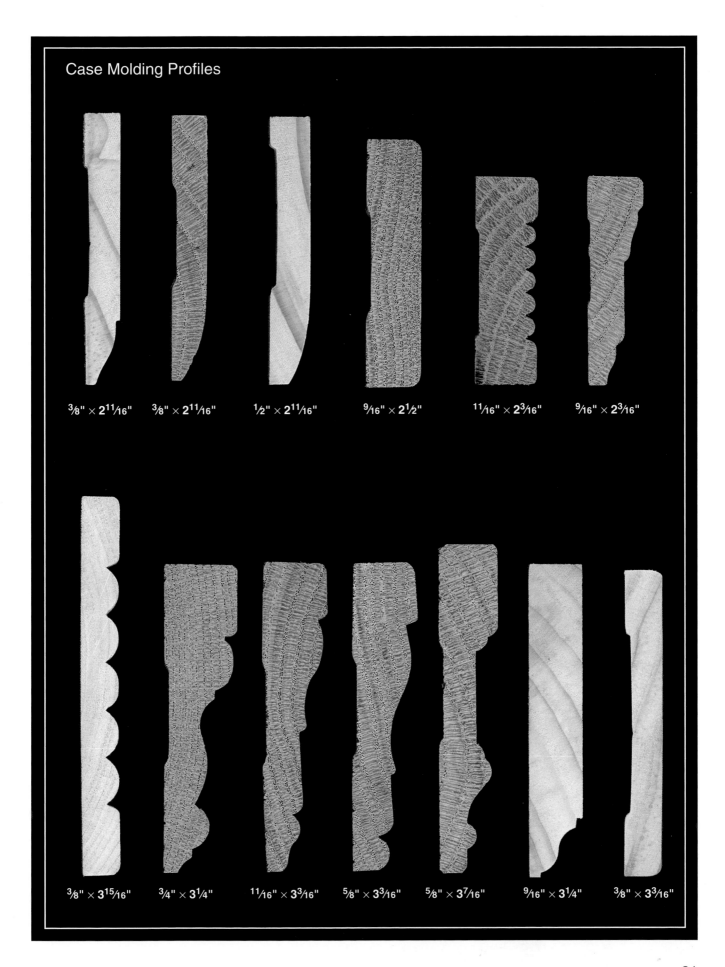

$\frac{3}{8}" \times 2\frac{11}{16}"$ $\frac{3}{8}" \times 2\frac{11}{16}"$ $\frac{1}{2}" \times 2\frac{11}{16}"$ $\frac{9}{16}" \times 2\frac{1}{2}"$ $\frac{11}{16}" \times 2\frac{3}{16}"$ $\frac{9}{16}" \times 2\frac{3}{16}"$

$\frac{3}{8}" \times 3\frac{15}{16}"$ $\frac{3}{4}" \times 3\frac{1}{4}"$ $\frac{11}{16}" \times 3\frac{3}{16}"$ $\frac{5}{8}" \times 3\frac{3}{16}"$ $\frac{5}{8}" \times 3\frac{7}{16}"$ $\frac{9}{16}" \times 3\frac{1}{4}"$ $\frac{3}{8}" \times 3\frac{3}{16}"$

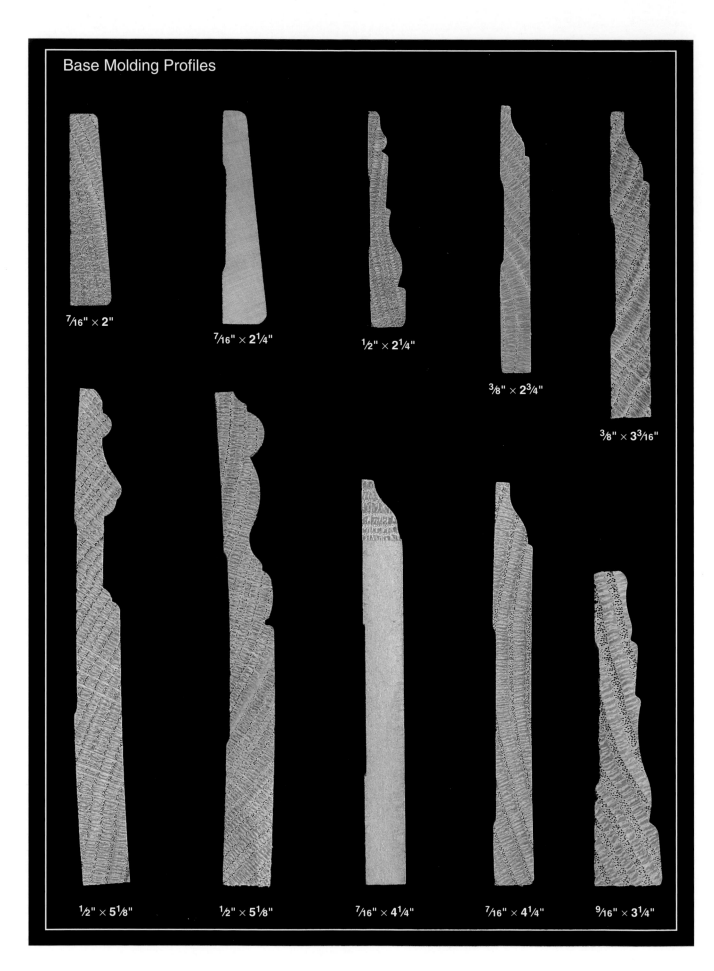

Base Molding Profiles

7/16" × 2"

7/16" × 2¼"

½" × 2¼"

⅜" × 2¾"

⅜" × 3³/₁₆"

½" × 5⅛"

½" × 5⅛"

7/16" × 4¼"

7/16" × 4¼"

9/16" × 3¼"

Cove Molding Profiles

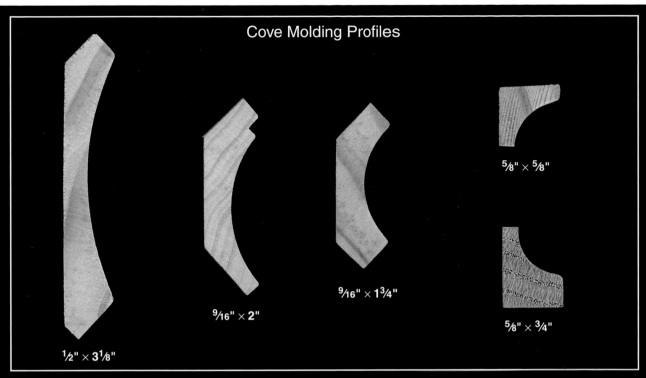

$1/2" \times 3\frac{1}{8}"$

$9/16" \times 2"$

$9/16" \times 1\frac{3}{4}"$

$5/8" \times 5/8"$

$5/8" \times 3/4"$

Cap Molding Profiles

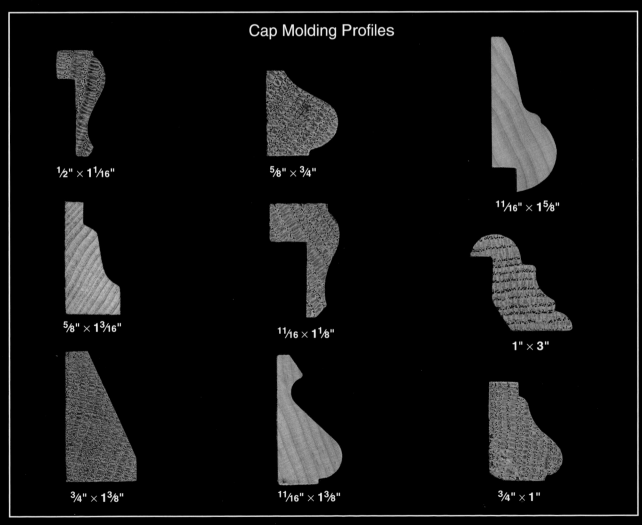

$1/2" \times 1\frac{1}{16}"$

$5/8" \times 3/4"$

$11/16" \times 1\frac{5}{8}"$

$5/8" \times 1\frac{3}{16}"$

$11/16 \times 1\frac{1}{8}"$

$1" \times 3"$

$3/4" \times 1\frac{3}{8}"$

$11/16" \times 1\frac{3}{8}"$

$3/4" \times 1"$

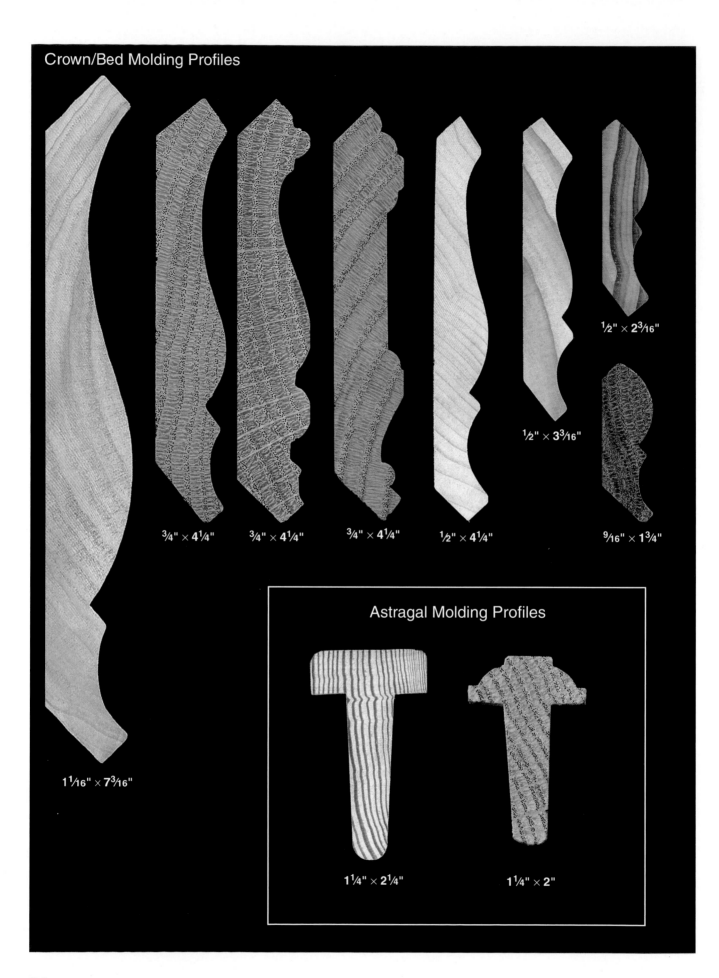

Crown/Bed Molding Profiles

¾" × 4¼"

¾" × 4¼"

¾" × 4¼"

½" × 4¼"

½" × 2³⁄₁₆"

½" × 3³⁄₁₆"

⁹⁄₁₆" × 1¾"

1¹⁄₁₆" × 7³⁄₁₆"

Astragal Molding Profiles

1¼" × 2¼"

1¼" × 2"

Quarter-round   Base Shoe

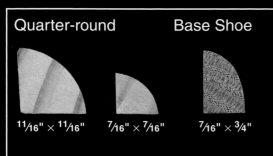

$^{11}\!/_{16}" \times ^{11}\!/_{16}"$ $^{7}\!/_{16}" \times ^{7}\!/_{16}"$ $^{7}\!/_{16}" \times ^{3}\!/_{4}"$

Stool Molding

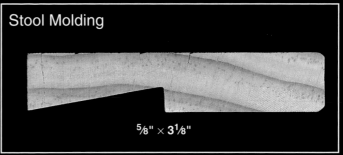

$^{5}\!/_{8}" \times 3^{1}\!/_{8}"$

Stop Molding Profiles

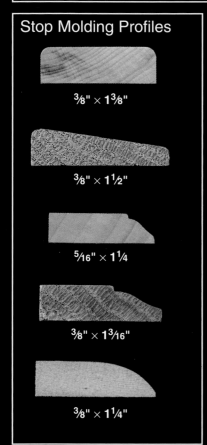

$^{3}\!/_{8}" \times 1^{3}\!/_{8}"$

$^{3}\!/_{8}" \times 1^{1}\!/_{2}"$

$^{5}\!/_{16}" \times 1^{1}\!/_{4}$

$^{3}\!/_{8}" \times 1^{3}\!/_{16}"$

$^{3}\!/_{8}" \times 1^{1}\!/_{4}"$

Corner Molding

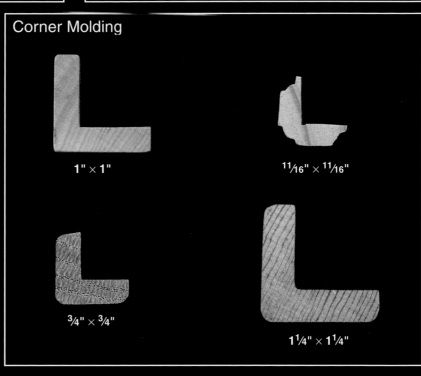

$1" \times 1"$ $^{11}\!/_{16}" \times ^{11}\!/_{16}"$

$^{3}\!/_{4}" \times ^{3}\!/_{4}"$ $1^{1}\!/_{4}" \times 1^{1}\!/_{4}"$

Picture Rail Molding

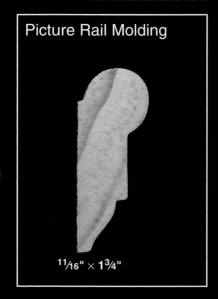

$^{11}\!/_{16}" \times 1^{3}\!/_{4}"$

Screen Retainer Profiles

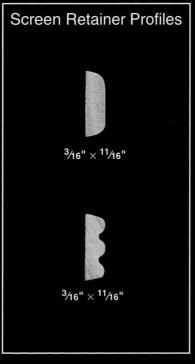

$^{3}\!/_{16}" \times ^{11}\!/_{16}"$

$^{3}\!/_{16}" \times ^{11}\!/_{16}"$

Shelf Edge Profiles

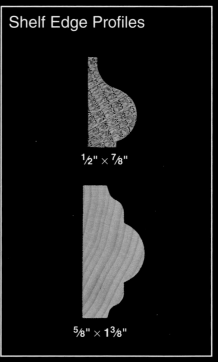

$^{1}\!/_{2}" \times ^{7}\!/_{8}"$

$^{5}\!/_{8}" \times 1^{3}\!/_{8}"$

Carpentry adhesives include carpenter's wood glue, exterior carpenter's glue, liquid hide glue, polyurethane glue, panel adhesive, construction adhesive, latex caulk, silicone caulk, and a hot glue gun with glue sticks.

Glues & Adhesives

Glues and adhesives are available at any hardware store or home center in many different specialty forms, depending upon the type of application. Use hot glue for lightweight trim projects, carpenter's glue for wood joints, and adhesive for strong bonds between panels or lumber.

Panel adhesive is used to install paneling, wainscoting, or other tongue-and-groove materials. Most adhesives are applied with a caulk gun, but some types are available in squeeze tubes for smaller applications. Caulks are designed to permanently close joints, fill gaps in woodwork, and hide subtle imperfections. Different caulks are made of different compounds and vary greatly in durability and workability. Latex caulks clean up with water and are paintable, but don't last as long as silicone-based products. Read the product la-

bel for adhesion quality to specific materials and ask a store representative for more information if you are uncertain which will work best for you.

If you are installing a trim project with a darker wood, such as walnut, or your trim has a dark finish applied, consider purchasing dark carpenter's glue for joint application. Dark glue dries at the same rate and with the same strength as regular carpenter's glue, but squeeze out from the joints will be less visible with a dark background. Exterior wood glue has a longer shelf life than regular glue and is a better multipurpose choice.

Polyurethane glue provides a high-strength bond between almost any materials; however, do not overapply. The dried product is difficult to remove from finished surfaces.

Screws & Nails

Screws and nails are the fasteners of choice for trim carpentry projects. Nails are the most common way of fastening trim in place, but screws are used for installing blocking, building up backing material, and installing trim in instances where nails don't have the holding power. Use box nails or long wallboard screws for rough framing of blocking, or backing for panels. For exterior trim projects and fastening door jambs, use casing nails. Finish nails are used for most trim installation because they have a slight head that is easy to countersink and conceal. To install smaller or thinner trim pieces that are prone to splitting, use brad nails. Brad nails are shorter and have a smaller gauge than finish nails for light trim work.

No matter what you are fastening, make sure the fasteners you choose are appropriate for your installation. Approximately half of the fastener should be embedded in the backing material when driven in place. It is a good idea to drill pilot holes in all materials before fastening them. Driving a fastener through wood without a pilot hole can split the wood fibers. These splits may not be visible when you are finished, but the integrity of your trim will be affected. Predrilling eliminates this splitting and creates stronger joints that last longer.

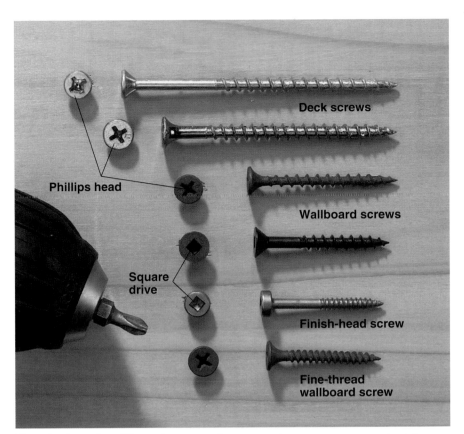

Use deck and wallboard screws for general-purpose, convenient fastening. Driving options include Phillips drive and square drive. Use finish-head screws to fasten trim to walls.

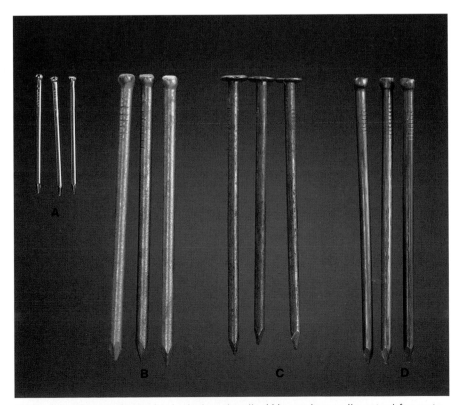

Nails for trim projects include brad nails (A), casing nails rated for exterior use (B), box nails (C), and finish nails (D).

Labels on image: Sanding block · Precut papers for power sanders · Foam-backed sandpaper

Sandpaper is available in a variety of styles for various applications: basic sheet sandpaper for general use, sponge sanding blocks for materials with light curves, and foam-backed paper for sanding tight curves and intricate details. Precut papers for power sanders include Velcro or adhesive backing.

Abrasives

Sandpaper is readily available from any hardware store or home center in a variety of styles, shapes, and sizes for just about any sanding task. Sandpaper is generally available in grits from 60 up to 220, but finer and coarser grits are also offered at some locations.

60-grit sandpaper is used to grind down badly scratched surfaces and is rarely needed for trim carpentry applications. 100-grit sandpaper is used for initial smoothing of wood. Stock moldings purchased from a home center or lumberyard may need a light initial sanding with 100-grit paper. Use 150-grit sandpaper to put a smooth finish on wood surfaces before painting or staining material. 220-grit sandpaper is useful for light sanding between coats of varnish, or to remove sanding marks left from power sanders.

No matter what you are sanding, begin with a lower-grit paper and work your way up the grit levels until you reach the desired smoothness for your project. Do not skip grit levels, especially 100-grit paper. Doing so will make it very difficult to remove scratches from previous sanding, and will leave some hardwoods with deep grain marks that will be visible through your finish.

Always wear a dust mask when sanding, particularly when using power sanders. The airborne particles created while sanding can cause serious health problems. The dust from some hardwoods, such as walnut, is known to cause serious allergic reactions in some people.

Sanding accessories for power drills include (clockwise from top right) disc sander for fast sanding, sanding drums, and flap sanders to smooth contoured surfaces.

Wood Fillers

No matter what type of finish you choose, painted or clear, wood fillers provide a convenient way to fill fastener holes quickly and effectively with minimal sanding or clean up. Each product differs in some way, including varying drying times, hardness when dry, and adhesion to specific materials. Read the packaging carefully to determine which product will best suit your needs.

Clear finishes require a filler that will either match the final finish color or stain similarly to the trim material. If you will be staining and varnishing your trim after it is installed, consider purchasing filler that will match when stained. Available in solvent and solvent-free form, these fillers apply easily with a putty knife, dry in a very brief amount of time, and sand with ease. Before applying stain-matching filler, use a scrap piece of trim to test the color.

If your trim will be finished prior to installation, use oil-based finishing putty to fill holes. This putty is available in numerous colors that can be mixed to achieve a nearly indistinguishable fill. Finish putty will never harden completely, so it's a good idea to apply one coat of varnish over the top to match the sheen of the finish.

Fastener holes in painted finishes can be filled with two main types of filling material. One is a premixed filler that is normally solvent based, such as plastic wood. The other requires mixing.

Solvent-based premixed fillers generally dry faster and harder than their water-based counterparts. Although premixed fillers are convenient to use, they have a shorter shelf life and are more expensive.

Fillers that require mixing are available in powder form for water-based products and two-part resin and hardener mixes for solvent-based products. Both work equally well in most circumstances; however, two-part resin and hardener mixes may emit dangerous fumes, and should be handled with caution.

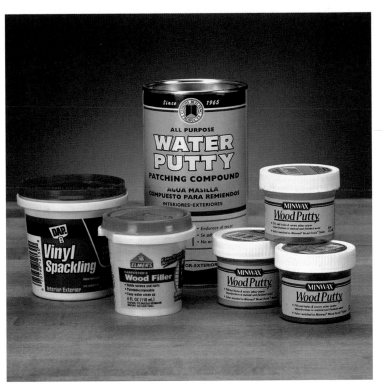

Wood fillers are available for two finish types: painted and clear finish. Based on the type of finish you choose and the fastener hole size to fill, these products provide many options for your filling needs.

Grain filler is available to brush on open-grained woods before finishing. These products fill in wood grain so that it does not mirror through the finish, creating a smoother appearance.

Clear finishing products include water- and oil-based polyurethane, water, and oil-based stain, wipe-on varnish and stain combinations, brush-on stain and varnish combinations, and spray lacquers.

Stain, Polyurethane & Lacquer

When choosing a clear-coat finish for your trim project, look for materials that best suit your needs. There are many things to consider before selecting a specific product, including dry time, application method, odor, and durability. With a virtual myriad of options available, it is easy to get confused about what the product you are looking at provides, much less what the ingredients are.

Polyurethane varnish is the clear choice for most trim carpentry projects. It dries quickly, is available in water- and oil-based varieties, and provides a very durable finish. Urethane can be wiped or brushed on, depending on what product you choose. Some urethanes are tintable, meaning stain can be or has been added to them, making application faster and easier. Just like paint, clear finishes are also available in a variety of sheen finishes ranging from satin to high gloss.

Options for wood stains are also available in water- and oil-based form. Keep in mind that water and oil don't mix. Whenever possible, use a water-based stain under a water-based urethane or an oil-based stain under an oil-based urethane. If you choose to mix oil and water, and the stain is not completely dried, you risk white splotches in your finish, called "bleed back." Bleed back occurs when the two non-similar finishes mix and separate as they dry. Bleed back may occur immediately, or it may take a week to appear. With newer urethanes and stain varieties available,

bleed back is less of an issue than it used to be, but if you plan on applying a water-based urethane over an oil-based stain, it is a good idea to allow at least 24 hours for the stain to dry.

Both stain and polyurethane are available in gel and wipe-on forms for easy application. If your trim has intricate detailing, do not choose a wipe-on finish. The gel is difficult to remove from tiny details, and brush application is simply faster.

For smaller projects, spray lacquer in an aerosol can is a convenient option. Lacquer is a common choice for professional finishers because it dries very quickly, allowing multiple coats in a matter of hours, and installation on the same day. With that speed comes a slight loss of durability in moist environments or locations with extreme humidity and heat.

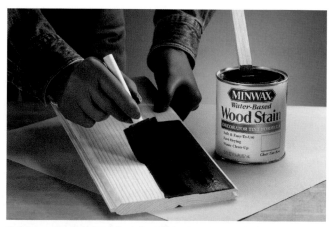

Some products blend stain with polyurethane to make application faster. These blends are available in many different colors. Stir the product frequently while applying to maintain color and consistency.

Paint comes in a variety of surface finishes, or sheens. Gloss enamel (A) provides a highly reflective finish for areas where washability is important. All gloss paints tend to show surface flaws. Alkyd enamels have the highest gloss. Medium-gloss latex enamel creates a highly washable surface with a slightly less reflective finish. Like gloss enamels, medium-gloss paints (B) tend to show surface flaws. Eggshell enamel (C) combines a softer finish with the washability of enamel. Flat latex (D) is an all-purpose paint with a soft finish that hides surface irregularities.

Paint

Paint is sold in latex (water-based) or alkyd (oil-based) varieties. Latex paint is easy to apply and clean up, and the improved chemistry of today's latexes makes them suitable for trim carpentry projects in any room of the house.

Paints come in various sheens ranging from flat to high-gloss enamels. Gloss enamels dry to a shiny finish and are commonly used for trim applications.

Paint prices are generally an accurate reflection of quality. As a general rule, buy the best paint you can afford. High-quality paints are easier to apply and often have better coverage than cheaper paints. Because they often require fewer coats, high-quality paints are usually less expensive in the long run.

Before applying the finish paint, prime all of the surfaces with a good-quality primer. Primer bonds well to all surfaces and provides a durable base that keeps the paint from cracking and peeling. If you plan on painting your trim with a paint that has a low-hide coverage, tint the primer to match the finish coat.

Trimwork is generally painted with a higher-gloss paint than the surrounding walls to highlight the trim of a room and draw attention to interesting features.

41

Calculating the lineal, or running, length of molding you need is one of the first steps in estimating your material needs. Take precise measurements, then add 10% to account for waste and improperly cut materials.

Making Plans
Estimating Material

Estimating material is an important part of any trim project. Taking the time to do a quality estimation of your needs will pay off with fewer trips to the lumberyard and little excess material. Estimating materials also helps keep your project in budget by only buying what you need to get the job done.

Begin by measuring the precise length needed for each piece of molding and marking the dimensions in your scale drawings. When all dimensions are measured, add the total lineal feet together. This number represents the minimum number of feet you need to purchase to complete the job.

To save yourself the difficulty of splicing in materials over every length, you may need to call the lumberyard or home center you are purchasing from to find out what dimensions the moldings are available in. Some moldings are sold in random lengths ranging from 1 ft to 16 ft. Others are only available in 8- or 10-ft. lengths. When you know the availability of the moldings you want, take the time to write out a detailed list, optimizing the lengths of material with the fewest number of joints.

Similar methods should be used to estimate paint, paneling, and plywood. Make a separate list for every trim element, molding, or sheet good needed. Separate lists help avoid confusion when ordering materials or picking the stock off the shelf. Consider purchasing a project calculator for easier estimating. Project calculators are preprogrammed with formulas for everything including estimating paint coverage, lineal feet for moldings, and calculating to the nearest 16th of an inch or better.

Project calculators simplify the math of square-foot coverage for paint, panel coverage for wainscoting, and lineal feet for trim components. The model shown calculates in fractions as well making precise measurement addition simple.

Make a detailed list for each trim component, listing which lengths can be cut from a stock dimension. Label the list clearly with the wood molding number and a description of the piece at the top of the page.

Planning a Deadline

Planning a deadline is just as important as buying the material for a trim project. Without a deadline, the other people around you don't know what to expect from the project. Because trim components are cosmetic, and not necessary for function of a home, trim projects have a tendency to become drawn out like no other. Planning a deadline gives you a specific point for completion as well as an overall goal to shoot for.

Do not sacrifice the quality of your installation to meet a deadline. Instead, choose a realistic timeline for certain components to be completed, altering the schedule as necessary. Remember that although the project may be exciting and fun now, there may come a time when it begins to feel like too much work. It is at this point that your schedule becomes your friend. No one wants to leave a project incomplete, but you need to make it a priority, or other things will pop up that sound more appealing, and your living room will look like a construction project for too long.

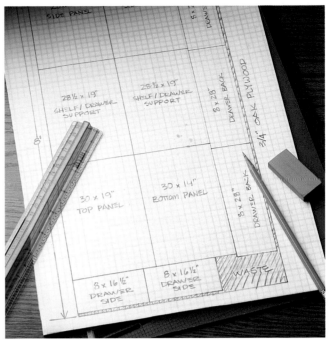

Draw cutting diagrams to help you make efficient use of materials. Make scale drawings of sheet goods on graph paper, and sketch cutting lines for each part of your project. When laying out cutting lines, remember that the cutting path (kerf) of a saw blade consumes up to 1/8" of material.

Laying out your project with scale drawings helps you anticipate what tools will be necessary and what the overall impact of your project will be as well as how it will affect your living space.

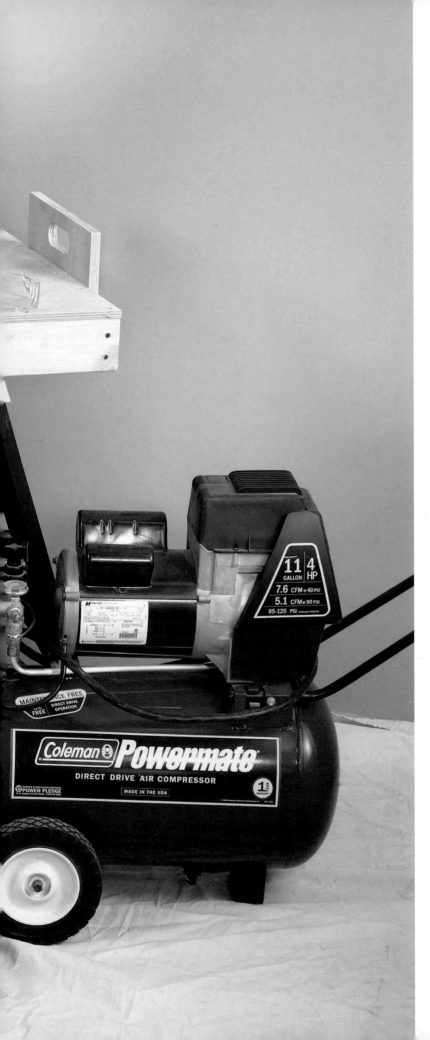

Basic Techniques

Prefinish your moldings. Always apply one coat to the backs of the moldings to seal the entire piece and help balance wood movement.

Finishing Trim

Even the best trim installation can look bad if the finishing is done poorly. That's why the type of finish and the quality of that finish makes such a big difference in the overall appearance of a room. Often, the finish of a trim project is overlooked entirely or done as an afterthought, and the installer may be so tired of working on the project that he or she does a lackluster job. To avoid this problem, finish as much of your trimwork as possible before you start to install. Paint-grade moldings should be primed on both sides and have one finish coat applied to the face. Stain-grade moldings should be stained and have two coats of polyurethane on the face and one coat on the backside. This way, after the moldings are installed, all you need to do is fill the nail holes and apply a final coat (and sometimes you can get away without the final coat).

Before you buy your material you need to decide what type of finish you will be using. The basic choice is between a painted finish and a clear finish over natural wood.

If you are a novice do-it-yourselfer, consider making your first trim project one with a painted finish. Installing decorative crown molding with a lustrous wood finish might have great appeal for you, but starting out with a painted baseboard installation in a bedroom or utility-type room is more realistic. This project will allow you to practice cutting joints and dealing with trimwork that can be easily filled and puttied, before attempting the more difficult stain-grade project.

Painted projects have appeal beyond simply being easier than stained projects. Paint-grade moldings are generally less expensive. For decorative multi-piece buildups, plywood can be substituted for solid lumber, and different pieces of trim can be made of different wood species.

Although stain-grade trim projects usually are more expensive and take longer to finish than painted projects, the natural warmth and appearance of wood grain cannot be recreated with paint. Stained projects show off the quality of the trim material rather than covering it up.

To properly prepare your moldings for finish, place them on sawhorses or a workbench where that are easy to reach. When finish sanding, always sand with the grain of the wood, stepping your way up to the coarser grits as you work (each finer grit smooths out the sanding marks from the previous grit). After sanding all the pieces smooth, wipe them down with a dry cloth (or better yet, a tack cloth) to remove dust.

After applying each coat of polyurethane, primer, or paint, examine each piece of trim for surface problems like dribbles, pooling, or skip marks. These areas need to be dealt with in a timely fashion so they do not telegraph through the final coat.

Regardless of the type of finish you choose, take the time to prepare and properly finish your moldings. In the end, you'll be glad you did—your trim will look better and the overall quality of your installation will improve.

Tips for Finishing Trimwork

Painted trim projects are easier for the novice do-it-yourselfer because nail holes and gaps in joinery (and other learning mistakes) are easier to conceal.

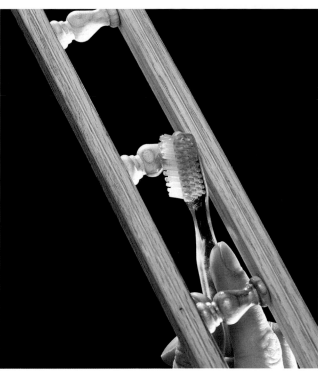

Use a soft toothbrush to apply brush-on finishes to hard-to-reach areas, like spindle-and-rail moldings and other ornamental trim pieces.

Gently but thoroughly stir clear topcoating products like polyurethane before and during application. Do not shake the product or air bubbles will develop in the liquid, leaving burst marks behind on the finished surface.

1. Attach waxed paper to wall before trim is nailed.

2. Pull waxed paper out after trim finish is applied and dry.

If you don't have time to prefinish your casings before installing, tape waxed paper to the walls before attaching the trim. Then when you apply your finish, the walls will already be masked off. Lap the seams so that any drips on the paper stay off the wall.

Sanding Trim Moldings

Use foam-backed sandpaper for curved or intricate trim pieces to avoid sanding down the high points of the molding.

Mark large blemishes with a pencil, designating them as scrap material. Don't bother to sand these areas smooth.

No matter what type of finish you apply, every piece of wood furniture requires sanding to ensure a smooth surface. Preparing trim pieces to accept stain, primer, or polyurethane is essentially the same process. The only difference is at which grit level you call the sanding complete.

Before you start sanding, do a visual check of each trim piece. Inspect the edges for splintering. Most splintering is easily sanded smooth, but larger splinters may need to be glued down. If you're installing clear-finished trim, look for large imperfections in the wood. The sections of trim containing these blemishes should not be used whenever possible. Mark the area of the molding around the blemish with pencil lines, and don't bother to sand it.

Most factory-made moldings are smooth enough off the shelf to start sanding at 100- or 120-grit. Grits below 100 are generally made for rough material removal, not sanding smooth. Trim used in painted projects generally is ready for primer after sanding at 120-grit. Stain-grade projects look better when the wood is sanded up to 150- or 180-grit.

Remember that the purpose behind sanding is to remove marks left from the machining process and leave a smooth surface to finish. Be careful to avoid rounding over the edges and any joint surfaces.

Choose tools and methods for sanding your trim pieces and use them consistenetly for all grit levels. Sand the trim with long, even strokes running in the grain direction, and reposition the paper frequently to expose new grit to the material. When you are finished sanding, wipe the pieces down with a dry cloth or tack cloth before applying the finish.

Tips for Sanding Trim

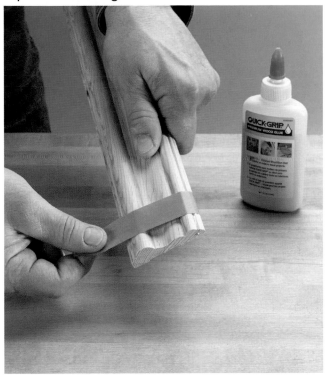

Repair large splinters with wood glue. Use masking tape to "clamp" the piece until the glue sets. Then remove the tape and sand the area smooth to remove excess glue.

Use a sanding block to smooth out flat surfaces evenly. Sanding blocks can also be made from scrap wood, such as a 2 × 4.

Wipe away the dust after the final sanding with a clean, dry cloth. Inspect the face of each piece one final time before applying the finish

Sand very lightly between finish coats with 220-grit paper. This scratches the surface just enough for the next coat to adhere properly, and also removes minor imperfections in the first finish coat.

Painting Trim Moldings

Paint-grade trim projects are easier to complete when the moldings have been prefinished. Although you will still need to apply the final topcoat after installation, this simplified method ensures that paint goes on evenly and helps avoid paint marks on finished walls and ceilings.

In their rush to get going on a trim project, many do-it-yourselfers completely skip coating the trim with primer and move right to finish paint. Primer is important. It creates a stronger bond with the raw material than paint alone, greatly reducing cracking and bubbling of the topcoats. Primer also costs less than good-quality finish paint and can be tinted to match the finish color, reducing the number of necessary finish coats.

Trimwork is generally primed on both the front and back to seal the entire piece, balancing the wood movement from humidity and temperature changes. After the primer is dry, two finish coats are applied to the face. When the finish coats are dry the molding can be installed. After installation, gaps in joints and fastener holes need to be filled. The final step is to apply a touchup coat to the filler areas.

Use a high-quality bristle brush to paint trimwork. Straightedge brushes around 2" are the tool of choice for many professional painters when painting moldings. Quality brushes have a shaped wooden handle and a sturdy, reinforced ferule made of noncorosive metal. Many also have flagged, or split, bristles with chiseled ends for precise work. If bristle marks are a concern, consider putting an additive in the paint. Paint additives thin the paint without affecting its durability or sheen. The end result is a paint that flows on smoother and lays out flatter when dry. Using an additive may require that you apply at least one additonal coat.

After each coat of primer or paint is applied, carefully inspect each piece for drips or clots. These problems need to be dealt with quickly, or they will mirror through the final coat. Remember that multiple thin layers of paint look better and last longer than one heavy coat. Heavy layers will also hide any intricate details or crisp edging, and could possibly make installation more difficult.

Paint trim moldings with a higher-sheen paint than the surrounding walls. Paint with higher gloss is more durable and highlights the trim, drawing attention to interesting details.

Pour a paint additive into the mix to reduce brush marks on the finished product. A "cut bucket" like the one above is easier to handle than a gallon pail and creates a convenient way to mix the products.

Tips for Painting Trim

Dip the brush into the paint, loading one-third to one-half of its bristle length. Tap the bristles against the inside of the can to remove excess paint. Do not drag the bristles against the top edge, or rub them against the lip of a one-gallon can.

Paint moldings with thin, even coats starting along the deeper grooves of the trim, and moving on to the smooth areas. This sequence will minimize drips into the detail of the molding.

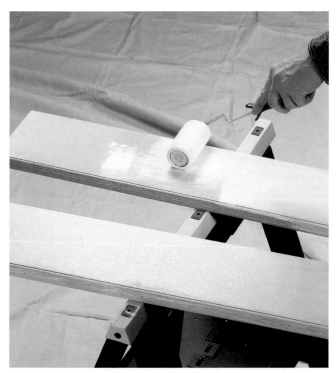

Use a small paint roller to coat long, straight strips of trim material. Rollers make for fast work and don't leave brush marks. If the paint is too thick or you roll too quickly, however, the roller can crate an orange peel effect that you may not like.

Clean the brush with mineral spirits when using oil-based paint, or with warm water when using water-based. Shake out the brush and let it dry. Always start subsequent coats with a clean, dry brush.

Clear-Coating Trim Moldings

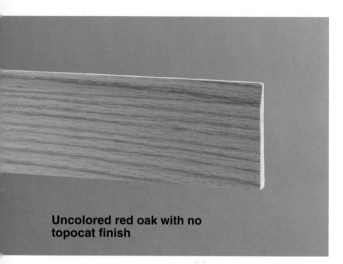

Water-based polyurethane over uncolored red oak

Uncolored red oak with no topocat finish

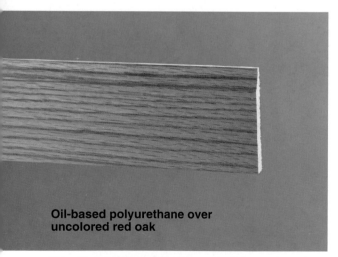

Oil-based polyurethane over uncolored red oak

The finished appearance of oil-based and water-based urethanes often differs. Oil-based products (bottom photo) tend to darken or yellow the trim, which can have the positive effect of highlighting grain characteristics. Water-based products (top photo) offer easier cleanup and faster drying times.

Water-based and oil-based finishes have a few basic differences in application and end result that you should be aware of so that you can make the best decision about which product is right for you.

Not long ago, oil-based polyurethanes were regarded as much more durable and capable of providing more even coverage than water-based products. Today, this is not always the case. The major differences between modern oil and water urethanes are not related to finish quality as much as secondary (but important) characteristics such as odor, finish appearance, and drying times. The durability of water-based products is no longer an issue. In fact, the most durable urethanes available are water-based.

Oil products emit fumes during drying that can linger for weeks. Pregnant women and young children should avoid these fumes altogether. Water-based products create minimal fumes, and are not dangerous under normal conditions with adequate ventilation.

According to most manufacturers, water-based products offer faster drying times than oil varieties. This literally means less time spent between coats. Water-based urethanes also clean up with soap and warm water, rather than mineral spirits. Easy clean-up can come in handy for large spills.

The biggest factor to consider when choosing a type of polyurethane is finish appearance. Although water-based products offer many more conveniences than oil, the end results can be quite different. When oil-based urethanes are applied, they add a warm amber color to trimwork that creates more visual depth and variety. Water-based products dry crystal clear. The color of the trim before the product is applied is similar to the finish product. Only a light color change appears. Keep in mind that most of the clear-finished trim in an older house is oil-based and water-based finishes will not match.

The following examples run through the steps of successful clear-coat finishing. These steps are a guideline to finishing only. Always follow the manufacturer's specific application directions. Drying times will vary, depending on temperature and humidity.

Everything You Need

Tools: bristle brush or foam brush, latex gloves, stir sticks, paint can opener. drop cloth or cardboard, sawhorses, plastic bag (optional).

Materials: trim material, polyurethane, stain (optional).

How to Apply a Clear Finish

1 Set up the work station area with a drop cloth or sheet of cardboard on the floor and two sawhorses. Place the trim pieces to be finished on the horses. Inspect each piece for large blemishes or flaws, repairing any large splinters (see page 49).

2 Sand each piece as necessary, finishing with a fine-grit paper. Wipe the moldings with a clean, dry cloth to remove any leftover dust.

3 If desired, apply a coat of stain to the moldings with a foam or bristle brush. For more even coverage of the stain, apply a pre-stain wood conditioner. Follow the manufacturer's instructions for stain drying time, and remove the excess with a clean rag.

4 Let the stain dry sufficiently and apply the first thin coat of polyurethane with a brush. Stir the polyurethane frequently before you begin, between coats, and during application. Let the finish dry for four to six hours.

5 After the finish has dried, lightly sand the entire surface with 220-grit sandpaper. This will ensure a smooth finish with a strong bond between layers. If the sandpaper gums up quickly, the moldings need more time to dry.

(continued next page)

6 Wipe down the moldings with a clean, dry rag to remove any dust. Apply a second layer of polyurethane. Check each piece for skipped areas and heavy drips of urethane. These areas need to be corrected as soon as possible or they may show through the final coat.

7 Let the moldings dry for four to six hours and lightly sand the entire surface with 220-grit sandpaper.

8 Apply a third and final coat of polyurethane to the moldings. Keep the third coat very thin, using only the tip of the brush to apply it. Lightly drag the tip across the molding on the flat areas. If the moldings have deep grooves or intricate details, skip these areas; two coats will be sufficient. Try to maintain constant pressure and avoid smashing the brush as this will create air bubbles in your finish. Allow the moldings to dry for a minimum of 12 hours (check manufacturer's recommended drying times).

Tips for Clear-Coat Finishing

Seal brushes in a plastic bag to avoid the necessity of cleaning the brush between coats. Wear latex gloves to protect your hands, especially when working with oil-based products.

Choose a brush that's well-suited for the application. If applying finish to round trim pieces with irregular surfaces, like the Victorian fretwork above, select a brush that's roughly the same width as the diameter of the workpieces.

Always stir urethane products to properly mix them. Never shake them. Shaking creates tiny air bubbles in the product that will follow to your project. Before opening the can, roll it gently upside down a few times to loosen the settled material from the bottom.

Apply urethane in a well-ventilated area. Lack of ventilation or heavily applied product will result in longer drying times. If you use a fan to increase ventilation, aim it away from the project: do not blow air directly on the project or dust and other contaminants will adhere to your finish.

In some trimwork projects, the most efficient way to accomplish the work is to convert the installation room into a temporary workshop.

Jobsite Preparation
The Work Area

Whether you are installing base trim in an entire house or just improving the appearance of window, with an additional molding, preparing the jobsite is an important step of your project. Remove as much furniture from the rooms you will be working in as possible so that you won't worry about getting sawdust on a nice upholstered chair, or damaging an antique furnishing with a scratch. Cover any items you cannot remove with plastic sheeting. You may also want to cover finished floors with cardboard or plastic as well to protect them from scratches or just to make clean-up easier.

Set up tools such as a power miter saw at a central workstation, to avoid walking long distances between where you are installing and where you are cutting material. This central location is key to professional results because measurements are easier to remember and quick trimming is possible without the added time of exiting and entering the house.

Make sure the work area is well lit. If you don't already own one, purchase a portable light (trouble light) to make viewing the workpieces easier.

Keep your tools sharp and clean. Accidents are more likely when blades are dull and tools are covered in dust and dirt.

Keep the work area clean and organized. A dedicated tool table for staging your tools is a great organizational aid. Tool tables also make it possible to conveniently keep tools from disappearing. If you only use the tools that you need and set them on the tool table when you aren't using them, tools stay off the floor and out of other rooms. Add a set of clamps to the table and you have a convenient space for fine-tuning the fit of each trim piece.

Organize your tools and avoid a bulky work belt by setting up a dedicated tool table where all of your project tools and materials can be staged.

Project Safety

Personal safety should be a priority when working on any project. Power tools and hand tools can cause serious injuries that require immediate attention. Be prepared for such situations with a properly stocked first aid kit. Equip your kit with a variety of bandage sizes and other necessary items such as antiseptic wipes, cotton swabs, tweezers, sterile gauze, and a first aid handbook.

To help you avoid using the first aid kit, read the owner's manuals of all power tools before operating them, and follow all outlined precautions. Protect yourself with safety glasses, ear protection, and dust masks and respirators when necessary.

Keep your work environment clean and free of clutter. Clean your tools and put them away after each work session, sweep up dust and any leftover fasteners, and collect scraps of cutoff trim in a work bucket. These scraps may come in handy before the end of the project, so keep them around until you are finished.

Maintain safety throughout your project, and remember that being safe is a priority. Everyone needs to use ear protection when operating loud tools. If you don't, you will lose your hearing. People don't just get used to loud noise. They lose their hearing and the noise doesn't seem as loud. The concept that safety applies to everyone but you is foolish. Take the necessary precautions to prevent injury to yourself and those around you.

Always wear safety glasses and ear protection when operating power tools. Use dust masks when necessary, and protect yourself from chemicals with a respirator. Work gloves save your hands when moving or handling large amounts of material. Knee pads are useful when working on floor-level projects such as baseboard.

Read the owner's manual before operating any power tool. Your tools may differ in many ways from those described in this book, so it's best to familiarize yourself with the features and capabilities of the tools you own. Always wear eye and ear protection when operating a power tool. Wear a dust mask when the project will produce dust.

Even trim that's been damaged should be removed carefully to avoid inflicting harm on innocent bystanders, like the baseboard behind the splintered base shoe above.

Removing Old Trim

Damaged trim moldings are an eyesore and a potentially dangerous splinter waiting to happen. There is no reason not to remove damaged moldings and replace them. Home centers and lumberyards sell many styles of moldings, but they may not stock the one you need, especially if you live in an older home. If you have trouble finding the trim you need, consider looking at home salvage stores in your area. They some-times carry styles no longer manufactured.

Removing existing trim so that it can be reused is not always easy, especially if you live in a home with intricate moldings. Age of the trim and the nailing sequence used to install it

greatly affect your ability to remove it without cracks or splits. Some moldings may be reusable in other areas of the home as well.

Whether you intend to reuse the trim or not, take your time and work patiently. It is always a good idea to remove trim carefully so you don't damage the finished walls, floor, or ceiling surrounding it.

Everything You Need

Tools: utility knife, flat pry bars (2), nail set, hammer, side cutters or end nippers, metal file.

Materials: scrap plywood or dimensional lumber.

How to Remove Painted Moldings

1 Before removing painted trim, cut along the top seam of the molding and the wall with a utility knife to free the molding from any paint buildup on the wall. Cut squarely on the top edge of the molding, being careful not to cut into the wallboard or plaster behind it.

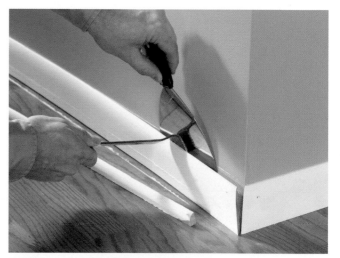

2 Work the molding away from the wall from one end to the other, prying at the nail locations. Apply pressure to the molding with your other hand to help draw it away from the wall. A wide joint compound or putty knife makes a good guard to insert bwteen the tool and the wall.

How to Remove Clear-finish Moldings

1 Remove the molding starting with the base shoe or the thinnest piece of trim. Pry off the trim with a flat bar using leverage rather than brute force, and working from one end to the other. Tap the end of the bar with a hammer if necessary to free the trim.

2 Use large flat scraps of wood to protect finished surfaces from damage. Insert one bar beneath the trim and work the other between the base and wall. Force the pry bars in opposing directions to draw the molding away from the wall.

How to Remove Nails

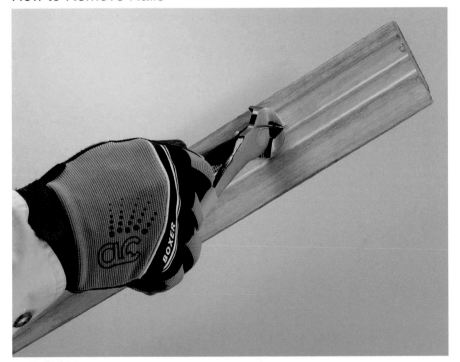

OPTION 1: Extraction. Use an end nips or a side cutters to pull the nails from the moldings. Take advantage of the rounded head of the end nippers, "rolling" the nail out of the molding rather than pulling it straight out.

OPTION 2: Reversing course. Secure the workpiece with a gap beneath the nail and drive the nail through the molding from the front with a nail set and hammer.

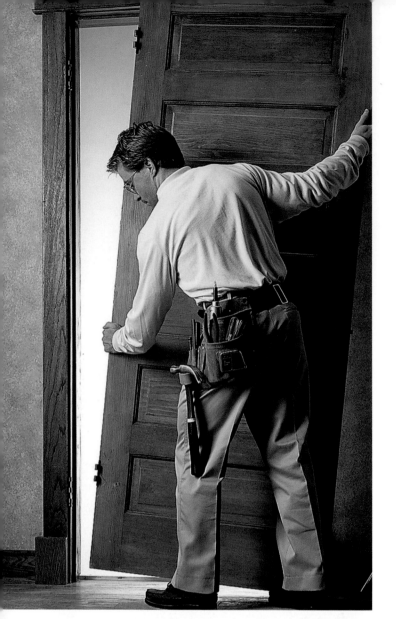

Removing Doors & Windows

Preparing properly for a trim project may include temporary removal of an existing door for easier access to the work area. Removing doors protects them from scratches and dents from materials and tools, and makes passage easier when you have your hands full. You may want to consider hanging sheet plastic over the opening to contain dust to the work area.

Removing a window makes tearing out existing moldings and any other demolition easier by providing a direct route out to a dumpster. The nails of removed trim are notorious for scratching finished hardwood floors or wallboard. If you are certain you won't need the moldings, get them out of the house promptly, or pull the fasteners as you go.

Remove a door by driving the hinge pins out with a screwdriver and a hammer. If you close the door first, you will be able to pull it from the hinges without a helper.

Remove a window to speed up your demolition work. Cover shrubs and flowers with plywood and adjoining lawn areas with plastic or canvas to simplify cleanup.

Locating Studs

Locating studs is an important step in preparing for any trim project. Studs define where you nail trim and locate trim seams. Marking the work area for stud locations is best done before you begin rather than searching by trial and error with a pneumatic nailer. Remember to mark the stud locations in the areas where you will be installing trim. Stud marks halfway up a wall are of little help when nailing down baseboard. If you are concerned about concealing marks after the trim is installed, consider using small Post-it Notes, or margin labels. These products adhere to clean surfaces well, but don't leave behind a residue.

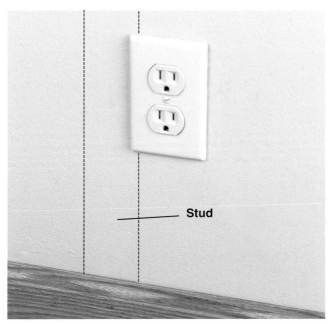

For temporary marking of stud locations, consider using Post-it Notes or margin locaters.

Use a studfinder to locate wall studs or ceiling blocking. These devices locate the edges of framing so you can determine the center of studs and joists.

Stud

Look along trim for nails to indicate framing locations. Electrical receptacles are typically installed on studs as well.

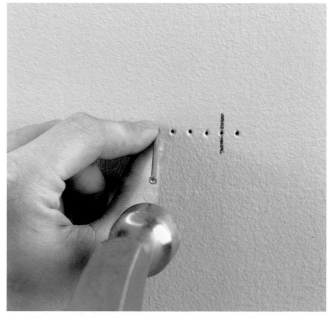

Confirm framing locations by driving a finish nail through the wall in an inconspicuous area. Locate and measure from the center point in 16" or 24" intervals to find neighboring members.

Establishing Level, Plumb & Square

Good carpenters strive to achieve three basic ideals in their work: plumb, level, and square. Go into any home, however, and you are bound to find walls that bow, floors that slope, and corners that don't form right angles. This doesn't always mean the carpenter did a poor job, but rather reflects the fact that wood and many building materials are natural products that expand, contract, and settle with the seasons. These natural movements do not always occur at the same rate, however, causing fluctuations that sometimes become permanent. That's why it's no surprise that older homes more commonly have larger fluctuations.

These movements can make installing a new trim project challenging. Level and plumb are hard concepts to apply to a wainscoting project where the floor slopes heavily and corners float in or out. Compounding the problem further is that power tools are made to cut and shape wood precisely. Preset angles on a compound miter saw don't include angles such as 47 degrees.

In most cases, your installation of chair rail, picture rail, or cornice molding will require compromises. Keep in mind the overall appearance of your project and remember that the concepts of plumb and level are only concepts. Strive to achieve them for quality joints, but don't insist on them when they affect the overall appearance of your project negatively. Here are a couple of fine pieces of advice to keep in mind:

• Level to the room is more important than level to the earth.

• Flat is more important than level.

A plumb bob is hung to establish a plumb (exactly vertical) line. Plumb can be difficult to visualize. Most chalk boxes can double as plumb bobs for rough use.

Window and door jambs are normally installed level and plumb, but if they aren't your casing should still follow an even reveal of $^3/_{16}$" to $^1/_4$" (about the thickness of a nickel) around the inside edge. Set the blade on a combination square to the depth of the reveal, then use the square as a guide for your pencil when marking. Install the casings flush with the mark.

Use a spacer block as a guide to install moldings near a ceiling. The spacer will allow you to easily follow any ups and downs of an uneven ceiling, making the trim run parallel to it rather than exactly level.

Install baseboard as close to level as possible, paying attention to areas where a floor dips or slopes over a longer length. In these instances, "cheat" the baseboard as close to level as you can, leaving a gap below it. You can only cheat the molding to less than the height of your base shoe, or quarter round. These trim pieces will cover the gap because they are thinner and easier to flex to the contour of your floor. Cheating the molding will also make cutting miters easier because they will require less of a bevel.

Use a T-bevel to measure for miter-cutting trim on out-of-square corners. Use a piece of scrap 1 × 4 to trace lines parallel to the corner walls. Place the T-bevel so the blade runs from the corner of the wall to the point where the lines intersect. Transfer this angle to your miter saw to cut your moldings.

Planning a Trim Layout

Planning the order, layout, and type of joint at each end of trim you will be installing is an important step before you actually start nailing things down. A good layout plan like the one shown below helps avoid frustration and errors during installation.

Generally, trim installations begin at the opposing wall to the entry to the room. The numbers in the sample layout plan below represent the order in which each piece is installed. Here, the first piece installed is butted at both ends, tight to the finished walls. Trim pieces are added to the installation, working back and forth around the room in both directions back toward the entry. The added trim is coped at all inside corners and mitered at outside corners. All window and door casings should be installed before any horizontal molding that will butt into it.

Minimize the number of joints necessary on each wall by using the longest pieces available.

For professional results, contoured molding is coped at inside corners with a coping saw. Fine-tune the cut with a metal file or rasp.

Keep in mind that the most visible spaces should have fewer joints whenever possible. Cut all joints so they face away from the direct line of sight from the room's entrance. If a piece will be coped on one end and mitered on the other, cut

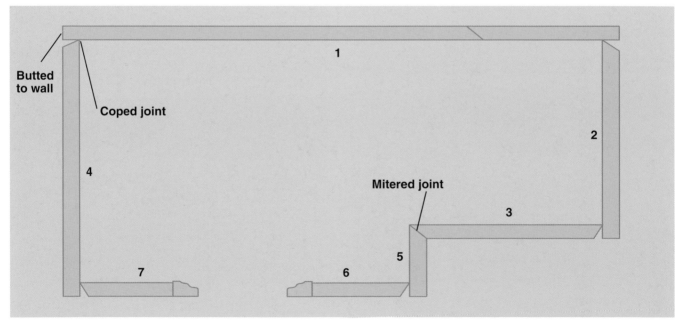

Plan the order of your trim installation to minimize the number of difficult cuts on individual pieces. Use the longest pieces of molding for the most visible walls, saving the shorter ones for less conspicuous areas. When possible, place the joints so they point away from the direct line of sight from the room's entrance. If a piece will be coped on one end and mitered on the other, such as no. 3 above, cut and fit the coped end first. Also keep in mind the nailing points—mark all framing members you'll be nailing into before starting the installation. At a minimum, all trim should be nailed at every wall stud, and every ceiling joist, if applicable. Install door and window casing before installing horizontal molding that will butt into it.

Standard Trim Joints

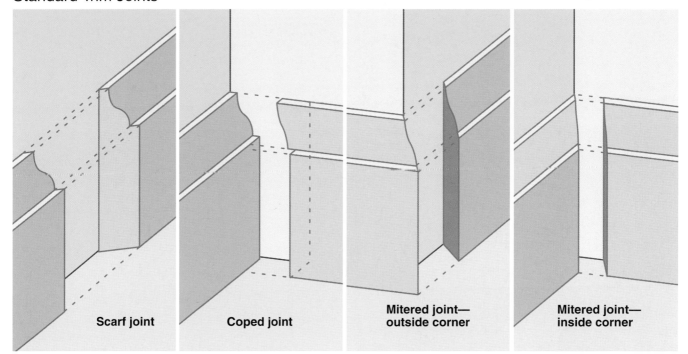

Scarf joint

Coped joint

Mitered joint—outside corner

Mitered joint—inside corner

The basic joints for installing most trim are shown here. A scarf joint joins two pieces along a length of wall. Coped joints join contoured molding at inside corners: the first piece is butted into the corner; the second piece is cut and fitted against the face of the first. Coped joints are less likely than mitered joints to show gaps if the wood shrinks. Mitered joints are used at outside and inside corners. They're typically made with two pieces cut at a 45° angle, but the angle may vary depending on the shape of the corner. Uncontoured moldings can also be butted together at inside corners.

and fit the coped end first. All nailing points should be clearly labeled before you begin. At a minimum, every piece of trim should be nailed at each wall stud and at every ceiling joist, if installing cornice molding.

If you have never installed trim before or if it is likely that you won't be able to complete the project all at once, consider making a layout plan like the one shown at the bottom of page 64. There is no absolutely right or wrong order for most tasks, but the chapters ahead dealing with the specific type of installation you'll be doing provide some helpful suggestions about sequencing your project. If you get confused about what to do next, or can't remember where you left off, the layout plan will guide you through the installation.

Miter outside corners, cutting each piece at 45°. Use a pattern with mitered ends to help position your workpieces. Fasten the first piece of each joint to within 2 ft. of the corner, leaving some flexibility for making adjustments when you install the adjoining piece.

Measuring & Marking Accurately

Measuring accurately is a very important aspect of every trim project. Make a mistake, and you potentially waste expensive material. Not only do you need to be able to read a tape measure, but also mark material so that when it is cut, it is the length you measured. This might seem obvious, but the two skills are not the same.

If you are unfamiliar with the increments on a tape measure, it is a good idea to purchase an easy-read variety (see next page, top left). This type of tape displays the actual fractions on the blade to avoid confusion. Do not use carpenter's pencils to mark trim for cutting. These pencils are meant for rough framing, not intricate work. Instead, use a standard-size writing pencil to mark moldings, and keep the tip sharp.

Whenever possible, use the same tape measure for the entire project. Blade hooks are easily bent and cause inaccurate readings from tape to tape, even when they are the same style and brand name. It is not important that your tape measure be dead-on accurate. It is important that you realize that the tape measure you use is the defining scale of your project. If you use multiple tape measures in a project that scale is thrown out of alignment and material will consistently be cut too long or short.

Measuring trim can be difficult, especially when working with mitered ends such as on a window or door casing. To simplify measuring, always measure to outside dimensions. For instance, to cut a head trim piece for a window, install the two side casings first and then measure from the outer edge of one side to the outer edge of the other.

Consistent measuring technique does nothing to improve your accuracy if your cutting technique fluctuates. Choose a method by trial and error for reading your marks for cutting and stick to the method. Some people choose to mark each piece with a "V" shape and then cut the "V" at its point. Others would prefer minimal marking of the workpiece to avoid having to sand off marks later. Whichever style you decide is right for you will work as long as you maintain it through your project.

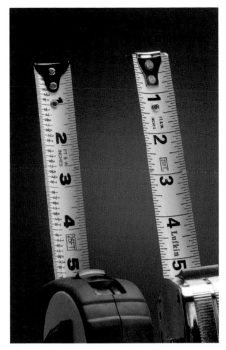

Purchase a solid 25-ft. tape measure for general trim projects. With the actual fractions printed on the tape, "easy-read" varieties are more user-friendly and help avoid confusion and cutting errors.

Use the trim piece as a measuring device, marking the cut line directly off the wall. Eliminating the tape measure reduces errors and makes it easier to visualize the cut.

To mark a line parallel to the edge of a board, lock the blade at the desired measurement, then hold the tip of the pencil along the edge of the blade as you slide the tool along the work piece. This is useful when marking reveal lines on window and door jambs.

Use a T-bevel to find the appropriate bevel angle for walls that are out of plumb and other angle measuring situations. Tighten the T-bevel and transfer the angle to your miter saw to cut the molding.

Scribe the back of a molding and check the mark with a square to determine whether or not the corner is plumb. If the scribe mark is not square, transfer the angle to your saw with a T-bevel and make a compound miter cut.

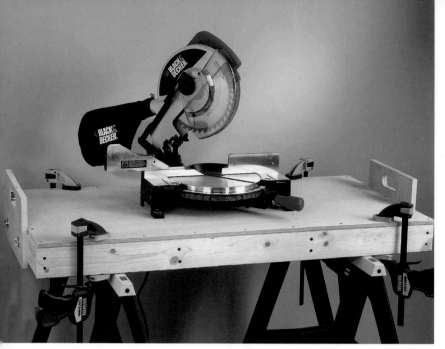

Building a Power Miter Saw Table

Build a custom-designed table platform for your power miter saw. The one shown here is roughly 2 ft. × 4 ft. and it features adjustable work supports at each end that double as handles for the lightweight platform. Instead of having legs, this table is clamped to sawhorses.

A portable table for your power miter saw is a great advantage in the field. You can design and build one yourself or purchase one at any building center.

Everything You Need

Tools: pencil, tape measure, circular saw, drill, socket set, 4-ft. level.

Materials: scrap ¾" and ½" plywood, 1 × 4, 2 × 4, wallboard screws, lag bolts with nuts and washers, lag screws, glue.

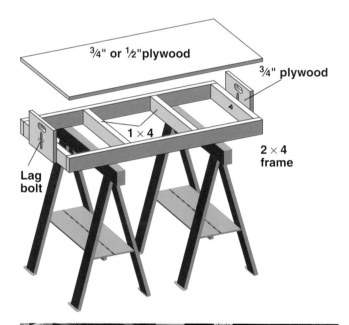

¾" or ½" plywood

¾" plywood

1 × 4

2 × 4 frame

Lag bolt

How to Build a Power Miter Saw Table

1 Build a 2 × 4 frame appropriate to your saw size. Add 1 × 4 stretchers to stiffen the frame. Cut a piece of plywood (½" or ¾") to size and glue and screw it to the frame with 1½" wallboard screws.

2 Center the miter saw on the platform. Mark the position of the bolt-down locations with a pencil and remove the saw. Drill bolt holes through the platform and attach the saw to the platform with lag bolts, using lag screws if you hit the 2 × 4 frame.

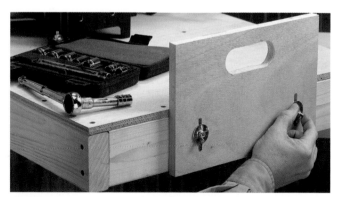

3 Cut end supports from ¾" plywood (the ones shown here are 8" × 12"). Make handle cutouts and cut grooves for the adjustable bolt connection with a ½" router bit. Bolt the work supports to the platform so the tops are level with the saw deck.

Building a Straightedge Guide

Making straight and accurate cuts on plywood or paneling is a challenge. Even the best carpenter can't always keep the blade on the cut line, especially over a longer span. A straightedge guide solves this problem as long as you keep the saw's base plate flush with the edge of the cleat.

The cleated edge of the guide provides an accurate anchor for the base plate of the saw as the blade passes through the material. You can make a straight cleat edge by ripping the first 2" off of an existing plywood panel and using the factory edge. Use a fine-toothed blade for rip cuts and a plywood blade for splinter-free crosscuts.

A straightedge guide overcomes the difficulty of making square rip cuts and other square cuts on long workpieces. The guide is built square, ensuring that any cuts made with it will be square as well.

Everything You Need

Tools: C-clamps, pencil, circular saw.

Materials: ¼" finish plywood base (10 × 96"), ¾" plywood cleat (2 × 96"), carpenter's glue.

How to Build a Straightedge Guide

1 Apply carpenter's glue to the bottom of the ¾" plywood cleat, then position the cleat on the ¼" plywood base, 2" from one edge. Clamp the pieces together until the glue dries.

2 Position the circular saw with its foot tight against the ¾" plywood cleat. Cut away the excess portion of the plywood base with a single pass of the saw to create a square edge.

3 To use the guide, position it on top of the workpiece, so the guide's square edge is flush with the cutting line on the workpiece. Clamp the guide in place with C-clamps.

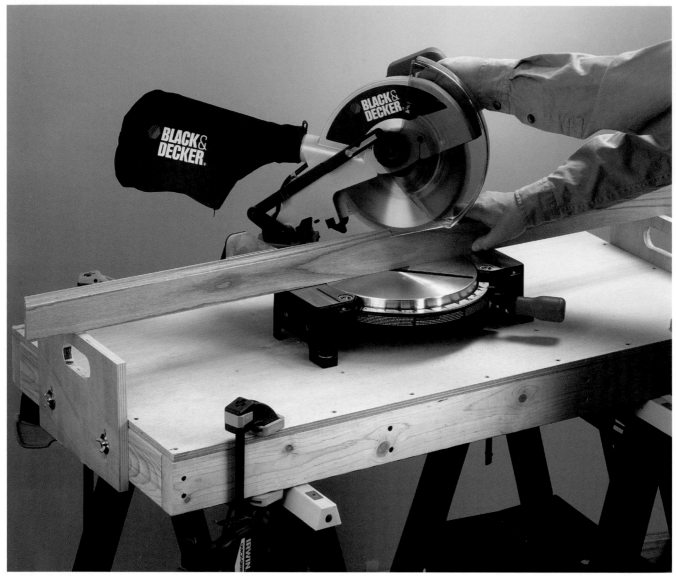

Careful cutting is the hallmark of good joinery, be it in making furniture or installing trim moldings. Used correctly, a power miter saw offers the speed and precision to make your project look like it was done by a pro.

Cutting & Fitting Joints

Cutting and fitting joints is a skill that requires patience, knowledge, and well-maintained equipment to achieve effective results. There are a few basic joints that are generally used for most trim applications: butt, inside and outside miter, scarf, and coped joints.

Although cutting trim joints accurately is the key function of a power miter saw, it is not the only tool necessary for quality joinery. Coped joints require a coping saw as well as a set of metal files. For some trim applications such as frame and panel wainscoting, fitting butt joints is simplified with the use of a biscuit jointer or a

pocket hole jig. These are specialty tools designed for joining wood.

Cutting and fitting joints during installation can be very frustrating, especially when it involves difficult walls that are not plumb and corners that are out of square. Take the time to read through the proper techniques of using a miter saw, as well as the correct method for cutting each individual joint. These techniques are described in detail to help you work through the imperfections found in every house and avoid common problems during installation.

Power Miter Saw Techniques

There are two main types of power miter saws. The basic style cuts mitered angles when material is placed against the fence or beveled angles when material is placed flat on the work surface. The second type is called a compound miter saw. Compound saws allow you to cut a miter and a bevel simultaneously. The compound angle is extremely helpful in situations where a corner is out of plumb and a mitered angle requires a bevel to compensate. Some compound saws are available with a sliding feature that allows you to cut through wider stock with a smaller blade size. This option raises the cost of the saw considerably.

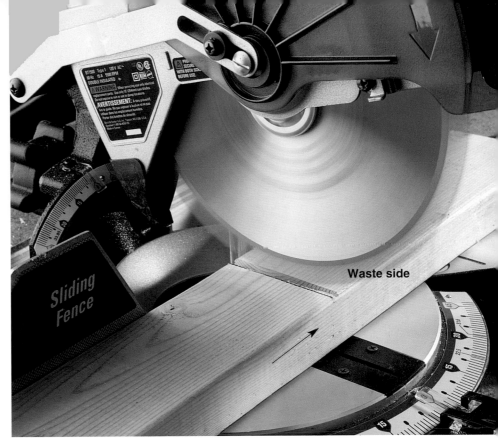

Waste side

Sliding Fence

Creep cuts. To avoid cutting off too much, start out by making a cut about ¼" to the waste side of the cutting line, then nibble at the workpiece with one or more additional cuts until you have cut up to the cutting line. Wait until the blade stops before raising the arm on every cut.

How to Make Repeat Cuts

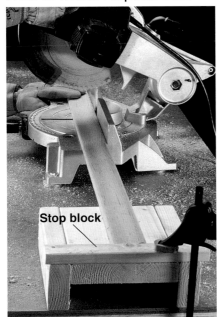

Stop block

To cut multiple pieces of stock to the same length, clamp a stop block to your support table at the desired distance from the blade. After cutting the first piece, position each additional length against the stop block and the fence to cut pieces of equal length.

How to Cut Wide Stock

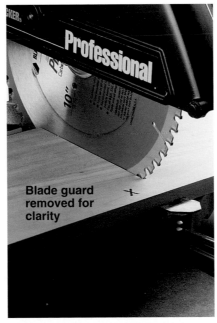

Blade guard removed for clarity

With a power miter saw: Make a full downward cut. Release the trigger and let the blade come to a full stop, then raise the saw arm. Flip the workpiece over and finish the cut

With a Sliding Compound Miter Saw: Equipped with a saw carriage that slides away from the fence, these saws have greater cutting capacity than a nonsliding saw so they can cut wider stock. They're also more expensive, but you may find it worth renting one.

Mitering Outside Corners

Cutting outside miters is one of the main functions of a power miter saw. Most saws have positive stops (called detents) at 45° in each direction, so standard outside corners are practically cut for you by the saw. Keep in mind that your saw must be accurately set up to cut joints squarely. Read the owner's manual for setting up your saw as well as for safety precautions. Before you begin, check the walls for square with a combination square or a framing square. If the corner is very close to square, proceed with the square corner installation. If the corner is badly out of square, follow the "Out of Square" procedure on the following page.

square corner installation. If the corner is badly out of square, follow the "Out of Square" procedure on the following page.

Everything You Need

Tools: combination square or framing square, miter saw, pencil, tape measure, pneumatic finish nail gun, air compressor, air hose, T-bevel.

Materials: molding, masking tape, 1 × 4.

How To Miter Square Outside Corners

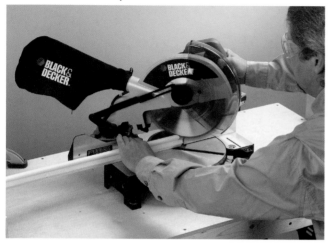

1 Set the miter saw to 45°. Position the first piece on-edge, flat on the miter box table, flush against the fence. Hold the piece firmly in place with your left hand and cut the trim with a slow, steady motion. Release the power button of the saw and remove the molding after the blade stops.

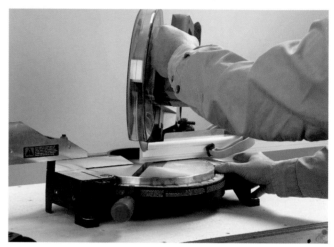

2 Set the miter saw blade to the opposing 45° positive stop. Place the second piece of molding on-edge, flat on the saw table, flush against the fence. Fasten the piece tightly in place with a hold-down or clamp. Cut the molding with a slow, steady motion.

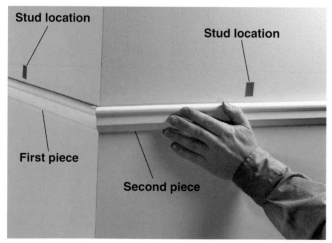

3 With the first piece of molding tacked in place, hold the second piece in position and check the fit of the joint. If the joint is tight, nail both pieces at stud locations.

4 If the corner joint does not fit tightly, shim the work piece away from the fence to make minor adjustments until the joint fits tightly. Shims should be a uniform thickness. Playing cards work well.

How to Miter Out-of-Square Outside Corners

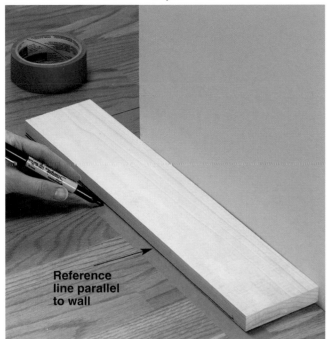

1 Draw a reference line off each wall of the corner using a straight 1 × 4. Put masking tape down on the finished floor to avoid scuffing it and to see your lines clearly. Trace along each wall, connecting the traced lines at a point out from the tip of the corner.

2 To find the angle you need to miter your moldings, place a T-bevel with the handle flush against one wall, and adjust the blade so that it intersects the point where your reference lines meet. Lock the blade in place at this angle.

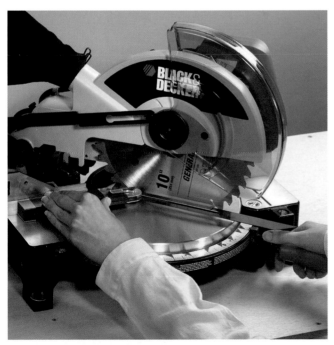

3 Transfer the angle of the T-bevel to the miter saw by locking the saw in the down position and adjusting the angle to match the angle of the T-bevel.

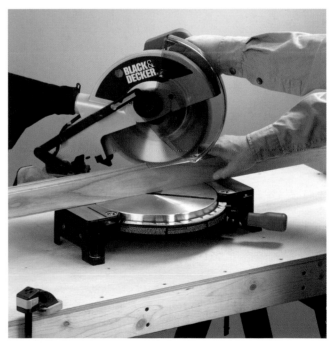

4 Position the molding on-edge, flat on the saw table and flush against the fence. Cut at your cutting mark. Tack the workpiece in place and repeat steps 2 through 4 to measure and cut the mating piece. Or, you can subtract the angle of the first cut (for example, 47°) from 90° to find the angle for the second cut (43° in this case). Using math is faster; taking direct measurements is more reliable.

Mitering Inside Corners

Although most professionals prefer to cope-cut inside corners, it is common to see moldings that are mitered to inside corners. These joints are more likely to separate over time and to allow gaps to show. For that reason it is not advised to use inside corner miters when installing a stain-grade trim product. The gaps will be visible and are very difficult to fill with putty. For paint-grade projects, mitering inside corners makes more sense because joints can be filled and sanded before the top coats of paint are applied.

Everything You Need

Tools: miter saw, pencil, tape measure, utility knife, pneumatic finish nail gun, air compressor, air hose.

Materials: molding.

How To Miter Square Inside Corners

1 Set the miter saw to 45° and place the first piece of trim on-edge, flat on the miter box table and flush against the fence. Hold the piece firmly in place with your left hand and cut the trim with a slow, steady motion. Release the power button and remove the molding after the blade stops.

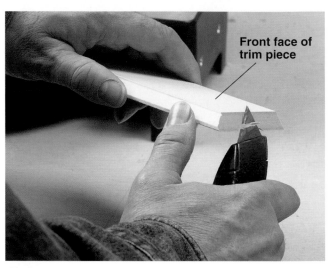

Front face of trim piece

2 Back-cut the inside edge of the trim piece with a utility knife so that the top corner will sit flush against the wall corner.

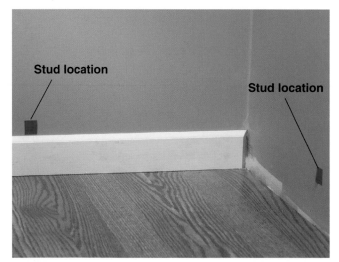

Stud location

Stud location

3 Butt the molding tightly against the wallboard and tack it into place.

4 Adjust the blade of the miter saw to the opposite 45° angle and cut the mating piece. Test the fit of the joint, adjusting the miter angle if necessary. Once the fit is tight, nail both pieces at stud locations.

Out-of-Plumb Corner Cuts

How to Make Out-of-Plumb Corner Cuts

Out-of-plumb walls are concave, convex, or simply not perpendicular to the floor and ceiling at one or more points. It is a common condition. In some cases, the condition is caused by the fact that wallboard sheets have tapered edges to make taping joints easier and the tapers fall at the edge of a work area where trim is installed. In other cases, the condition may be caused by wall framing issues. In either case, you'll find that it's easier to adapt your trim pieces to the wall than to try and straighten out the finished wall surface. To do this, the trim pieces need to be cut to match the out-of-plumb area, to compensate for the taper in the panel. Another option is to install a running spacer along the bottom edge and cut your molding square, as on the previous page.

Stud location

Stud location

1 Place a T-bevel into the corner and press the blade flush to the wall surface. Tighten the adjustment knob so the blade conforms to the angle of the profile of the wall.

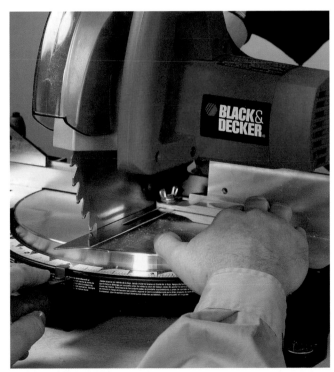

2 Transfer the angle of the T-bevel to the miter saw blade by locking the saw in the down position and adjusting the angle to match the angle of the T-bevel. Cut the molding to match the angle.

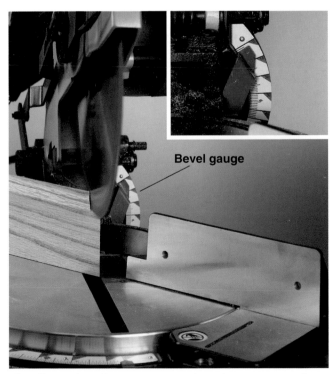

Bevel gauge

Tip: Occasionally, a compound cut is necessary for cutting miters on out-of-plumb corners. When this situation arises, set the bevel of the miter saw to match the out-of-plumb wall (inset photo) and miter the angle at the appropriate degree. Compound cuts can be difficult to get right the first time, so test the fit with a piece of scrap material first.

Coping is a tricky skill to learn, but a valuable capability to possess once you've got the process down. With very few exceptions, a coped cut can be made only with a hand saw (usually, a coping saw like the one shown in the photo above).

Making Coped Cuts

At first glance, coping moldings appears to be difficult work that only a professional would attempt. But, in actuality, coping only requires patience and the right tools. Whether a molding is installed flat against the wall, or is sprung to fill an inside corner junction, as with crown molding, the concept of coping is the same. It is essentially cutting back the body of a trim piece along its profile. This cutting is done at an angle so that only the face of the molding makes direct contact with the adjoining piece.

For beginners, coping a molding requires a coping saw, a utility knife, and a set of metal files with a variety of profiles. The initial cope cut is made with the coping saw and the joint is fitted with a utility knife and files. This fitting can be a long process, especially when working with intricate crown moldings, but the end results are superior to any other method.

Everything You Need

Tools: miter saw, metal files or rasp set, utility knife, pencil, tape measure, pneumatic finish nail gun, air compressor, air hose.

Materials: molding.

How to Cope-Cut Moldings

1 Measure, cut, and install the first trim piece. Square-cut the ends, butting them tightly into the corners, and nail the workpiece at the marked stud locations.

2 Cut the second piece of molding at a 45° angle as if it were an inside miter. The cut edge reveals the profile of the cope cut.

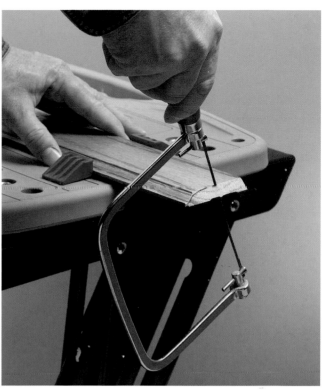

3 Starting with the most delicate edge of the molding, cut along the front edge of the molding with a coping saw, following the contour exactly. Bevel the cut at 45° to create a sharp edge along the contour.

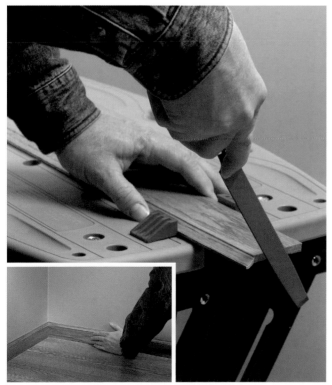

4 Test-fit the piece (inset photo) and use a metal file to fit the joint precisely. When the joint is properly fitted, nail the coped piece in place.

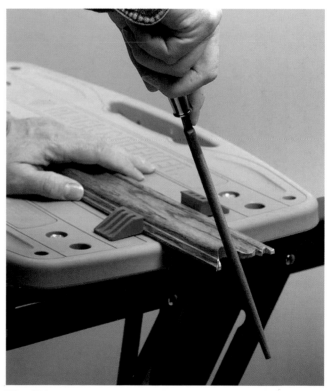

Tip: Trim components such as this chair rail can be complex to cope properly. A variety of rasps or metal files with different profiles is the key to fitting these joints tightly.

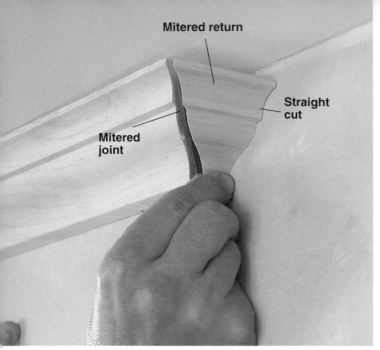

Mitered return

Straight cut

Mitered joint

Mitered returns finish molding ends that would otherwise be exposed. Miter the main piece as you would at an outside corner. Cut a miter on the return piece, then cut it to length with a straight cut so it butts to the wall. Attach the return piece with wood glue.

Everything You Need

Tools: combination square, utility knife, power miter saw, miter box and back saw, pencil, tape measure, pneumatic finish nail gun, air compressor, air hose, T-bevel.

Materials: molding, wood glue.

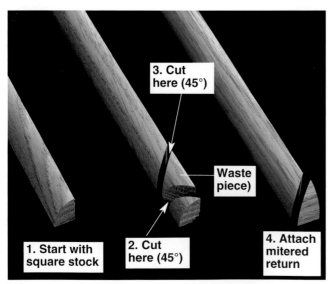

3. Cut here (45°)

Waste piece)

1. Start with square stock

2. Cut here (45°)

4. Attach mitered return

Returns are made from two 45° angle cuts. The scrap piece is removed and the return piece is glued into place.

Cutting Mitered Returns

Mitered returns are a decorative treatment used to hide the end grain of wood and provide a finished appearance when molding stops prior to the end of a wall. Mitered returns range from tiny pieces of base shoe up to very large crown moldings. They are also commonly used when installing a stool and apron treatment or on decorative friezes above doors.

Bevel returns are another simple return option for chair rails, baseboards, and base shoe. A bevel return is simply a cut at the end of the molding that "returns" the workpiece back to the wall at an angle. The biggest advantage to using mitered returns rather than bevel returns is that mitered returns already have a finish applied. Bevel returns require more touchups.

Cutting mitered returns for small moldings, such as quarter round, or for thin stock, such as baseboard, can be tricky when using a power miter saw. The final cut of the process leaves the return loose where it can sometimes be thrown from the saw due to the air current of the blade. Plan on using a piece of trim that is long enough to cut comfortably, or you will find yourself fighting the saw.

How to Cut Mitered Base Shoe Returns

1 Measure and mark the molding to length. Adjust the miter saw blade to 45° and back-miter the molding, cutting the front edge to the desired overall length of the trim. Nail the back-mitered piece in place using a square to line it up flush with the edge of the door casing.

2 Adjust the blade of the miter saw to the opposite 45° angle and miter-cut the molding using a slow, steady stroke.

Mitered return

3 Hold the mitered molding against the baseboard at a right angle above the installed base shoe. Mark the molding at the depth of the installed base shoe. Square-cut the molding at the cutoff mark. Because making this cut with a power saw is very dangerous, use a miter box and a back saw. The cut-off piece will be the mitered return piece.

Mitered return

4 Check the fit of the return against the baseboard. If it is too small repeat steps 3 and 4, making the piece slightly larger. If the return is too large, trim it to fit with a utility knife or sandpaper. Once the return fits properly, glue it in place with wood glue.

Beveled return

OPTION: Beveled returns are a quick and simple alternative to mitered returns. They require finish touchup after the trim is installed.

A scarf joint is a glorified butt joint that's used to join two pieces of trim that are the same profile and are in line with one another. Scarf joints are easier to conceal than butt joints and also less prone to opening and showing gaps when humidity or temperature change.

Cutting Scarf Joints

Scarf joint is a technical term for the miter joint used to join two pieces of trim over a long length. This joint is not difficult to cut, but should always be laid out over a stud location so it can be properly fastened.

Whenever possible, position scarf joints so they point away from the main entry to the room (or another area from which the joint is most likely to be viewed). Doing so will hide the joint from view at a quick glance.

When forming scarf joints in moldings that will be painted, lightly sand the mating surfaces of the joint to flush out any imperfections and fill any resulting gaps with filler. Prefinished stain-grade materials need to be tightly fitted and the nail holes filled with putty.

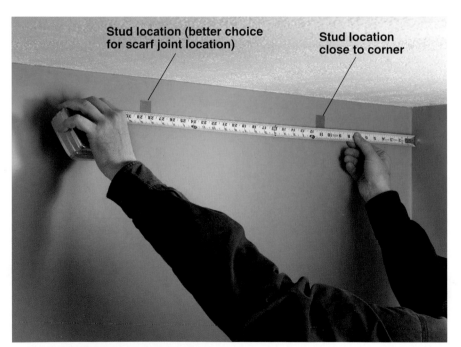

Stud location (better choice for scarf joint location)

Stud location close to corner

Layout tip. Determine the stud where the scarf joint will be located along the length of the run before cutting any of your stock. Divide the run as evenly as possible while optimizing material yield. In other words, avoid creating a joint too close to the end of the run because it can look unbalanced. Measure the length for the first piece of molding from the corner to the center of the stud location.

Everything You Need

Tools: miter saw, pencil, tape measure, pneumatic finish nail gun, air compressor, air hose.

Materials: molding.

TIP: Use a sliding compound miter saw to make scarf joint cuts on wide pieces of stock. These saws may be rented at most tool rental centers.

How to Cut a Scarf Joint

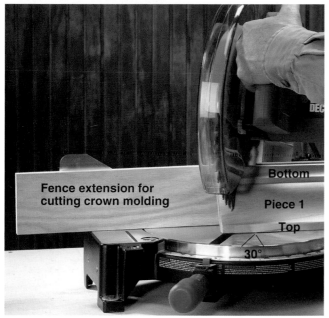

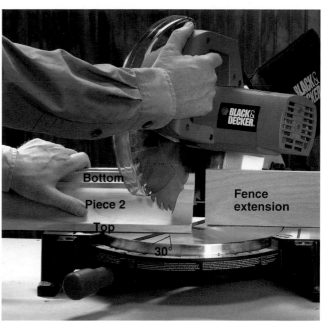

1 Cut the first piece of molding a couple of inches longer than its planned length, at a 30° angle. This angle should be back-beveled or back-mitered so the molding will fit over the open-cut end of the second piece. If you are cutting crown molding and the molding is taller than the fence of your power miter saw, attach a wood fence extension to the fence so you can position the molding properly on the saw table (see "Installing Crown Molding," p. 104).

2 Measure and cut the second piece of trim to length (so it will fall over a stud when installed—see tip, page 80), leaving the saw set at its original 30° angle. Make sure the second piece of molding is in the same orientation as the first (bottom edge up in photos above).

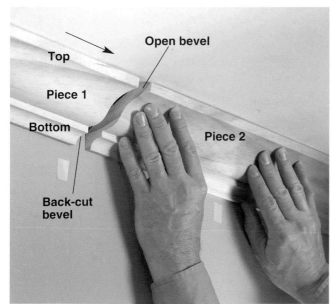

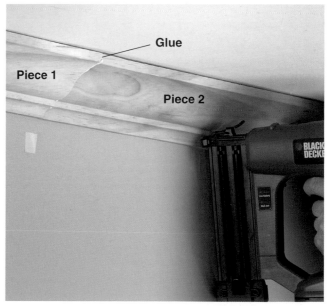

3 Test-fit the scarf joint on the wall (a helper is a great asset here). Have one person hold the piece with the open bevel (Piece 2 above) in position while the other person places the piece with the back-cut bevel over it. Check for a tight joint and then mark the back-cut piece for trimming to final length (if both ends of the run are inside corners, you'll have to overlap the open-cut piece and mark for cutting to length).

4 Tack the piece with the open bevel in position and apply wood glue (high-tack trim and molding glue are perfect here) to the open bevel. Reform the scarf joint and tack the back-cut piece in position. Finish nailing around the joint and then work your way toward each end with the nailer.

 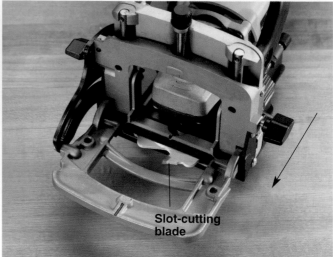

A biscuit joiner (also called a plate joiner) has a small circular blade tucked into a housing at the front of the saw. When you press the spring-loaded tool against the edge of a board, the self-registering blade emerges from the housing and engages the board edge, cutting a perfect slot.

Using A Biscuit Joiner

A biscuit joiner, also known as a plate joiner, is a specialty power tool used, along with football-shaped wood biscuits, to join two pieces of wood with a butt joint. Biscuit joiners have a horizontal circular saw blade that is safely hidden inside the body of the tool. When the tool is pressed against the edge of a board the blade emerges from its housing and cuts a semicircular slot in wood stock. A matching slot is then cut into an adjoining piece of wood, and a biscuit is coated with glue and inserted. The biscuit swells up in the opening and when the glue dries, helps to keep the boards in perfect alignment.

Biscuit joiners can be set to very precise cutting depths and heights, making them a versatile joining choice for a variety of applications. They are commonly used to join wood face frames as well as wood parts for furniture and cabinets.

Biscuit joints are similar in strength to traditional wood dowel joints but they are simpler and faster to make.

In order to produce strong joints with a biscuit joiner, the two surfaces to be joined should be cut squarely. Materials that are not square do not clamp properly and result in a loose joint that is easily broken.

Biscuits are available in three common sizes for different-sized joints (#0, #10, and #20, from smallest to largest). Any stock narrower than 2" should be joined with an alternative joining method such as pocket holes.

How to Use a Biscuit Joiner

1 Lay out the two mating pieces of material on a flat surface. Holding the material together with moderate hand pressure, draw a line midway across the joint with a pencil. When joining materials that have already been finish sanded, make small marks to avoid excess sanding.

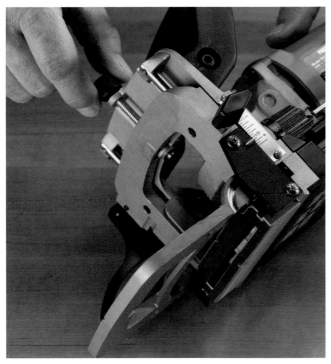

2 Set the height of the fence on the biscuit joiner to one-half of the thickness of the material to be joined (⅜" for ¾"-thick stock).

3 Turn the blade depth adjustment knob to the appropriate biscuit size for the project. The size (#20 shown above) is written on the face of the biscuit for easy reference.

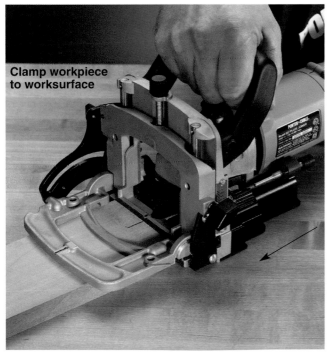

Clamp workpiece to worksurface

4 Clamp the first workpiece to a flat worksurface, and align the registration mark on the biscuit joiner with the cutting line drawn in Step 1. Cut the first biscuit slot by pressing the joiner firmly into the edge of the workpiece, keeping a firm grip on both to avoid slipping out of alignment. Cut a slot in the mating workpiece the same way.

5 Spread wood glue into both slots and press a biscuit into one of the slots. Slide the second piece over the remaining edge of the biscuit, lining up the reference marks from Step 1. Clamp the pieces in place until the glue dries.

Pocket hole screws require a pocket hole jig to be used effectively, but if you plan on doing a lot of trim carpentry or cabinetry you'll be glad you made the investment. This joinery method is fast, strong, and virtually foolproof.

Using a Pocket Hole Jig

A pocket hole jig is a specialty joining tool that allows you to join two pieces of square stock quickly and efficiently. There are a variety of pocket hole systems available, from fully automated machines to inexpensive plastic or aluminum body jigs. The smaller versions are most common among hobby woodworkers and do-it-yourselfers.

Pocket hole jigs utilize any power drill to drill angled holes through a workpiece. The workpiece is then clamped in place and a special pocket hole screw is driven through the angled hole into the mating workpiece. The resulting joint is strong, but when combined with wood glue and allowed to dry, the joint becomes extremely durable, especially when joining materials of ¾" thickness or greater.

Pocket hole jigs offer a few distinct advantages over other methods of joinery, including biscuit joining. The greatest advantage of a pocket hole jig is clamp time. Pocket hole joints don't require any clamping, so once two pieces are joined you can move on to installing them or adding additional joints. There is no need to wait for the glue to dry or to clamp the assembly overnight.

Another advantage of a pocket hole jig is that it can be used to join pieces as small as 1" wide. Unlike a biscuit joiner, which is limited to the size of biscuit available, pocket joints only need room for a single screw to be driven in place.

Pocket hole joints are also extremely quick and easy to produce. Traditional joinery methods require time and patience. Pocket joints only need a power drill and jig.

Because pocket holes are highly visible, they normally are used only in areas that will be hidden from view. A good example would be the face frame of a cabinet. The pocket holes are buried inside the cabinet where they generally won't be seen. Some manufacturers offer pocket hole plugs to match commonly used wood species. These plugs are inserted into glued pocket holes. When the glue dries, the plugs are cut off and sanded smooth.

Everything You Need

Tools: drill with bits, pocket hole jig

Materials: carpenter's glue, square wood stock, pocket hole screws.

How to Use a Pocket Hole Jig

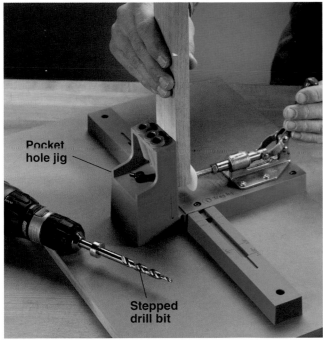

Pocket hole jig

Stepped drill bit

1 Insert the specialty stepped drill bit into your drill and tighten the chuck. Place the edge or end of the workpiece to be joined in the bottom of the pocket hole jig with the back facing the drill bit guide holes. Tighten the clamp, holding the workpiece firmly in place.

2 Place the tip of the stepped bit into the drill guides and drill out the holes, making sure the bit bottoms out on the workpiece. The guide will position the bit automatically. Do not try to change the path of the bit.

Mating work-piece requires no predrilling

Pocket holes

3 Apply wood glue to the edge of the pieces and arrange them on a flat work surface. Place a clamp over the seam of the joint, clamping the pieces down to the table so they are flush in height and tightly together.

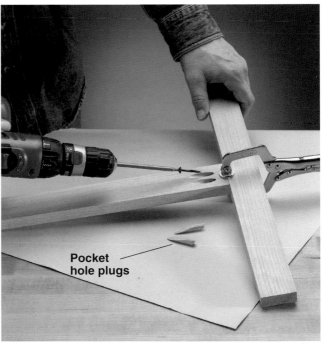

Pocket hole plugs

4 Change the drill bit to a long-neck square drive bit. Place a pocket screw on the bit and drive it into one of the holes until glue squeezes from the joint. Drive the second screw, remove the clamp, and wipe away any excess glue with a damp rag. Glue plugs into the pocket holes if you wish.

Fitting Trim Around Obstructions

Cutting and fitting joints between workpieces can be a challenge, but that challenge increases when dealing with obstructions such as electrical outlets, HVAC system components, and plumbing or cable TV lines. These obstructions feed the rooms of our homes with the systems we want or need, and many times are crudely installed as if they were an afterthought. Installing new trim allows you the unique opportunity to make these obstructions part of the room again. With thoughtful trimwork, electrical outlets will become less of an eyesore and cable TV lines will appear as if they are supposed to be there, not as if they were thrown in quickly and hastily.

In many instances, the new trim you are installing will need to be form-fitted around an obstruction. If the new trim would completely encompass the obstruction area, consider cutting a hole in the trim for the object to pass through. Building up a backer collar for an obstruction is also a decorative option. All of these adjustments are easily made with power tools such as a belt sander, drill with bits, or a jig saw. These tools make quick work out of difficult alignment issues.

For ideas on dealing with heat vents and cold air returns see page 95.

This baseboard molding has been trimmed to allow a floor transition molding to run underneath it. The technique is similar to making a coped cut (see p. 76).

Mitered returns (left) and beveled returns (right) are techniques used to terminate a molding with an exposed end where it meets an obstruction, such as the base shoe that runs into the door casing above (see pages 78 to 79).

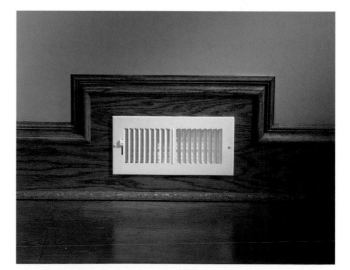

Building out is one way to handle a larger obstruction, like the wall-mounted heat register shown above (see page 95 for other methods of dealing with heat registers). When using the build-out approach, strive to keep the spacing around the added trim as symmetrical as possible so it does not look unplanned.

Tips for Fitting Trim Around Obstructions

To cut holes in trim to fit around obstructions, trace the outline of the area to be cut out on the finished piece. Start the cutout by drilling a hole in the corner of the outline and then trim out the area with a jig saw. Stay just inside the cutting lines and finish removing material to the lines using a wood file.

Cutting switchplate covers is easier than making cutouts in door and window casing. Do not remove more than ¼" or so of the coverplate material. If you do need to make a small cutout in case molding, a rotary cutting tool can do the job while the molding is still on the wall.

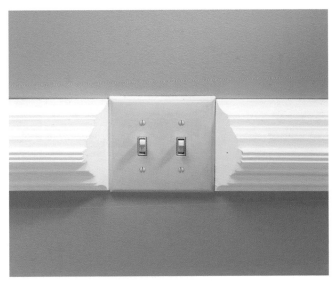

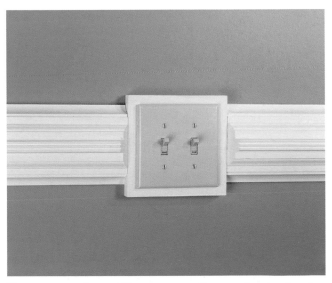

When electrical cover plates fall in the installation path of a trim component, consider returning the molding to the wall with a bevel-cut return similar to the base shoe returns seen on page 86. Bevel returns look cleaner than square edges and are simple to create with a power miter saw.

For a more decorative approach, construct a backing board to place behind the obstruction, and return the moldings into the board. Backing boards can be made from 1× material if the trim is ¾" thick or thinner. Cut edge profiles on the backing board with a router for a more decorative edge.

Installing Trimwork

Baseboard doesn't need to be fancy to be effective. Without a shoe or a cap, a plain, one-piece base molding makes a neat transition from floor to wall.

Everything You Need

Tools: pencil, tape measure, power miter saw, T-bevel, coping saw, metal file set, pneumatic finish nail gun & compressor.

Materials: moldings, pneumatic fasteners, carpenter's glue, finishing putty.

Installing One-piece Base Molding

Baseboard trim is installed to conceal the joint between the finished floor and the wallcovering (a necessary feature of a house). Installing plain, one-piece baseboard such as ranch-style base or cove base is a straightforward project. Outside corner joints are mitered, inside corners are coped, and long runs are joined with scarf cuts.

The biggest difficulty to installing base is dealing with out-of-plumb and nonsquare corners. However, a T-bevel makes these obstacles easy to overcome.

Plan the order of your installation prior to cutting any pieces and lay out a specific piece for each length of wall. It may be helpful to mark the type of cut on the back of each piece so you don't have any confusion during the install.

Locate all studs and mark them with painter's tape 6" higher than your molding height. If you need to make any scarf joints along a wall, make sure they fall on the center of a stud. Before you begin nailing trim in place, take the time to prefinish the moldings. Doing so will minimize the clean-up afterward.

How to Install One-piece Base Molding

1 Measure, cut, and install the first piece of baseboard. Butt both ends into the corners tightly. For longer lengths, it is a good idea to cut the piece slightly oversized (up to 1/16" on strips over 10 ft. long) and "spring" it into place. Nail the molding in place with two nails at every stud location.

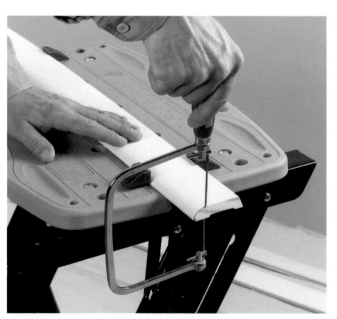

2 Cut the second piece of molding oversized by 6" to 10" and cope-cut the adjoining end to the first piece. Fine-tune the cope with a metal file and sandpaper. Dry fit the joint adjusting it as necessary to produce a tight-fitting joint.

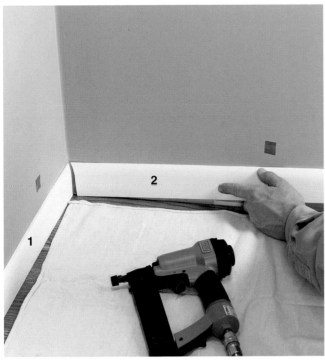

3 Check the corner for square with a framing square. If necessary, adjust the miter cut of your saw. Use a T-bevel to transfer the proper angle. (see page 73). Cut the second piece (coped) to length and install it with two nails at each stud location.

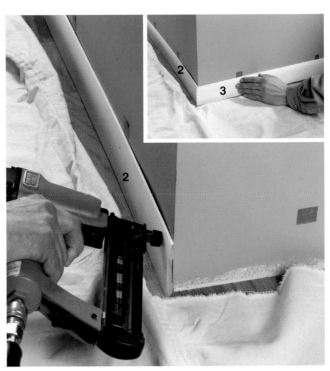

4 Adjust the miter angle of your saw to cut the adjoining outside corner piece. Test fit the cut to ensure a tight joint (inset photo). Remove the mating piece of trim and fasten the first piece for the outside corner joint.

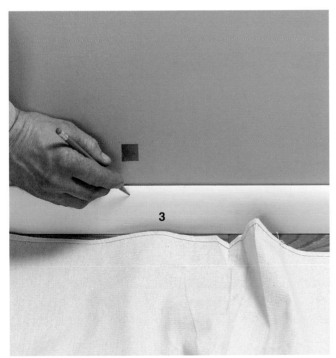

5 Lay out any scarf joints by placing the piece in position so that the previous joint is tight, and then marking the center of a stud location nearest the opposite end. Set the angle of your saw to a 30° angle and cut the molding at the marked location (see pages 80 to 81).

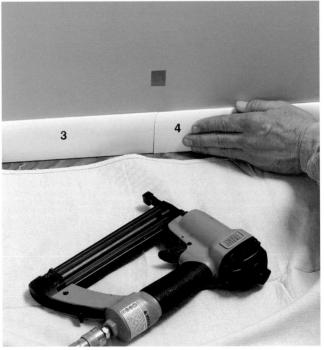

6 Nail the third piece in place, making sure the outside corner joint is tight. Cut the end of the fourth piece to match the scarf joint angle and nail it in place with two nails at each stud location. Add the remaining pieces of molding, fill the nail holes with putty, and apply a final coat of finish.

Installing a Built-up Base Molding

Built-up base molding is made up of several strips of wood (usually three) that are combined for a particular effect. It is installed in two common scenarios: to match existing trim in other rooms of a house; or to match a stock, one-piece molding that is not available.

Installing a built-up base molding is no more difficult than a standard one-piece molding, because the same installation techniques are used. However, built-up base molding offers a few advantages over standard stock moldings. Wavy floors and walls are easier to conceal, and the height of the molding is completely up to you, making heat registers and other obstructions easier to deal with.

In this project, the base molding is made of high-grade plywood rather than solid stock lumber. Plywood is more economical and dimensionally stable than solid lumber and can be built up to any depth, as well as cut down to any height. Keep in mind that plywood molding is less durable than solid wood, and is only available in 8 and 10-ft. lengths, making joints more frequent.

Everything You Need

Tools: pneumatic finish nail gun, air compressor, air hose, miter saw, pencil, tape measure, hammer, nail set, table saw or straight edge guide and circular saw, sandpaper, power sander.

Materials: ¾" finish-grade oak plywood, base shoe molding, cap molding, 2" finish nails, wood putty.

92

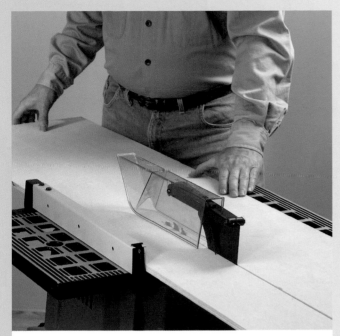

Cut the plywood panel into 6" strips with a table saw or a straightedge guide and a circular saw. Lightly sand the strips, removing any splinters left from the saw. Then, apply the finish of your choice to the moldings and the plywood strips.

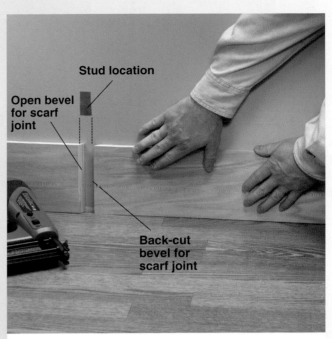

Stud location

Open bevel
for scarf
joint

Back-cut
bevel for
scarf joint

Install the plywood strips with 2" finish nails driven at stud locations. Use scarf joints on continuous runs, driving pairs of fasteners into the joints. Cut and install moldings so that all scarf joints fall at stud locations.

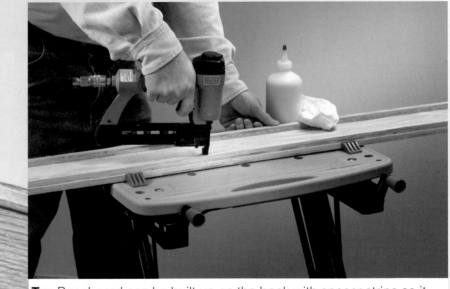

TIP: Baseboard can be built up on the back with spacer strips so it will project further out from the wall. This can allow you to match existing casings, or to create the impression of a thicker molding. However, the cap rail needs to be thick enough to cover the plywood edge completely, or the core of the panel may be visible.

Tips for Installing Built-up Base Molding

Test-fit inside corner butt joints before cutting a workpiece. If the walls are not square or straight, angle or bevel the end cut a few degrees to fit the profile of the adjoining piece. The cap molding will cover any gaps at the top of the joint. See illustration, page 92.

Miter outside corners squarely at 45°. Use wood glue and 1¼" brad nails to pull the mitered pieces tight, and then nail the base to the wall at stud locations with 2" finish nails. Small gaps at the bottom or top of the base molding will be covered with cap or base shoe.

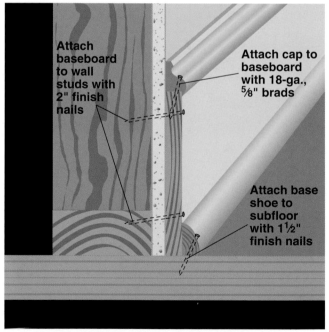

Use a brad nailer with 18-gauge, ⅝" brads to install the cap and base shoe moldings along the edges of the plywood base. Fit scarf joints on longer lengths, coped joints on inside corners, and miter joints on outside corners. Stagger the seams so that they do not line up with the base molding seams, following the suggested nailing pattern above. Set any protruding nails with a nail set and fill all nail holes with putty.

Built-up baseboard requires more attention to the nailing schedule than simple one-piece baseboards. The most important consideration (other than making sure your nails are all driven into studs or other solid wood), is that the base shoe must be attached to the floor, while the baseboard is attached to the wall. This way, as the gap between the wall and floor changes, the parts of the built-up molding can change with them.

Options with Heat Registers

Installing base molding around heat registers and cold-air returns can sometimes be challenging. Register thickness and height vary, complicating installation. Here are a few methods that can be employed for trimming around these obstructions. See pages 86 to 87 for more information on working around obstructions that impede your trim project.

Adjust the height of your base molding to completely surround the heat register opening, then cut a pocket out of the base for the heat register to slide into. Install the base shoe and cap trim molding continuously across the edges of the base molding.

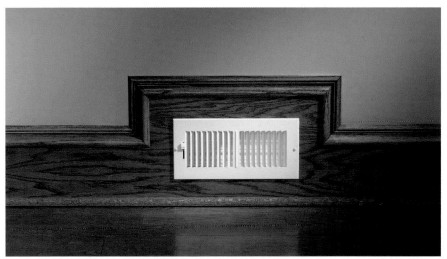

Install a taller backer block to encompass larger register openings. Cut a hole the same size as the duct opening in the backer block and cover the edges of the plywood with cap rail, mitering at the corners. Butt the base molding into the sides of the register. Cut and install returns for the base shoe flush with the ends of the register.

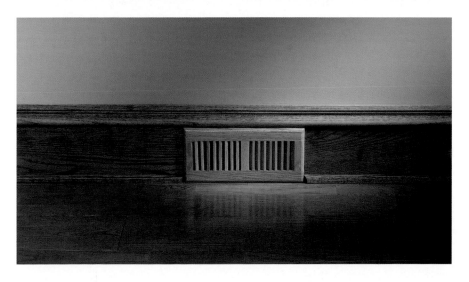

Install a wooden heat register for a less noticeable appearance. Wooden registers can be finished to match your trim and are available through most hardwood floor retailers. Butt the base molding into the ends of the register cover and bevel the front edges of the base shoe to match the depth of the register.

Installing Picture Rail

Picture rail molding is a specialty molding that was installed in many older homes so the homeowners could avoid making nail holes in the finished walls. Picture rail molding is a simple but elegant way to add style to any room. Special picture hanging hooks slide over the molding and artwork may be hung with a cord over the hook. Picture rail molding also provides its own decorative touch, breaking up the vertical lines from floor to ceiling. For this reason, it is also installed as a decorative touch by itself.

Picture rail molding is easy to install but should be reinforced with screws, not brads or nails, especially if you are hanging large, heavy items. Depending upon the style of your home, picture rail can be hung anywhere from 1 ft. to a few inches down from the ceiling. In some homes, picture rail is added just below the cornice or crown molding to add an additional layer of depth. When applied this way, it is commonly referred to as a frieze board.

In the example shown, the picture rail is installed using a level line to maintain height. If your ceiling is uneven, you may choose to install picture rail a set distance from the ceiling to avoid an uneven appearance.

Everything You Need

Tools: ladder, pencil, stud finder, tape measure, power miter saw, T-bevel, pneumatic finish nail gun & compressor, 4-ft. level or laser level, drill with bits.

Materials: painter's tape, moldings, pneumatic fasteners, 1⅝" wallboard screws, hole filler.

How to Install Picture Rail Molding

1 Measure down the desired distance from the ceiling and draw a level reference line around the room using a pencil and a 4-ft. level (or, take advantage of modern technology and use a laser level). While you are up there, use a stud finder to locate the framing members, and mark the locations on the walls with blue painter's tape.

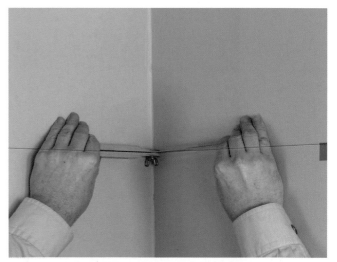

2 Use a T-bevel to measure the angle of the corner, tightening the lock nut with the blade and the handle on the reference line. Place the T-bevel on the table of your power miter saw and adjust the miter blade so that it matches the angle. See page 73.

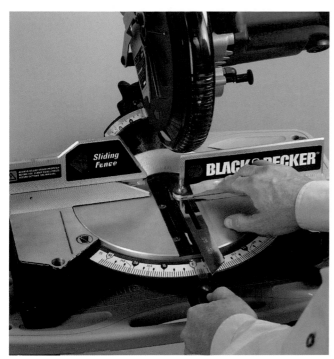

3 Most corners are close to 90°, but to cut a tight inside corner, the actual angle must be divided exactly in half. With the T-bevel tight to the fence, read the angle the saw is set to when it aligns with the T-bevel. If the blade is angled to the right of zero degrees the angle is larger than 90; to the left, smaller.

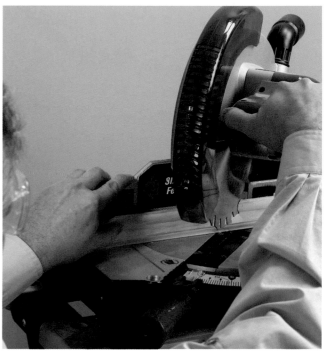

4 Read the angle from the miter saw table, divide the number by two, and add or subtract that number from 45 degrees to find the proper cutting angle for each corner. Cut each molding slightly longer than the measured length.

5 Nail the molding at the stud locations covering the level line around the room (if you're using a laser level, you simply keep it in position and turned on to cast a reference line you can follow). After each molding is completely nailed in place, go back to each stud location and drive 1⅝" wallboard screws into the molding through counter-bored pilot holes.

6 Fill nail holes with wood filler. Let the filler dry and sand it smooth. Then apply a final coat of paint over the molding face.

Chair rail once was installed to protect fragile walls from chair backs, but today it is mainly installed as a decorative accent that breaks up dull walls visually.

Installing Chair Rail

Chair rail molding typically runs horizontally along walls at a height of around 36" (the rule of thumb is to install it one-third of the way up the wall). Originally installed to protect walls from collisions with chair backs, today chair rail is commonly used to divide a wall visually. Chair rail may cap wainscoting, serve as a border for wallpaper, or divide two different colors on a wall. Or, more interesting chair rail profiles can be effective alone on a one-color wall.

Stock chair rail moldings are available at most lumberyards and home centers. However, more intricate and elaborate chair rails can be crated by combining multiple pieces of trim. Keep in mind the height of your existing furnishings when installing a chair rail. It is not good to find out that the new molding has a bad visual effect with your couch or chair backs when the project is completed.

Everything You Need

Tools: pencil, stud finder, tape measure, power miter saw, 4-ft. level, air compressor, finish nail gun, metal file set.

Materials: moldings, pneumatic fasteners, painter's tape, carpenter's glue, finishing putty, finishing materials.

How to Install Chair Rail

1 On the starting wall of your installation, measure up the desired height at which you plan to install the chair rail, minus the width of the molding. Mark a level line at this height around the room. Locate all studs along the walls and mark their locations with painter's tape below the line.

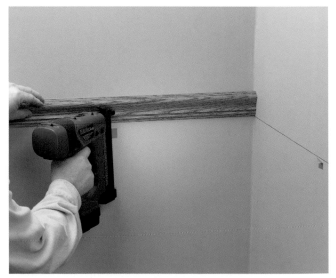

2 Measure, cut, and install the first piece of chair rail with the ends cut squarely, butting into both walls (in a wall run with two inside corners). Nail the molding in place with two 2" finish nails at each stud location.

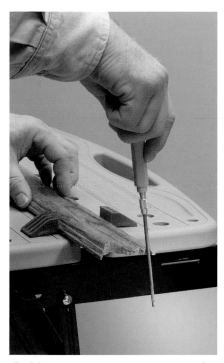

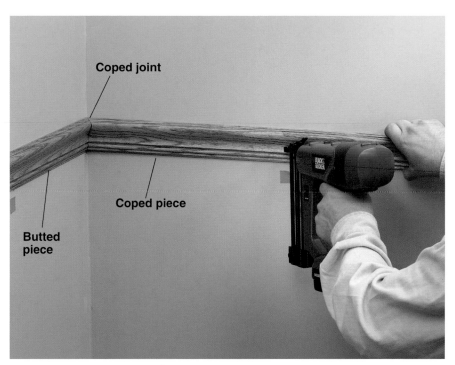

Coped joint

Coped piece

Butted piece

3 Miter-cut the second piece of molding with a power miter saw and then cope the end with a coping saw. Clean up the edge of the cope cut with a metal file to ensure a tight fit. Dry-fit the piece to check for any gaps in the joint.

4 When the coped joint fits tightly, measure, mark, and cut the opposing end of the second piece of trim squarely with a miter saw. Nail the second piece in place with two nails at each stud location. Follow the level line with the bottom edge of the molding.

5 Install the third piece of chair rail with a cope cut at one end. Use a butt joint where the molding runs into door and window casings. Fill all nail holes with putty and apply a final coat of finish to the molding.

Option: Cut a mitered return for the chair rail in areas where it will end without joining into another molding. Cut the return with a miter saw and glue it in place, using painter's tape to hold it until the glue dries.

Installing a Built-up Chair Rail

Designing and installing a built-up chair rail can be a very creative project that adds a considerable amount of style to any room. For the project shown, five smaller pieces of trim are combined with a 1 x 4 filler strip to create a bold, strong chair rail. If you are considering a larger built-up chair rail, make sure the existing base and crown moldings of the room will not be overshadowed. A good scale rule to remember is that chair rail should always be smaller than the crown or base.

If you plan to design your own molding, the choices are just about endless. It is a good idea to mimic the style of your existing moldings so that the new chair rail will not look out of place. If the room you are installing in currently has no chair rail, consider new wall finishes as well. Two-tone painted walls will emphasize the transition of a chair rail, as will changing the finish from paint to wallpaper or wainscoting.

A built-up chair rail is made up of several styles of moldings, so the design options are virtually unlimited. The profile shown here features a strip of screen retainer on top of two pieces of profiled door stop. The stop molding is attached to a 1 x 4 filler that is then softened at the top and bottom edges with cover molding.

Choosing a Chair Rail Return

Before you begin installing the molding pieces of the built-up chair rail, decide what type of return you will use. Returns are finish details that occur in areas where different moldings meet at perpendicular angles, or quit in the middle of a wall. A **beveled return (left)** is a bit difficult to produce but has a clean look. On some built-up chair rail, you can take advantage of the depth of the molding by butting the back moldings up to the obstructions but running the cap moldings onto the surface **(right)**.

How to Install a Built-Up Chair Rail

1 On the starting wall of your installation, mark the desired height of the first chair rail component you will install (here, the 1 × 4 filler strip). At this height, mark a level line around the room. Locate all studs along the walls and mark their locations with painter's tape above the line.

2 Cut and install the 1 × 4 filler strip so that the top edge of the strip follows the level line around the room. Fasten the strip with two, 2½" finish nails driven at every stud location. Butt the ends of the filler strip together, keeping in mind that the joints will be covered by additional moldings.

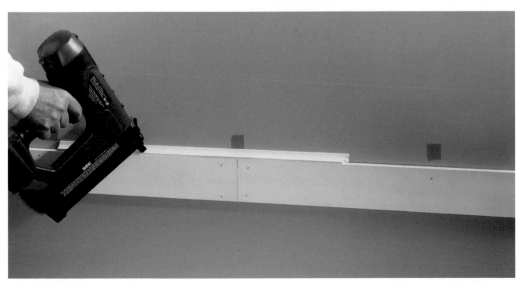

3 Cut and install the upper piece of cove molding around the room, nailing it flush to the top edge of the 1 × 4 filler strip. Use scarf joints on long runs, coped joints at inside corners and mitered joints on outside corners. Drive one nail at every stud location into the wall and one nail between each stud down into the filler strip.

(continued next page)

How to Install a Built-up Chair Rail (continued)

4 Install the lower piece of cove molding flush with the bottom edge of the filler strip. Use the same nailing sequence as with the upper cove molding. Cut scarf joints on long runs, coped joints at inside corners, and mitered joints on outside corners.

5 Measure, cut, and install the upper piece of stop molding around the room, driving two 2½" finish nails at each stud location. Cut scarf joints, coped joints, and mitered joints as necessary for each piece. Stagger the seams of the scarf joints on the stop molding so that they do not line up with the scarf joints of the cove moldings.

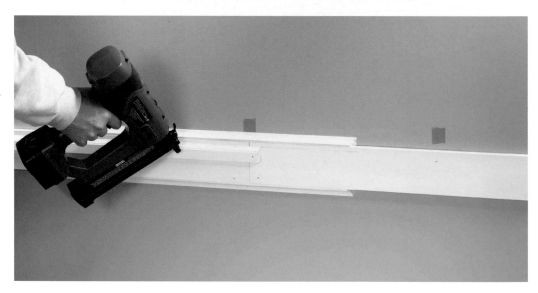

6 Install the lower piece of stop molding around the room, keeping the edge of the molding flush with the bottom edge of the filler strip. Fit each joint using the appropriate joinery method. Drive two nails at each stud location.

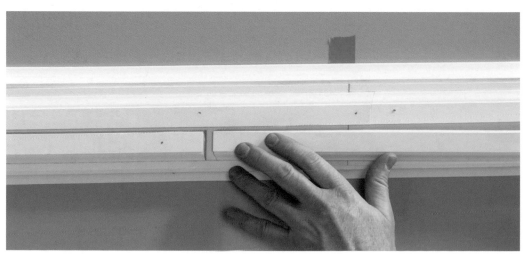

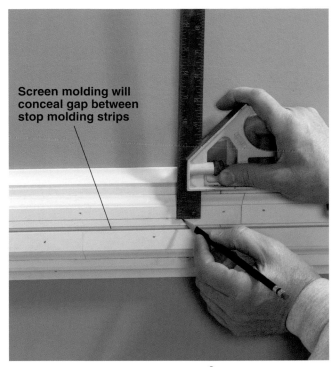

Screen molding will conceal gap between stop molding strips

7 Set a combination square to 1⅜". Rest the body of the square on the top edge of the upper stop molding and use the blade of the square as a guide to mark a reference line around the room. This line represents the top edge of the screen molding.

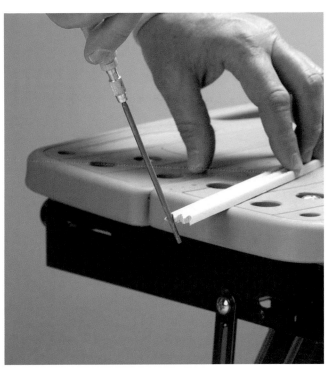

8 Install the screen retainer molding, as with the other moldings, using the appropriate joints necessary. Fine-tune the cope cuts using a round metal file. Nail the molding in place with a brad nailer and 1⅝" brad nails. Keep the top edge of the molding flush with the reference line from step 7.

9 Set any nail heads with a nail set and fill all the nail holes with paintable wood filler. Check for any gaps in the joinery and fill them as well. Let the filler dry and sand it smooth with 180-grit sandpaper. Wipe the moldings with a dry cloth to remove any dust.

10 Use a paintbrush to apply a final coat of paint to the moldings. Cover the finished floor with a drop cloth and protect the lower portion of the wall from drips by masking it off with plastic if necessary.

Basic crown molding softens the transitions between walls and ceilings. If it is made from quality hardwood crown molding can be quite beautiful when installed and finished with a clear topcoat. But historically, it is most often painted—either the same color as the ceiling (your eye tends to see it as a ceiling molding, not a wall molding) or with highly elaborate painted and carved details.

Installing Basic Crown Molding

Simply put, crown molding is angled trim that bridges the joint between the ceiling and the wall. In order to cover this joint effectively, crown moldings are "sprung." This means that the top and bottom edges of the molding have been beveled, so when the molding is tilted away from the wall at an angle the tops and bottoms are flush on the wall and ceiling surfaces. Some crown moldings have a 45° angle at both the top and the bottom edges; another common style ("38° crown") has a 38° angle on one edge and a 52° angle on the other edge.

Installing crown molding can be a challenging and sometimes confusing process. Joints may be difficult for you to visualize before cutting, and wall and ceiling irregularities can be hard to overcome. If you have not worked on crown molding joints before, it is recommended that your first attempt be made with paint-grade materials. Stain-grade crown is commonly made of solid hardwood stock, which makes for expensive cutting errors, and difficulty concealing irregularities in joints.

Inside corner joints of crown molding should be cope cut, not mitered, except in the case of very intricate profile crown that is virtually impossible to cope (and must therefore be mitered). While mitering inside corners may appear to save time and produce adequate results, after a few changing seasons the joints will open up and be even more difficult to conceal.

Although many people install crown molding with nails driven directly into the ceiling and wall framing, irregularities in the surfaces are easier to overcome and adjustments are easier to make if the molding is nailed to a backing board. Backing boards or angled cleats are a convenient way to anchor crown molding without concern for stud or joist locations. They also eliminate the need for construction adhesive along the joint between the ceiling and the molding, on walls that are parallel with ceiling joists. Nailing the crown to a solid backer will allow you to hide many irregularities in the walls and ceiling, but not all of them. To fill gaps ⅛" or smaller use paintable caulk. To fill in gaps on clear-coat

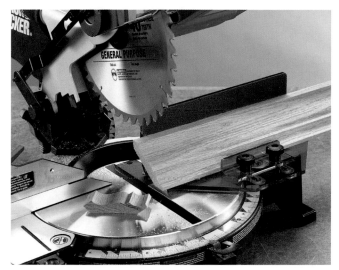

Cutting compound miters is tricky. Throughout this book, crown molding is shown being mitered with the workpiece held against a fence or fence extension. This hand-held approach is quick and effective, but takes some getting used to. A practically foolproof option is to use an adjustable jig, such as the compound miter jig shown here.

finishes, tape off the edge of the molding with painter's tape and fill the gap with wallboard compound.

There are two methods to cutting crown molding on a power miter saw. The first is to hold the molding in a sprung position against the fence

with the top edge of the molding against the saw table, or upside down. In this set-up, the position of the molding relative to the saw table and fence is the same as it will be relative to the wall and ceiling.This may sound difficult to do accurately, but with a 10" or a 12" saw it works quite well for basic crown moldings.

If you have a larger molding that does not fit under the blade of your saw in the sprung position, you'll need to cut this molding flat on the saw table with a compound saw. Many power miter saws have positive stops on both the miter and the bevel gauge that make it possible to cut crown molding at compound angles while it is lying flat on the saw table.

Everything You Need

Tools: pencil, tape measure, circular saw, straightedge guide, drill with bits, coping saw, power miter saw, pneumatic finish nail gun, framing square or combination square, nail set, hammer, metal files.

Materials: 2 × 4 material for backing, 3" wallboard screws, carpenter's glue, crown molding, 2", 1½" finish nails, fine-grit sandpaper, hole filler, paint and brushes.

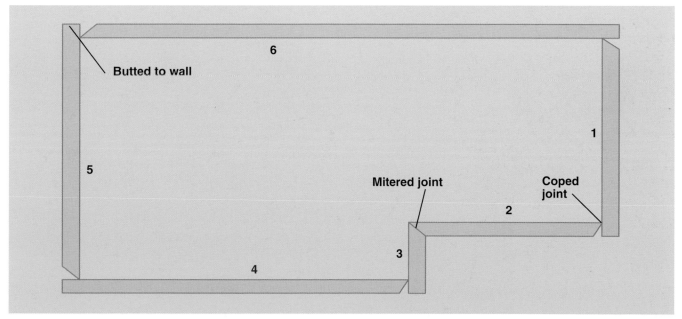

Plan the order of the installation to minimize the number of difficult joints on each piece and use the longest pieces for the most visible sections of wall. Notice that the left end of first piece is cope-cut rather than butted into the wall. Cope-cutting the first end eliminates the need to cope-cut both ends of the final piece, and places the cuts in the same direction. This simplifies your installation, making the method to cut each piece similar.

How to Use Backers to Install Crown Molding

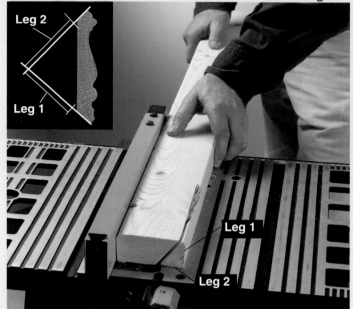

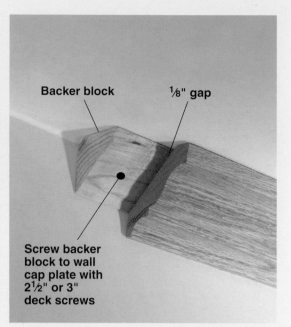

Backer block

⅛" gap

Screw backer block to wall cap plate with 2½" or 3" deck screws

1 Installing crown molding is greatly simplified if you first attach triangular backers in the crotch area between the walls and ceilings. You can run the backers continuously along all walls or you can space them at regular intervals for use as nailers. To measure the required length for the triangle legs, set a piece of the crown molding in the sprung position in a square in an orientation like the inset photo above. Rip triangular backer strips from 2× stock on your table saw, with the blade set at 45°.

2 Locate the wall studs with a stud finder and mark the locations on the wall with blue painter's tape. Secure the backer block to the wall by driving 2½" or 3" deck screws at an angle through the block and into the top plate of the wall. Now, your crown molding can be attached to the backers wherever you'd like to nail it. Install crown according to the following instructions.

How to Install Basic Crown Molding

Test cope cuts against this profile

1 Cut a piece of crown molding about 1-ft. long with square ends. Temporarily install the piece in the corner of the last installation wall with two screws driven into the blocking. This piece serves as a template for the first cope cut on the first piece of molding.

2 Place the first piece of molding upside down and sprung against the fence of the miter saw. Mark a reference line on the fence for placement of future moldings, and cut the first coped end with an inside miter cut to reveal the profile of the piece.

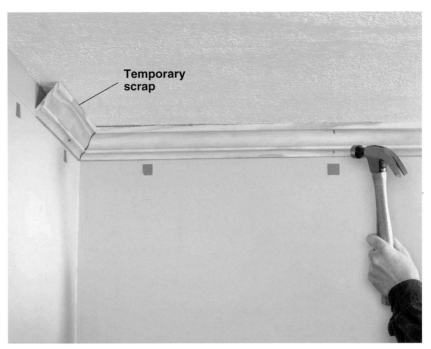

Temporary scrap

3 Cope-cut the end of the first piece with a coping saw. Carefully cut along the profile, angling the saw as you cut to back-bevel the cope. Test-fit the coped cut against the temporary scrap from Step 1. Fine-tune the cut with files and fine-grit sandpaper.

4 Measure, cut to length, and install the first piece of crown molding, leaving the end near the temporary scrap loose for final fitting of the last piece. Nail the molding at the top and bottom of each stud location.

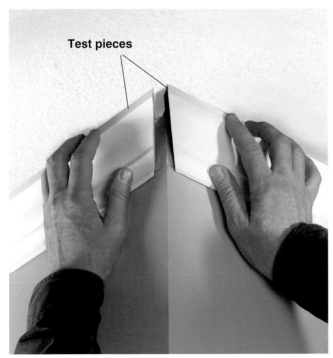

Test pieces

5 Cut two test pieces to check the fit of outside corners. Start with each molding cut at 45°, adjusting the angles larger or smaller until the joints are tight. Make sure the test moldings are properly aligned and are flush with the ceiling and walls. Make a note of your saw settings once the joint fits tightly.

6 Position the actual stock so a cut end is flush against the wall at one end and, at the other end, mark the outside corner on the back edge of the molding. Miter-cut the piece at the mark, according to the angles you noted on the test pieces.

(continued next page)

How to Install Basic Crown Molding (continued)

7 Measure and cut the third piece with an outside corner miter to match the angle of your test pieces. Cut the other end squarely, butting it into the corner. Install the piece with nails driven at stud locations. Install the subsequent pieces of crown molding, coping the front end and butting the other as you work around the room.

8 To fit the final piece, cope the end and cut it to length. Remove the temporary scrap piece from Step 3, and slide the last molding into position. Nail the last piece at the stud locations when the joints fit well, and finish nailing the first piece.

How to Make a Scarf Joint Using Crown Molding

Use scarf joints when necessary, laying out the joint so it falls over a stud location. Keep the saw at the same angle to cut the second piece, and apply a bead of glue to the joint before nailing the molding in place. See pages 80 to 81 for more information.

Lightly sand the face of the scarf joint with fine-grit sandpaper to smooth out the face of the joint.

9 Fill all nail holes (use spackling compound if painting; wait until the finish is applied and fill with tinted putty for clear finishes). Use a putty knife to force spackling compound or tinted wood putty into loose joints and caulk gaps ⅛" or smaller between the molding and the wall or ceiling with flexible, paintable, latex caulk.

10 For gaps larger than ⅛" between the molding and the wall or ceiling, use a wallboard knife and compound to skim coat the wall and fill in the gap. Protect the finished surface of the molding with painter's tape.

11 Lightly sand the filled nail holes and joint gaps with fine sandpaper. Sand the nail hole flush with the surface of the moldings and apply a final coat of paint to the entire project.

Stop molding

Crown molding

Baseboard

Creating a Built-up Cornice

Designing your own cornice molding is a creative and fun process. A cornice is basically an elaborate crown molding, decorating the area where the wall meets the ceiling. Traditional cornices are made of plaster, one continuous solid molding piece, or a combination of simple molding pieces—called a built-up cornice. Built-up types are the most common today because the individual moldings are much cheaper and easier to install than one large piece. Built-up moldings also allow you to create a custom-designed molding that fits with the style of your room. To design your own cornice, visit a well-stocked lumberyard or home center and gather several molding samples of different types: baseboard, stop, crown, and bed moldings, as well as smaller trims, like quarter rounds and coves. Bring the samples home and arrange them in different combinations and positions to find the best design.

As you design your cornice, be careful not to overwhelm the room with a large, complicated molding. A good general rule is to try to match the size of the cornice to the overall size of your baseboard. Baseboard creates a visual balance with cornice when the two are proportionate.

Backing is another serious issue to consider when designing a built-up cornice. Whenever possible, install blocking inside the wall or ceiling. When blocking is not an option, consider using a backer block fastened directly to the wall studs as done in the project "Installing Crown Molding" (page 104). A backer block allows you to firmly nail moldings in place when there are no joists in the ceiling to nail to. In the event you do not have framing or a blocking to nail to, use a bead of construction adhesive to adhere the molding to the ceiling and drive nails at opposing angles to hold the molding in place until the adhesive dries.

The cornice shown in this project starts with a $1\frac{3}{8}$" colonial stop installed along the ceiling, and a band of $3\frac{1}{2}$" baseboard run along the wall. A simple crown molding is then fastened to the two moldings to complete the cornice.

Everything You Need

Tools: pencil, tape measure, chalk line, power miter saw, pneumatic finish nailer, nail set, hammer.

Materials: molding, 2" and $1\frac{1}{4}$" finish nails, carpenter's glue, construction adhesive.

How to Create a Built-up Cornice

1 Cut a 4"- to 6"-long piece from each type of molding. Glue or nail the pieces together in the desired arrangement to create a marking template. Position the template flush with the wall and ceiling and mark along the outside edges of the ceiling and wall moldings. Mark at both ends of each wall.

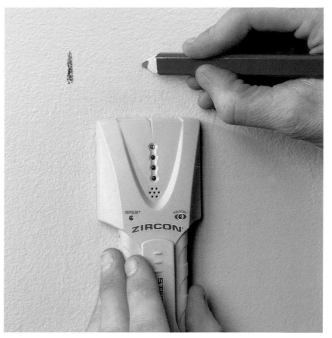

2 Locate and mark all of the wall studs and ceiling joists, marking in areas that will be hidden by the crown molding.

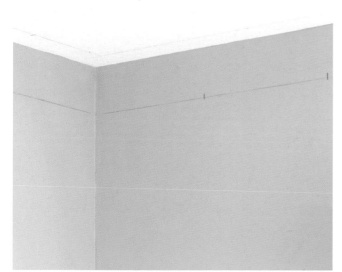

3 Locate and mark all of the wall studs and ceiling joists, marking in areas that will be hidden by the crown molding. Snap chalk lines between the template marks you made in Step 2 (you can also mark with a pencil and level). If the ceiling has a deep texture, scrape off the texture just behind the chalk lines, using a drywall taping knife.

4 Install the ceiling trim, aligning its outside edge with the chalk line. Nail into the joists with 2" (6d) finish nails, and miter the joints at the inside and outside corners. Wherever possible, place the nails where they'll be hidden by the crown molding.

(continued next page)

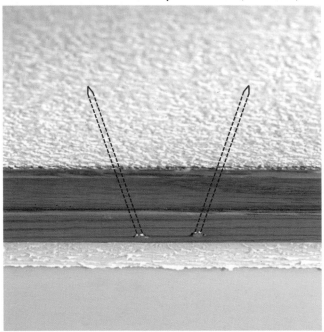

5 Where walls run parallel to the ceiling joists, and there are no joists to nail into, apply a bead of construction adhesive to the trim and nail it in place with pairs of nails driven at opposing angles. If you're handnailing, drill oversized pilot holes and secure the trim with coarse-thread drywall screws. Let the adhesive dry before starting the next step.

6 Install the vertical band trim along the walls, nailing into each stud with two 2" nails. Miter the band at outside corners.

7 Cope the molding at inside corners by first cutting a 45° angle on the piece. Then cope-cut the angle with a coping saw. Cut along the front edge of the molding, following the contour. Test-fit the cut and fine-tune it with a metal file if necessary.

8 Add the crown molding, fastening it to the ceiling trim and wall band with 1¼" (3d) nails. Miter the molding at outside corners, and miter or cope the inside corners. Use a nail set to set all nails that aren't countersunk.

CORNICE VARIATIONS

Use picture rail (page 96) to enhance a cornice molding. Standard height for picture rail is about 10" to 12" below the ceiling, but you can place it at any level. For a simple variation of the project shown, use square-edged stock for the band (since the bottom edge will mostly be hidden), and add picture rail just below the band. Be sure to leave enough room for placing picture hooks.

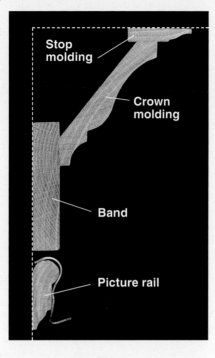

Stop molding

Crown molding

Band

Picture rail

Install blocking to provide a nailing surface and added bulk to a built-up cornice. In this simple arrangement, a 2 × 2 block, or nailing strip, is screwed to the wall studs. A facing made from 1 × 2 finish lumber is nailed to the blocking and is trimmed along the ceiling with quarter-round. The crown molding is nailed to the wall studs along the bottom and to the nailer along the top.

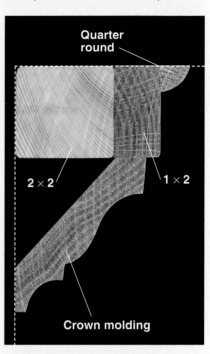

Quarter round

2 × 2

1 × 2

Crown molding

This highly detailed Victorian-style built-up cornice is made up of several pieces of stock trim and solid stock ripped down to different widths. The right-angle component of this cornice may be screwed directly to the wall, to serve both a decorative function as well as serve as a nailer for the other trim elements. The screw holes are covered when the crown molding is installed.

Built up cornice treatments can be as simple or complex as you would like. This Arts & Crafts variation is made up of flat solid stock ripped down to specific dimensions. Two pieces of 1 × 2 stock are fastened together to form an "L" shaped angle. The angle is then screwed to the wall at the stud locations. An additional piece of 1" wide stock is nailed in place so the top edge is flush with the installed angle. This configuration creates a stepped cornice with a simpler appearance than the traditional sprung moldings. Notice that the "L" angle is nailed together with a slight gap at the back edge. This is done to compensate for irregularities in the corner joint.

Installing Polymer Crown Molding

Polymer moldings come in a variety of ornate, single-piece styles that offer easy installation and maintenance. The polystyrene or polyurethane material is as easy to cut as softwood, but unlike wood, the material won't shrink, and it can be repaired with vinyl spackling compound.

You can buy polymer moldings preprimed for painting, or you can stain it with a nonpenetrating heavy-body stain or gel. Most polymers come in 12-ft. lengths, and some have corner blocks that eliminate corner cuts. There are even flexible moldings for curved walls.

Everything You Need

Tools: drill with countersink-piloting bit, power miter saw or hand miter box and fine-tooth saw, caulk gun, putty knife.

Materials: crown molding, finish nails, 150-grit sandpaper, rag, mineral spirits, polymer adhesive, 2" drywall screws, vinyl spackling compound, paintable latex caulk.

How to Install Polymer Crown Molding

1 Plan the layout of the molding pieces by measuring the walls of the room and making light pencil marks at the joint locations. For each piece that starts or ends at a corner, add 12" to 24" to compensate for waste. If possible, avoid pieces shorter than 36", because short pieces are more difficult to fit.

2 Hold a section of molding against the wall and ceiling in the finished position. Make light pencil marks on the wall every 12" along the bottom edge of the molding. Remove the molding, and tack a finish nail at each mark. The nails will hold the molding in place while the adhesive dries. If the wall surface is plaster, drill pilot holes for the nails.

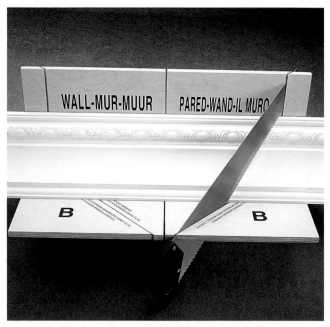

3 To make the miter cuts for the first corner, position the molding faceup in a miter box. Set the ceiling side of the molding against the horizontal table of the miter box, and set the wall side against the vertical back fence. Make the cut at 45°.

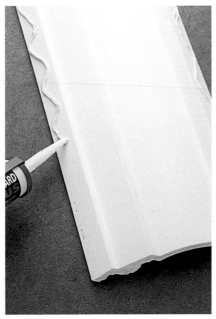

4 Check the uncut ends of each molding piece before installing it. Make sure mating pieces will butt together squarely in a tight joint. Cut all square ends at 90°, using a miter saw or hand miter box.

5 Lightly sand the backs of the molding that will contact the wall and ceiling, using 150-grit sandpaper. Slightly dampen a rag with mineral spirits, and wipe away the dust. Run a small bead of polymer adhesive (recommended or supplied by the manufacturer) along both sanded edges.

6 Set the molding in place with the mitered end tight to the corner and the bottom edge resting on the nails. Press along the molding edges to create a good bond. At each end of the piece, drive 2" drywall screws through countersunk pilot holes through the flats and into the ceiling and wall.

7 Cut, sand, and glue the next piece of molding. Apply a bead of adhesive to the end where the installed molding will meet the new piece. Install the new piece, and secure the ends with screws, making sure the ends are joined properly. Install the remaining molding pieces, and let the adhesive dry.

8 Carefully remove the finish nails and fill the nail holes with vinyl spackling compound. Fill the screw holes in the molding and any gaps in the joints with paintable latex caulk or filler, and wipe away excess caulk with a damp cloth or a wet finger. Smooth the caulk over the holes so it's flush with the surface.

Installing Crown Molding Lighting

Flexible, low-voltage rope lights hidden above a crown molding create a soft, comforting light effect that is much more relaxing than direct lighting. When combined with light-colored walls and ceilings, this system provides cool, balanced lighting, with no eye-straining glare. A stand-alone run along a wall can be used to draw attention to a room's focal point.

Rope lights can be easily adapted to any length of lighting run. Connect one rope to another by simply removing the end caps and inserting male/female connectors into the ends. You can also trim rope lighting to length at marked cutting lines located every 18".

Everything You Need

Tools: stud finder, pencil, chalk line, drill, tape measure, bevel gauge, table saw or circular saw, miter saw, square, jig saw, hammer, nail set.

Materials: crown molding, rope lighting, 2 × 2 lumber, 3" wallboard screws, 6d finish nails, mounting clips for rope lighting (optional).

How to Install Crown Molding Lighting

1 Use a stud finder to locate studs in the installation area. Mark the stud locations with light pencil marks near the ceiling, making sure the lines will be visible when the trim is in place. Plan the layout order of the molding pieces so as to minimize cuts and avoid noticeable joints. Also keep in mind the location of the receptacle that you plan to plug the rope lighting into.

2 Determine the location for your molding. To maximize light reflection from the walls and ceiling, position the molding 3" to 12" from the ceiling. Measure from the ceiling and mark a point to represent the bottom edge of the molding. Mark at the ends of each wall that you plan to work on, then snap a chalk line between the marks.

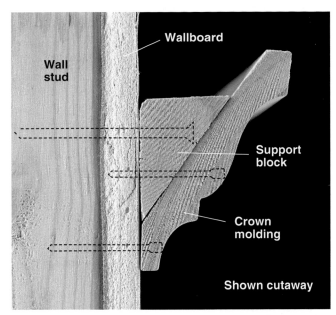

Wall stud

Wallboard

Support block

Crown molding

Shown cutaway

3 Because the crown molding will not be fastened at the top, it is necessary to install support blocking. Use a bevel gauge to determine the precise angle of your crown molding. Rip 2 × 2 lumber to this angle, using a table saw or circular saw. Fasten the supports to wall studs using 3" screws. The supports can be installed in long strips or cut into 6" blocks and attached at each molding joint and every 4 ft. on long runs of molding.

4 Set the molding in place along the chalk line. Have a helper hold the molding in place as you drill pilot holes and fasten it with 6d finish nails. Drive one nail into the stud along the lower edge of the molding and one into the support blocking. Use a nail set to recess the nail heads slightly.

5 Install the remaining sections of molding. When you are above the receptacle you will use to power the rope lighting, cut a small notch in the molding with a jig saw and lay the cord in the notch before fastening the molding to the wall.

6 Follow the manufacturer's instructions to join or cut any segments of rope lighting to the proper length. Lay the rope light in the trough between the wall and molding and work it around the entire installation. You may want to use mounting clips (sold separately) to keep the rope lighting lying flat. Plug in the light to activate it.

Variation: Flip the molding upside down and attach it to the wall for a cornice lighting effect. Attach the rope lighting to the top of the cornice with mounting clips sold separately by the manufacturer.

Finishing Window & Door Openings

Window Casing Styles

Window and door casings are the one of the most defining elements of trim in every home. Casing and base trim are commonly the foundation on which all other elements of trim are based. This means they play a crucial role in defining the style of your home.

Take your time deciding on a particular style of casing. When you have made your decision, follow that style throughout your home for a balanced appearance. The following few pages are included to help you choose a casing style. Window casings are covered first, followed by door treatments. Some of the styles shown are projects in the book. The other styles provided use similar installation techniques with different combinations of trim.

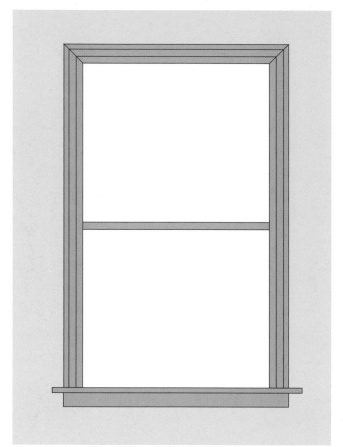

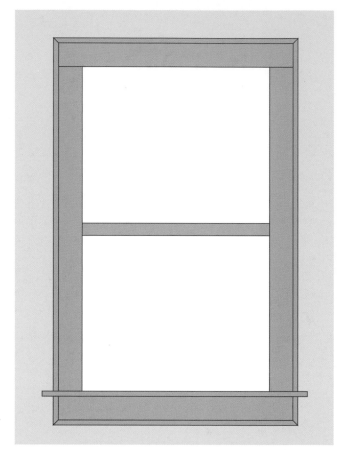

A built-up **Victorian** window casing consists of two pieces of stock molding with a solid 1" band around the perimeter. The two stock moldings are stacked together and capped with the square stock. Built-up casings such as these are easier to install when they are preassembled on a work surface and installed as one piece because all three moldings can be mitered at the same time. This treatment would be mitered at the top corners and butt into a stool at the base of the window. The stool treatment is plain square stock so it will not draw attention away from the more elaborate casing.

Arts & Crafts casings have many different variations that all have one thing in common: straight clean lines with emphasis on wood grain. In the example shown, a solid 1 × 4 piece is used with butt joints as casing. It is then capped with a back band molding that is mitered at the corners. The apron treatment maintains the back band edge as a continuation of the lines from the casing, interrupted only by a plain piece of flat 1× stock used as a stool. Top corner joints of this treatment are commonly joined with a biscuit (page 82) to aid in alignment and strength of the joint, but use of a biscuit is not mandatory. Quartersawn white or red oak is frequently used for this style to show off grain pattern, but painted moldings are also acceptable. Installation of this trim style is on pages 130 and 131.

A common **Neoclassical** window treatment is fluted casings with a decorative head cap. The fluted casings are butted into an ordinary stool and apron at the sill and finished off with a built-up cap similar to the one on page 138. This style is very similar to Victorian fluted casings, but uses a decorative cap rather than rosette blocks at the upper corners.

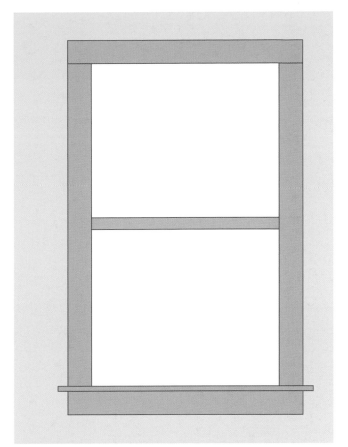

Modern casings may sound dull compared to the curvy style of Victorian casings; however, similar to Arts & Crafts, Modern trim emphasizes smooth straight lines. In the example shown, 3½" birch plywood strips are clear coated to show off the end grain of the product. The casings are butted together at the top corners, with the head capping the legs, and the stool and apron are made entirely of plywood, with no effort made to conceal the plies of the product. Other examples of Modern window treatments include clamshell moldings and plain wallboard without casing.

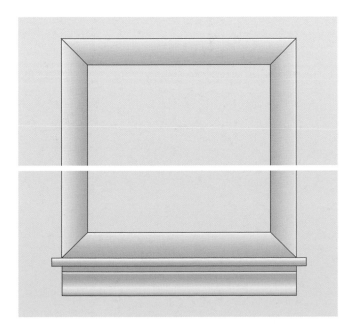

Traditional style casings are also frequently installed to add visual variety to windows or doors in rooms with mixed styles. The example shown, a stock molding with a mix of curves and straight angles, helps to blend together different styles. A standard stool of square stock is finished off with an apron built up from base molding and base cap stacked together.

Door Casing Styles

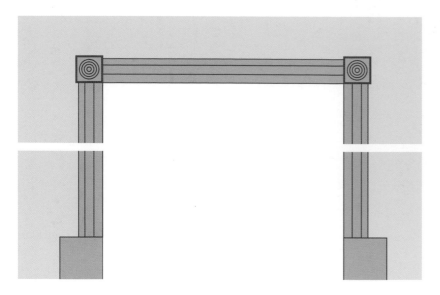

Victorian door treatments include a distinctive style made up of fluted casings with plinth blocks at the floor, and rosette blocks at the top corners. This is a classic Victorian trademark that holds many advantages for the do-it-yourselfer. Most notably, this style eliminates mitering and uses style treatments with butt joints at each corner, making installation easy and quick.

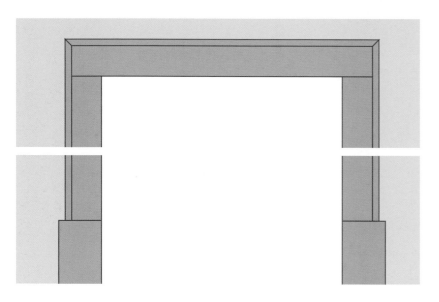

A thicker head casing in an **Arts & Crafts** installation creates a reveal across the bottom edge of the header, making it easier to deal with irregular walls. A slight miter to the ends of the head casing creates visual appeal. 5/4 milled stock for the head casing is available at most lumberyards or hardwood suppliers.

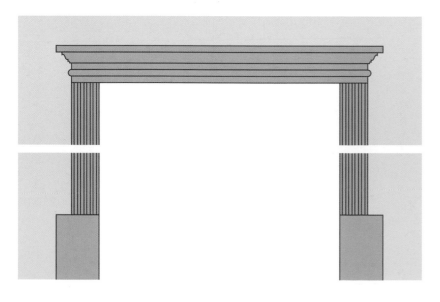

A crossette corner is a **Neoclassical** style with Georgian roots. Crossette corners, or "shoulders," can be built up to any size. The corner shown is made up of standard 1× material with a 1" wide 6" to 10" long extension placed at the top of each leg. The head casing caps the tops of the legs and a thicker piece of molding is applied as a back band. In the image shown, exterior brick molding is cut down with a table saw and butted to the edges of the casings, mitered in the corners. Winged casings are easier to build on a work surface prior to installation. Paint-grade material is recommended to hide the seam between the casing and the casing extension.

A basic installation of clamshell or ranch-style casing is a good example of **Modern** style. These casings are generally made of soft woods and painted to blend in with their surroundings. While basic clamshell moldings don't give you a lot to look at visually, if the room has busy faux painted walls or other features you want to highlight, clamshell casings are a simple and inexpensive alternative.

Traditional-style door casings mix well with many different styles and include extensive built-up casings as well as off-the-shelf moldings with little adaptation. In the first traditional example, a solid 1 × 4 is installed with butt joints. A stop molding is installed over the perimeter face of the 1 × 4 with mitered joints. Finally, a cove molding is applied to the outer edge of the 1 × 4 to cover the seam along the perimeter. This style of molding may be stain or paint grade.

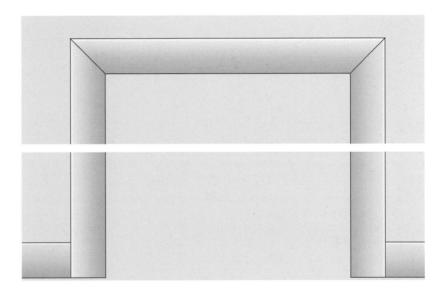

Casing a Window or Door

Stock wood casings provide an attractive border around window and door openings while covering the gaps between the wall surface and the window jamb. Install casings with a consistent reveal between the inside edges of the jambs and the edges of the casings.

In order to fit casings properly, the jambs and wall surfaces must be in the same plane. If one of them protrudes, the casing will not lie flush. To solve this problem, you may need to shave the edges of the jambs down with a block plane. Or you may need to attach jamb extensions to the window or door to match the plane of the wall. For small differences where a wallboard surface is too high, you can sometimes use a hammer to compress the wallboard around the jambs to allow the casings to lie flush.

Wallboard screws rely on the strength of untorn face paper to support the panel. If the paper around the screws becomes torn, drive additional screws nearby where the paper is still intact.

Everything You Need

Tools: tape measure, drill, pencil, nail set, hammer or pneumatic nailer, level, combination square, straightedge, miter saw.

Materials: casing material, baseboard molding and corner blocks (optional), 4d and 6d finish nails, wood putty.

How to Install Mitered Casing on Windows & Doors

1 On each jamb, mark a reveal line ³⁄₁₆" to ¹⁄₄" from the inside edge. The casings will be installed flush with these lines.

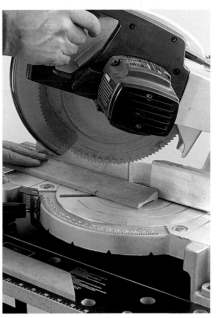

2 Place a length of casing along one side jamb, flush with the reveal line. At the top and bottom of the molding, mark the points where horizontal and vertical reveal lines meet. (When working with doors, mark the molding at the top only.)

3 Make 45° miter cuts on the ends of the moldings. Measure and cut the other vertical molding piece, using the same method.

4 Drill pilot holes spaced every 12" to prevent splitting, and attach the vertical casings with 4d finish nails driven through the casings and into the jambs. Drive 6d finish nails into the framing members near the outside edge of the casings.

5 Measure the distance between the side casings and cut top and bottom casings to fit, with ends mitered at 45°. If window or door unit is not perfectly square, make test cuts on scrap pieces to find the correct angle of the joints. Drill pilot holes and attach with 4d and 6d finish nails.

6 Locknail the corner joints by drilling pilot holes and driving 4d finish nails through each corner, as shown. Drive all nail heads below the wood surface, using a nail set, then fill the nail holes with wood putty.

125

Installing Stool & Apron Window Trim

Stool and apron trim brings a traditional look to a window, and is most commonly used with double-hung styles. The stool serves as an interior sill; the apron (or the bottom casing) conceals the gap between the stool and the finished wall.

In many cases, such as with 2 × 6 walls, jamb extensions made from 1× finish-grade lumber need to be installed to bring the window jambs flush with the finished wall. Many window manufacturers also sell jamb extensions for their windows.

The stool is usually made from 1× finish-grade lumber, cut to fit the rough opening, with "horns" at each end extending along the wall for the side casings to butt against. The horns extend beyond the outer edge of the casing by the same amount that the front edge of the stool extends past the face of the casing, usually under 1".

If the edge of the stool is rounded, beveled, or otherwise decoratively routed, you can create a more finished appearance by returning the ends of the stool to hide the end grain. A pair of miter cuts at the rough horn will create the perfect cap piece for wrapping the grain of the front edge of the stool around the horn. The same can be done for an apron cut from a molded casing.

As with any trim project, tight joints are the secret to a successful stool and apron trim job. Take your time to ensure all the pieces fit tightly. Also, use a pneumatic nailer—you don't want to spend all that time shimming the jambs perfectly only to knock them out of position with one bad swing of a hammer.

TIP: "Back-cut" the ends of casing pieces where needed to help create tight joints, using a sharp utility knife.

Everything You Need

Tools: tape measure, straightedge, circular saw or jig saw, handsaw, plane or rasp, drill, hammer, pneumatic nailer (optional).

Materials: 1 × finish lumber; casing; wood shims; 4d, 6d, and 8d finish nails.

How to Install Stool & Apron Window Trim

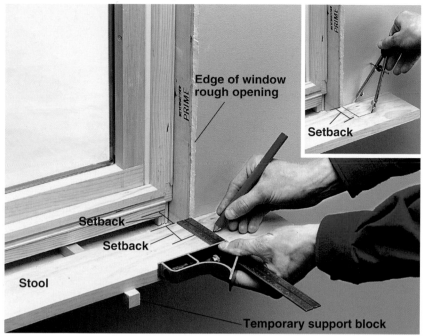

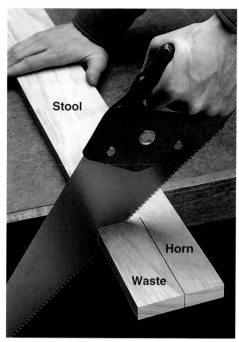

1 Cut the board for the stool to length, with several extra inches at each end for the horns. Temporarily position the stool in the window opening, pressed against the wall and centered on the window. Use a combination square to measure the setback distance from the window frame to the near edge of the stool. Mark the setback onto the stool at each edge of the window rough opening (if the measurements are different, use the greater setback distance for each end). Then, use a compass and pencil to scribe the profile of the wall onto the stool to complete the cutting line for the horn (inset photo).

2 Cut out the notches to create the stool horns. For straight lines, you can use a large handsaw, but for the scribed line use a more maneuverable saw like the jig saw or a coping saw. Test-fit the stool, making any minor adjustments with a plane or a rasp so it fits tightly to the window frame and flush against the walls.

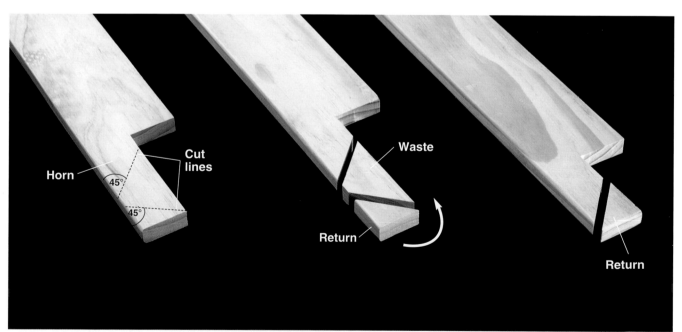

3 To create a return at the horn of the stool, miter-cut the return pieces at 45° angles. Mark the stool at its overall length and cut it to size with 45° miter cuts. Glue the return to the mitered end of the horn so the grain wraps around the corner. NOTE: Use this same technique to create the returns on the apron, but make the cuts with the apron held on-edge, rather than flat.

(continued next page)

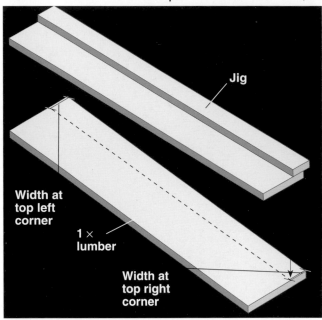

TIP: Where jamb extensions are needed, cut the head extension to its finished length—the distance between the window side jambs plus the thickness of both side extensions (typically 1× stock). For the width, measure the distance between the window jamb and the finished wall at each corner, then mark the measurements on the ends of the extension. Use a straightedge to draw a reference line connecting the points. Build a simple cutting jig, as shown.

4 Clamp the jig on the reference line, then rip the extension to width, using a circular saw; keep the baseplate tight against the jig and move the saw smoothly through the board. Reposition the clamp when you near the end of the cut. Cut both side extensions to length and width, using the same technique as for the head extension (see TIP).

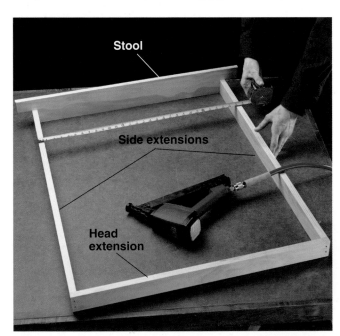

5 Build a box frame with the extensions and stool, using 6d finish nails and a pneumatic nailer. Measure to make sure the box has the same dimensions as the window jambs. Drive nails through the top of the head extension into the side extensions, and through the bottom of the stool into side extensions.

6 Apply wood glue to the back edge of the frame, then position it against the front edge of the window jambs. Use wood shims to adjust the frame, making sure the pieces are flush with the window jambs. Fasten the frame at each shim location, using 8d finish nails driven through pilot holes. Loosely pack insulation between the studs and the jambs, or use minimal-expanding spray foam.

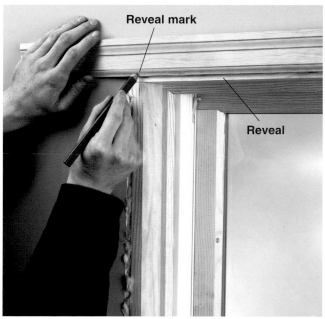

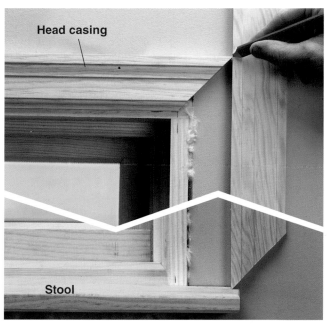

7 On the edge of each jamb or jamb extension, mark a ³⁄₁₆" to ¼" reveal. Place a length of casing along the head extension, aligned with the reveal marks at the corners. Mark where the reveal marks intersect, then make 45° miter cuts at each point. Reposition the casing at the head extension and attach, using 4d finish nails at the extensions, and 6d finish nails at the framing members.

8 Cut the side casings to rough length, leaving the ends slightly long for final trimming. Miter one end at 45°. With the pointed end on the stool, mark the height of the side casing at the top edge of the head casing.

9 To get a tight fit for side casings, align one side of a T-bevel with the reveal, mark the side extension and position the other side flush against the horn. Transfer the angle from the T-bevel to the end of the casing, and cut the casing to length.

10 Test-fit the casings, making any final adjustments with a plane or rasp. Fasten the casing with 4d finish nails at the extensions, and 6d finish nails at the framing members.

11 Cut the apron to length, leaving a few inches at each end for creating the returns (step 3). Position the apron tight against the bottom edge of the stool, then attach it, using 6d finish nails driven every 12".

Installing Arts & Crafts Casing

The Arts & Crafts style is similar to the overall look and feel of Mission furniture, as can be seen in this relatively simple oak window casing.

Everything You Need

Tools: tape measure, straightedge, power miter saw, circular saw or jig saw, hand saw, plane or rasp, drill hammer, pneumatic nailer, combination square, compass, nail set.

Materials: 1 × 4 finish lumber; back band trim; wood shims; 4d, 6d, and 8d finish nails; finishing putty.

Traditional Arts & Crafts casings are made of simple, flat materials with little to no decorative molding trimmed out of the stock. Add nonmitered corners to the mix and this casing becomes as plain as possible. The back band installed on the perimeter of this project is optional, but it adds depth to the window treatment while maintaining simple style.

Traditionally, the wood used for this style of trim is quartersawn oak. The term "quartersawn" refers to the method of milling the material. Quartersawn oak is easily distinguishable from plain-sawn oak by its tight grain pattern laced with rays of lighter color also known as rifts. Quartersawn oak is more expensive than plain oak, and may only be available at lumberyards or hardwood supply stores, depending upon your area. Either plain sawn or quartersawn oak will fit the style of this casing.

To begin the installation of this trim style, refer to pages 125 and 126 to read the step-by-step process for installing jamb extensions, if necessary, and the stool portion of this project.

How to Install Arts & Crafts Casing

Follow the step-by-step process on pages 128 to 129 to install the stool and jamb extensions. Set a combination square to ³⁄₁₆" or ¼" and mark a reveal line on the top and side jambs.

To find the length of the head casing and apron, measure the distance between the reveal lines on the side jambs and add twice the width of the side casings. Cut the head casing and the apron to length. Install the head casing flush with the top reveal line. Use a scrap piece of trim to line up the head casing horizontally.

Measure and cut the side casings to length. Install them flush with the reveal lines. Make sure the joints at the top and bottom are tight. Measure the distance to the end of the stool from the outer edge of the side casing. Install the apron tight to the bottom of the stool at the same dimension from the end of the stool.

Measure, cut, and install the back band around the perimeter of the window casings, mitering the joints at the corners. Continue the back band around the edge of the apron, mitering the corners. Nail the back band in place with 4d finish nails.

Installing a Window Shelf

Shelves may be hung above windows as novelty top treatments to showcase plants and collections. They can be used alone or in combination with other window treatments, such as curtains. In that case, mount the shelf with brackets hidden under the valance.

Although the end pieces in this project act as supports for the shelf, also secure the shelf to a horizontal support piece. Then, attach the whole unit to the wall with wood screws. If heavy items are to be displayed, drill more pilot holes for the wood screws to be closer together for added strength.

Whatever the size of the items to be displayed, you can adjust the depth of the shelf unit to accommodate them.

Everything You Need

Tools: hammer, drill and bits, circular saw, jig saw, router, sander, nail set.

Materials: 1 x 8 and 1 x 2 lumber, 2" wood screws, 6d casing nails, paint or stain.

Shelf Variations

Add larger supports at the shelf ends to accommodate a dowel for hanging dried flowers and herbs. A coordinating "backsplash" provides a way to attach the shelf to the wall. Attach hooks to the underside of the shelf to hang other collectibles or keepsakes.

How to Build a Window Shelf

1 Cut the 1 × 8 shelf board and the 1 × 2 horizontal support piece the same length as the total width of the window unit, including the outer casing. Attach the shelf to the support at a 90° angle, using 2" wood screws spaced every 6" to 10".

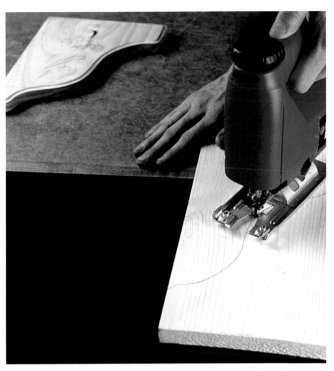

2 Cut out the two end pieces from 1 × 8 lumber. If the design has only straight lines, use a circular saw. If it includes curves, use a jig saw.

3 Add a design to the end supports, using a router. Sand smooth the faces and edges that will be exposed. Attach end supports to shelf unit using wood glue and 6d casing nails. Use a nail set to recess the nail heads. Finish the unit by staining or painting.

4 Drill pilot holes in the support piece every 6" to 10", avoiding screws attaching the shelf to the horizontal support. Attach shelf unit to wall just above window casing, using 2" wood screws driven through pilot holes. Plug and finish screw holes, if desired.

Because they are set into thick foundation walls, basement windows present a bit of a trimming challenge. But the thickness of the foundation wall also lets you create a handy ledge that's deep enough to hold potted plants or even sunning cats.

Trimming a Basement Window Opening

Basement windows bring much-needed sunlight into dark areas, but even in finished basements they often get ignored on the trim front. This is partly because most basement foundation walls are at least 8" thick, and often a lot thicker. Add a furred-out wall and the window starts to look more like a tunnel with a pane of glass at the end. But with some well designed and well-executed trim carpentry, you can turn the depth disadvantage into a positive.

A basement window opening may be finished with wallboard, but the easiest way to trim one is by making extrawide custom jambs that extend from the inside face of the window frame to the interior wall surface. Because of the extra width, plywood stock is a good choice for the custom jambs. The project shown here is created with veneer-core plywood with oak veneer surface. The jamb members are fastened together into a nice square frame using rabbet joints at the cor-

ner. The frame is scribed and installed as a single unit and then trimmed out with oak casing. The casing is applied flush with the inside edges of the frame opening. If you prefer to have a reveal edge around the interior edge of the casing, you will need to add a solid hardwood strip to the edge of the frame so the plies of the plywood are not visible.

Everything You Need

Tools: pencil, tape measure, table saw, drill with bits, 2-ft level, framing square, utility knife, straightedge.

Materials: finish-grade $\frac{3}{4}$" oak plywood, spray-foam insulation, composite or cedar wood shims, $1\frac{1}{4}$, 2" finish nails, $1\frac{5}{8}$" drywall screws, carpenter's glue.

How to Trim a Basement Window

1 Check to make sure the window frame and surrounding area are dry and free of rot, mold or damage. At all four corners of the basement window, measure from the inside edges of the window frame to the wall surface. Add 1" to the longest of these measurements.

2 Set your table saw to make a rip cut to the width arrived at in step 1. If you don't have a table saw, set up a circular saw and straightedge cutting guide to cut strips to this length. With a fine-tooth panel-cutting blade, rip enough plywood strips to make the four jamb frame components.

Miter gauge

3 Cross-cut the plywood strips to correct lengths. In our case, we designed the jamb frame to be the exact same outside dimensions as the window frame, since there was some space between the jamb frame and the rough opening.

$3/8 \times 3/4$" rabbet

4 Cut $3/8$"-deep × $3/4$"-wide rabbets at each end of the head jamb and the sill jamb. A router table is the best tool for this job, but you may use a table saw or hand saws and chisels. Inspect the jambs first and cut the rabbets in whichever face is in better condition. To ensure uniformity, we ganged the two jambs together (they're the same length). It's also a good idea to include backer boards to prevent tear-out.

(continued next page)

5 Glue and clamp the frame parts together, making sure to clamp near each end from both directions. Set a carpenter's square inside the frame and check it to make sure it's square.

6 Before the glue sets, carefully drill three perpendicular pilot holes, countersunk, through the rabbeted workpieces and into the side jambs at each corner. Space the pilot holes evenly, keeping the end ones at least ¾" in from the end. Drive a 1⅝" drywall screw into each pilot hole, taking care not to overdrive. Double check each corner for square as you work, adjusting the clamps if needed.

7 Let the glue dry for at least one hour (overnight is better), then remove the clamps and set the frame in the window opening. Adjust the frame so it is centered and level in the opening and the exterior-side edges fit flush against the window frame.

8 Taking care not to disturb the frame's position (rest a heavy tool on the sill to hold it in place if you wish), press a steel rule against the wall surface and mark trimming points at the point where the rule meets the jambs at each side of all four frame corners, using a sharp pencil.

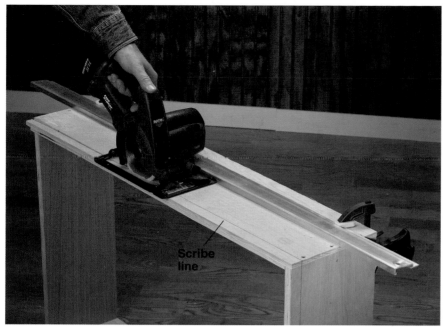

9 Remove the frame and clamp it on a flat work surface. Use a straight-edge to connect the scribe marks at the ends of each jamb frame side. Set the cutting depth of your circular saw to just a small fraction over ¾". Clamp a straightedge guide to the frame so the saw blade will follow the cutting line and trim each frame side in succession. (The advantage to using a circular saw here is that any tear-out from the blade will be on the nonvisible faces of the frame).

10 Replace the frame in the window opening in the same orientation as when you scribed it and install shims until it is level and centered in the opening. Drive a few finish nails (hand or pneumatic) through the side jambs into the rough frame. Also drive a few nails through the sill jamb. Most trim carpenters do not drive nails into the head jamb.

11 Insulate between the jamb frame and the rough frame with spray-in polyurethane foam. Look for minimal-expanding foam labeled "window and door" and don't spray in too much. Let the foam dry for a half hour or so and then trim off the excess with a utility knife. Tip: Protect the wood surfaces near the edges with wide strips of masking tape.

12 Remove the masking tape and clean up the mess from the foam (there is always some). Install case molding. We used picture-frame techniques to install fairly simple oak casing.

Installing a Decorative Door Header

Adding a decorative head casing to a door is a simple way to dress up your existing trim. Although head treatments are more common over doors, this project will work for window trim as well. Designing your own decorative molding can be creative and fun, but try not to overwhelm the room with an elaborate piece, or it may detract from the décor.

Standard stock door casings have an outer-edge thickness of approximately $1\frac{1}{16}$". Build your custom header around this thickness. Use it to create a reveal line to a thinner piece of trim, or build out from the edge for a bolder, more substantial appearance. In the project shown, a bed molding, or smaller piece of crown molding, is used to build out the header away from the wall. The ends of the molding are returned to the wall, and the entire piece is capped with a piece of lattice molding. Installing a decorative header of this style on an interior door may require the installation of additional blocking. For installation over an exterior door or a window, nail the pieces in place directly to the load-bearing framing in the wall above the opening.

Replacing plain head casing on a door or window with a decorative built-up version is a quick and easy way to add some sophistication to any ordinary feature of your home.

Everything You Need

Tools: pencil, tape measure, power miter saw, finish nail gun, brad nail gun.

Materials: moldings, wood glue.

How to Install a Decorative Door Header

1 Measure the width of your door casing and rough-cut a piece of bed or crown molding 6" longer. Use the casing width dimension to layout cut marks on the bottom edge of the molding. Start the marks 2" from the end to allow space for cutting the mitered ends.

2 With the molding upside down and sprung against the fence, cut a 45° outside corner miter angle at each end, on the casing reference marks from step 1. See pages 104 to 105 for more information on miter-cutting crown molding.

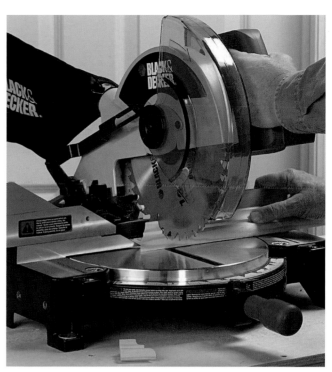

3 Cut mitered returns for the molding using the left-over piece. Set the angle of the power miter saw to the opposing 45° angle and cut the returns with the molding upside down and sprung against the fence. Dry-fit the pieces, recutting them if necessary. Apply glue to the return pieces and nail them to the ends of the head molding with 1" brad nails.

4 Nail the new header in place with 2½" finish nails driven at an angle through the bed molding and into the framing members of the wall.

5 Cut lattice molding 1" longer than the length of the bed molding and nail it in place with ⅝" brad nails so that it has a uniform overhang of ½" Fill all nail holes with spackle and sand them with fine-grit sandpaper. Apply the final coat of finish.

Before

Passthrough openings between rooms often are left very plain by the builders, especially in more modern homes. Not only is this a dull design statement, it also exposes the edges of the wallboard openings to damage. A little bit of door casing and new jambs can bring new life to the opening (and protect it as well).

Trimming a Wall Opening

Trimming out a wallboard opening is an easy way to add style to any room transition using decorative trim. Although this project may be done with paint-grade materials, clear finish adds detail and inviting wood grain, showcasing the opening.

In the project shown, solid wood trim is used to cover the wallboard jambs of the opening. This technique can also be accomplished with plywood jambs. However, to maintain a constant reveal with the rest of the room, a thin strip of solid oak material should be applied to the edges of the plywood to cover the visible plies. This application should be done prior to installing the jambs to avoid fastening difficulties.

The odds are good that the finished wallboard corners are irregular, causing some minor differences in wall thickness along the jambs of the

opening. When these irregularities are minor, (less than $3/16$ "), it is best to cut the jamb material at the widest jamb measurement and let the casing bridge the difference. When wall thickness varies a lot ($3/16$" or more), it is better to cut tapered jambs to cover the difference.

Everything You Need

Tools: pry bar, side cutters, pencil, tape measure, circular saw and straightedge guide, 4-ft. level, pneumatic finish nail gun, power miter saw, framing square.

Materials: jamb material (lumber or plywood), case moldings, base moldings, 2½" finish nails, wood glue, shims, scrap 2 × 4 material.

How to Trim a Wall Opening

1 Remove the existing base molding with a pry bar and hammer. Be careful not to mar the surface of the moldings as you remove them. Pull the nails out of the moldings through the back face with an end nippers or side cutters.

2 Measure the width and length of the head jamb and the width of each side jamb. Measure each jamb at both ends as well as in the middle of each run. Take note of the measurements. If a jamb differs in width by more than ³⁄₁₆", install a tapered length (see TIP, below).

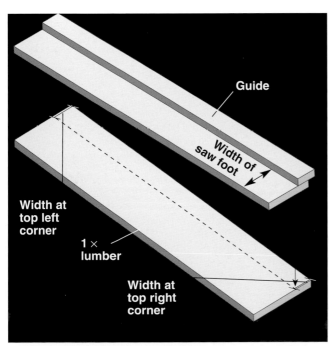

Guide

Width of saw foot

Width at top left corner

1 × lumber

Width at top right corner

TIP: Jambs that do not taper can be cut on a table saw, but if you have enough variation in your jamb widths that a taper is called for, make a simple cutting jig and taper-cut the jambs to width with a circular saw. Then, lay out the dimensions on the head jamb using the measurements from step 2. The head jamb should run the full length of the opening

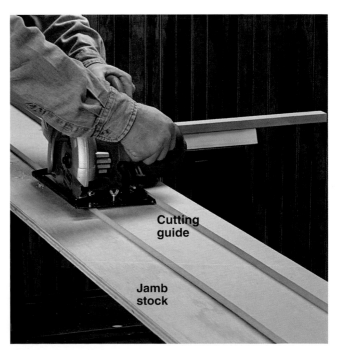

Cutting guide

Jamb stock

3 Clamp a straightedge guide (TIP, left) to the head jamb on the reference line from the measurements of Step 2, and cut the piece to width with a circular saw. Keep the base plate tight against the fence and move the saw smoothly through the board. Reposition the clamp when you near the end of the board.

(continued next page)

4 Position the head jamb at the top of the opening, flush with the edges, and nail it in place starting in the middle. Before nailing the ends of the head jamb, check it for square with the walls of the opening, adjusting with shims if necessary. Drive a pair of 2" finish nails every 16".

5 Place a T-bevel on the floor at the bottom of each side jamb to check for any angled cuts necessary to follow the pitch of the floor. The handle of the bevel should rest against the outer face of the wall, with the blade across the floor.

6 Transfer the angle from the T-bevel in step 5 to a power miter saw and cut the side jambs to length. The top end of the jamb should be cut square (90°). Each jamb should butt against the head jamb and fit tightly to the finished flooring.

7 Nail the side jambs in place using pairs of 2" finish nails driven every 16" along the jamb. Check the edges of the jamb pieces as you go to make sure they are flush with the surface of the wall.

8 Install casing around the opening. Maintain a consistent $\frac{3}{16}$" to $\frac{1}{4}$" reveal around the opening.

9 Measure, cut, and reinstall the existing baseboard so that the ends butt into the sides of the casing. Cut and reinstall the base shoe using mitered or beveled returns (page 79).

10 Fill all nail holes with finishing putty and apply a final coat of polyurethane or your finish of choice (try to match existing trim in the room).

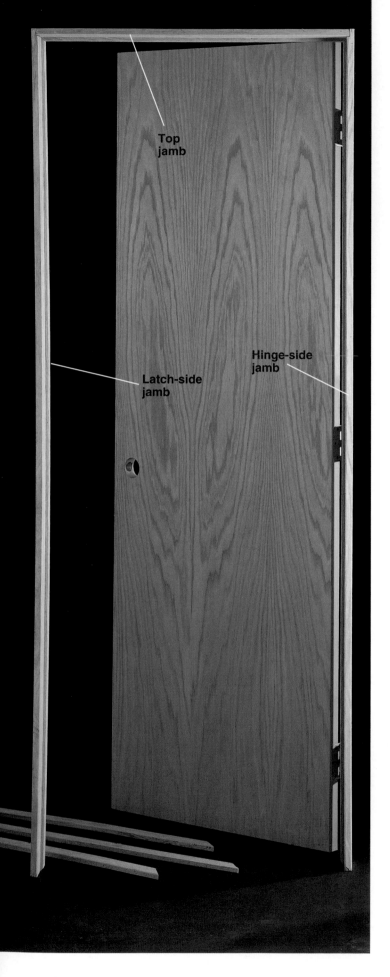

Top jamb

Hinge-side jamb

Latch-side jamb

Hanging Interior Prehung Doors

Prehung doors come as single units with the door already hung on hinges attached to a factory-built frame. To secure the unit during shipping, most prehung doors are braced or nailed shut with a couple of duplex nails driven through the jambs and into the door edge. These nails must be removed before you install the door.

The key to installing doors is to plumb and fasten the hinge-side jamb first. After that's in place, you can position the top and latch-side jambs by checking the reveal—the gap between the closed door and the jamb.

Standard prehung doors have 4½"-wide jambs and are sized to fit walls with 2 × 4 construction and ½" wallboard. If you have thicker walls, you can special-order doors to match, or you can add jamb extensions to standard-size doors.

Everything You Need

Tools: 4-ft. level, nail set, handsaw.

Materials: prehung door unit, wood shims, 8d and 10d casing nails.

Solid-core interior doors are heavier than hollow-core doors and may cause the jamb to bow, throwing the unit out of alignment. To fix this problem, loosely nail the top and bottom of the hinge-side jamb in place. Use a pry bar on the bottom of the door to lift the weight off the jamb. While the weight is lifted, drive two 10d casing nails near the top hinge. This will relieve the weight of the door and you may continue installation as with a hollow-core unit.

How to Install a Prehung Interior Door

1 Set the door unit into the framed opening so the jamb edges are flush with the wall surfaces and the unit is centered from side to side. Using a level, adjust the unit so the hinge-side jamb is plumb.

2 Starting near the top hinge, insert pairs of shims driven from opposite directions into the gap between the framing and jamb, sliding shims in until they are snug. Check the jamb to make sure it remains plumb and does not bow inward. Install shims near each hinge and the top and bottom of the jamb.

3 Anchor the hinge-side jamb with 8d casing nails driven through the jamb and shims and into the framing. Drive nails only at the shim locations.

4 Insert pairs of shims into the gap between the framing members and the top jamb and latch-side jamb, aligning them roughly with the hinge-side shims. With the door closed, adjust the shims so the reveal is consistent. Drive casing nails through the jambs and shims and into the framing members.

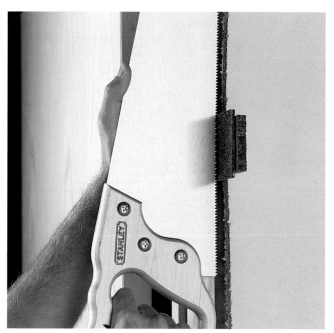

5 Set all nails below the surface of the wood with a nail set, then cut off the shims flush with the wall surface, using a handsaw or utility knife. Hold the saw vertically to prevent damage to the door jamb or wall. See page 124 to install the door casing.

Miterless moldings are gaining in popularity because they are so simple to install. Instead of making tricky miter cuts or cope cuts, you simply butt each piece of trim to a corner block or transition block.

Installing Plastic & Miterless Molding

Although traditional moldings are made from solid wood, your options (especially for paint-grade projects) do not end there. There is a wide variety of plastic molding available as well as molding made from wood products such as medium density fiberboard, or MDF. These alternative moldings are sold at home centers near the solid wood products.

One of the biggest advantages of alternative materials for trim moldings is cost. Intricate detailed moldings are considerably less expensive than their wood counterparts. Larger, more elaborate trim that is not available in solid wood (because it would be too expensive), is available in an assortment of styles right off the shelf, or custom ordered. Ceiling medallions and decorative corbels are examples of other plastic products that would otherwise not be commonly available. Ready-to-assemble mantels and decorative door caps are also offered. These products add style to any room immediately and are simple to install.

Another advantage of some plastic material and MDF is dimensional stability. With the change of humidity and temperature in the seasons, solid wood products expand and contract at varying rates. This causes joints to open up over time and, in some cases, split around a fastener. Some alternative materials are known to expand and contract less than wood. These materials are more dimensionally stable, which means that your project will most likely look better with tighter joints for a longer period of time.

For the most part, solid wood alternatives can be cut, machined, and installed just as solid wood products are. Many plastics will not split when fastened like wood, making installation easier. Some products may melt when cut slowly with a power saw, so it's a good idea to make cuts with moderate speed at a uniform rate.

Be cautious when purchasing plastic trim. Each material has pros and cons that you should be aware of. For example, some plastics such as polystyrene are less expensive but less durable than solid wood. They are also available with a prefinished wood grain appearance, unlike most other plastic products. Consult a home center specialist to help you choose the best material for your particular application.

Miterless moldings are another option that is commonly available with alternative materials. Miterless moldings utilize corner "blocks" and transition moldings to eliminate the need for complex cuts at corners or between pieces of molding. Plastic blocks may be used along with plastic molding or in combination with solid wood. After the project is painted, the difference in materials will be unnoticeable. Miterless moldings are available in solid wood as well. Plinth blocks and corner posts are available for base trim installation. Door and window casings can be trimmed out with rosette corners or decorative head treatments that cap the legs of the casing.

146

Plastic moldings can be cut, machined, and nailed just like wood moldings. Unlike wood moldings, plastics won't split when nailed near an edge.

Prefabricated MDF moldings are very dimensionally stable compared to solid wood products and sand easily. For best results, prime and paint the molding prior to installation.

Ornamental corbels don't have any practical value, but they provide strong visual appeal and can also be used to create small decorative shelves.

Rosettes made from wood products or urethane can be installed at the corners of window and door openings to eliminate the need for precise miter angles.

Hanging French Doors

Traditionally, French doors open onto the patio or lush garden of a backyard. But you can create stylish entrances inside your home by bringing French doors to formal dining rooms, sitting rooms or dens, and master suites.

French doors are made up of two separate doors, hinged on opposing jambs of a doorway. The doors swing out from the center of the doorway and into or out from a room. Like most

doors, French doors are typically sold in prehung units, but are also available separately. They are generally available only in wood, with a variety of designs and styles to choose from.

Before purchasing a prehung French door unit, determine the size of doors you will need. If you are planning to install the doors in an existing doorway, measure the dimensions of the rough opening, from the unfin-

ished framing members, then order the unit to size—the manufacturer or distributor will help you select the proper unit.

You can also pick the prehung unit first, then alter an existing opening to accommodate it (as shown in this project). In this case, build the rough opening a little larger than the actual dimensions of the doors to accommodate the jambs. Prehung units typically require adding 1" to the width and ½" to the height.

If the doorway will be in a load-bearing wall, you will need to make temporary supports, and install an appropriately sized header. Sizing the header (depth) is critical: it's based on the length of the header, the material it's made from, and the weight of the load it must support. For actual requirements, consult your local building department.

When installing French doors, it is important to have consistent reveals between the two doors and between the top of the doors and the head jamb. This allows the doors to close properly and prevents the hinges from binding.

Everything You Need

Tools: tape measure, circular saw, 4-ft. level, hammer, handsaw, drill, utility knife, nail set.

Materials: prehung French door unit, 2 × 4 and 2 × 6 lumber, ½" plywood, 10d & 16d common nails, wood shims, 8d finish nails.

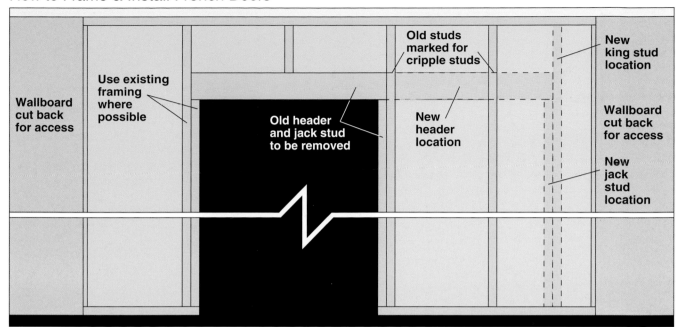

1 Shut off power and water to the area. Remove the wall surfaces from both sides of the wall, leaving one stud bay open on each side of the new rough opening. Also remove or reroute any wiring, plumbing, or ductwork. Lay out the new rough opening, marking the locations of all new jack and king studs on both the top and bottom plates. Where practical, use existing framing members. To install a new king stud, cut a stud to size and align with the layout marks, toenail to the bottom plate with 10d common nails, check for plumb, then toenail to the top plate to secure. Finally, mark both the bottom and top of the new header on one king stud, then use a level to extend the lines across the intermediate studs to the opposite king stud. If using existing framing, measure and mark from the existing jack stud.

2 Cut the intermediate studs at the reference marks for the top of the header, using a reciprocating saw. Pry the studs away from the sole plates and remove—the remaining top pieces will be used as cripple studs.

3 To install a jack stud, cut the stud to fit between the sole plate and the bottom of the header, as marked on the king stud. Align it at the mark against the king stud, then fasten it in place with 10d common nails driven every 12".

(continued next page)

4 Build the header to size and install, fastening it to the jack studs, king studs, and cripple studs, using 16d common nails. Use a handsaw to cut through the bottom plate so it's flush with the inside faces of the jack studs. Remove the cutout portion.

5 Finish the walls before installing the doors, then set the prehung door unit into the framed opening so the jamb edges are flush with the finished wall surfaces and the unit is centered from side to side.

6 Using a level, adjust the unit to plumb one of the side jambs. Starting near the top of the door, insert pairs of shims driven from opposite directions into the gap between the framing and the jamb, sliding the shims until they are snug. Check the jamb to make sure it remains plumb and does not bow inward.

7 Working down along the jamb, install shims near each hinge and near the floor. Make sure the jamb is plumb, then anchor it with 8d finish nails driven through the jamb and shims and into the framing. Leave the nail heads partially protruding so the jamb can be readjusted later if necessary.

8 Install shims at the other side jamb, aligning them roughly with the shims of the first jamb. With the doors closed, adjust the shims so the reveal between the doors is even and the tops of the doors are aligned.

9 Shim the gap between the header and the head jamb to create a consistent reveal along the top when the doors are closed. Insert pairs of shims every 12". Drive 8d finish nails through the jambs and shims and into the framing members.

10 Drive all the nails fully, then set them below the surface of the wood with a nail set. Cut off the shims flush with the wall surface, using a handsaw or utility knife. Hold the saw vertically to prevent damage to the door jamb or wall. Install the door casing.

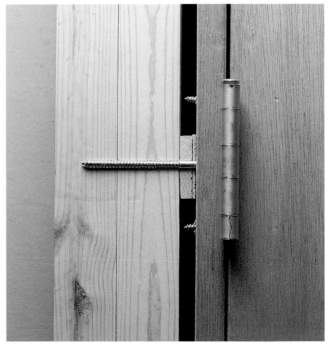

OPTION: Replace the center mounting screw on each hinge with a 3" wood screw to provide extra support for door hinges and jambs. These long screws extend through the side jambs and deep into the framing members. Be careful not to overtighten screws—overtightening will cause the jambs to bow.

Installing Decorative Wall & Ceiling Elements

Tongue-and-groove wainscoting boards are milled with smooth faces, or contoured to add additional texture to your walls. For staining, choose a wood species with a pronounced grain. For painting, poplar is a good choice, since it has few knots and a highly consistent grain.

Installing Wainscoting with Tongue & Groove Boards

A wainscot, by definition, is a wall treatment covering the lower portion of a wall. Virtually any material can be used as wainscoting, but the most common by far is wood. In most applications, the wainscot is covered along the bottom by a baseboard and along the top by a cap molding, rail, or shallow shelf.

Wainscots are useful not only for decoration but also as protective surfaces. Standard wainscot heights are between 32" and 36", a range at which the top cap can serve as a chair rail to protect the wall from furniture collisions. In hallways, mudrooms, and other functional areas, wainscots may run 48" and higher.

Wood wainscoting is available in a variety of species and styles. For price and ease of installation, the best types for do-it-yourselfers are 4 × 8-ft. sheets and tongue-and-groove boards, commonly called *beadboard*. Standard materials include paint-grade pine (and other softwoods); hardwood veneers, such as oak and birch; molded polymers; and fiberboard.

There are two basic methods for installing wainscoting. Sheets and thinner boards (up to ⅜", in most cases) can be attached to drywall with construction adhesive and nails, or with nails alone. Thicker boards usually must be nailed,

preferably blind-nailed—the technique of driving angled nails along the base of the tongue so the groove of the next board hides the nail heads. Thinner boards may have to be face-nailed to avoid splitting the wood.

Wainscoting that is fastened only with nails must have blocking or backing to serve as a nailing surface. If the framing is exposed, you can install plywood backing over the wall studs in the area of the wainscot, then cover the rest of the wall with drywall of the same thickness (make sure the local building code permits installing wood directly over wall framing). You can also install 2 × 4 blocks between the studs, at 12" to 16" intervals, before hanging the drywall.

The project on pages 158 to 159 shows you specific methods for installing tongue-and-groove beadboard, such as dealing with electrical outlets and trimming around windows. Pages 160 and 161 deal with installing sheet paneling with traditional moldings applied to the top and bottom edges. Because of its height, and tall baseboard, this wainscot is especially suited to mudroom or hallway walls that receive some abuse, but it can work well in bathrooms as well. Install hooks for coats or towels along the rail or add a shelf for additional storage.

How to Prepare for a Wainscoting Project

Measure to make a plan drawing of each wall in your project. Indicate the locations of fixtures, receptacles, and windows. Use a level to make sure the corners are plumb. If not, mark plumb lines on the walls to use as reference points.

Condition the planking by stacking it in the room where it will be installed. Place spacers between the planks to let air circulate around each board, allowing the wood to adjust to the room's temperature and humidity. Wait 72 hours before staining or sealing the front, back, and edges of each plank.

Remove the baseboard moldings, along with any receptacle cover plates, vent covers, or other wall fixtures within the area you plan to cover. Before you begin, turn off the electricity to the circuits in the area.

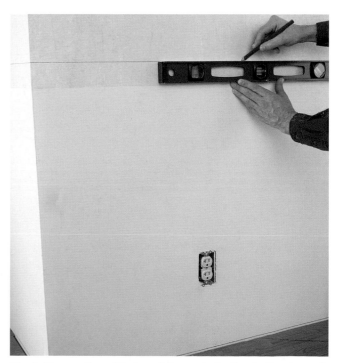

Mark the walls with level lines to indicate the top of the wainscoting. Mark a line ¼" from the floor to provide a small gap for expansion at the floor.

(continued next page)

How to Prepare for a Wainscoting Project (continued)

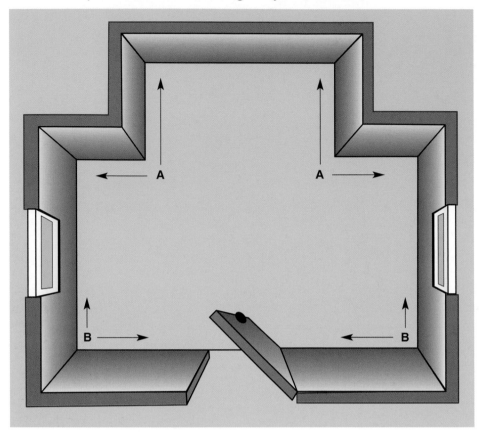

Begin installation at the corners. Install any outside corners (A) first, working your way toward the inside corners. In sections of a room that have no outside corners, start at the inside corners (B), and work your way toward the door and window casings. Calculate the number of boards required for each wall, using the measurements on the drawing you created earlier (length of wall ÷ width of one plank). When making this calculation, remember that the tongues are removed from the corner boards. If the total number of boards for a wall includes a fraction of less than ½ of a board, plan to trim the first and last boards to avoid ending with a board cut to less than half its original width.

How to Install Wainscoting at Outside Corners

1 Cut a pair of boards to the widths indicated in the calculations you developed during the planning process.

2 Position the boards at the corner, butting them to create a plumb corner. Facenail the boards in place, then nail the joint, using 6d finish nails. Drive the nails to within ⅛" of the face of the boards, then finish with a nail set.

3 Position a piece of corner trim and nail it in place, using 6d finish nails. Install the remaining boards (opposite, steps 5 and 6).

How to Install Wainscoting at Inside Corners

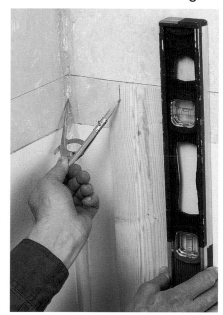

1 Hold a level against the first board and hold the board flush with the corner. If the wall is out of plumb, trim the board to compensate: hold the board plumb, position a compass at the inside corner of the wall, and use it to scribe a line down the board.

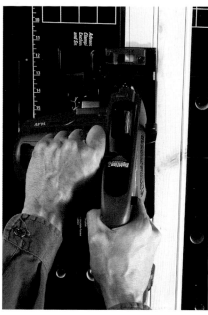

2 Cut along the scribed line with a circular saw.

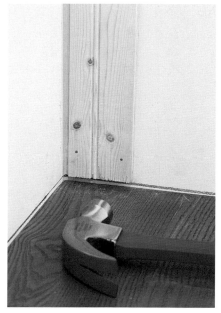

3 Hold the first board in the corner, leaving a ¼" gap for expansion, and facenail into the center of the board at each nailer location, using 6d finish nails. Drive the top nails roughly ½" from the edge so they'll be hidden from view once the cap rail is attached.

4 Install a second board at the corner by butting it against the first one, then facenailing in at least two locations. Nail to within ⅛" of the face of the board, then use a nail set to finish.

5 Position subsequent boards. Leave a ¹⁄₁₆" gap at each joint to allow for seasonal expansion. Use a level to check every third board for plumb. If the wainscoting is out of plumb, adjust the fourth board, as necessary, to compensate.

6 Mark and cut the final board to fit. If you're at a door casing, cut the board to fit flush with the casing (trim off at least the tongue). If you're at an inside corner, make sure it is plumb. If not, scribe and trim the board to fit.

How to Make a Cutout

1 Test the receptacle (inset) to make sure the power is off. Then, unscrew and remove the receptacle from the box. Coat the edges of the electrical box with bright-colored chalk.

2 Press the back of the board that will be installed over the receptacle directly against the electrical box, to create a cutting outline.

3 Lay the board face-down and drill a large pilot hole near one corner of the outline. Use a jig saw fitted with a fine-tooth woodcutting blade to make the cutout. Be careful not to cut outside the lines.

4 Facenail the wainscoting to the wall, then reattach the receptacle with the tabs overlapping the wainscoting so the receptacle is flush with the opening. You may need longer screws.

TIP: When paneling around a receptacle with thick stock, you will need to attach a receptacle box extender to the inside of the box, then reconnect the receptacle so it is flush with the opening in the paneling.

How to Install Wainscoting Around a Window

On casement windows, install wainscoting up to the casings on the sides and below the window. Install ½" cove molding or other trim to finish the edges.

On double-hung windows, install wainscoting up to the side casings. You can notch the wainscoting to fit around the stool, or remove the stool and notch it to fit over the wainscoting. Remove the apron (below the stool) and reinstall it over the wainscoting.

How to Finish a Wainscoting Project

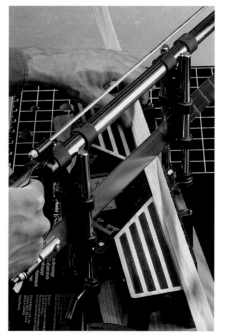

1 Cut baseboard moldings to fit over the wainscoting and attach them by nailing 6d finishing nails at the stud locations. If you plan to install base shoe, leave a small gap at the floor.

2 Cut the cap rail to fit as you would contoured baseboard. At doors and windows, install the cap rail so its edge is flush with the side casings.

3 Attach the cap rail by nailing 4d finish nails through the flats of the moldings at the stud locations. Set the nails with a nail set.

How to Install a Wainscot with Sheet Paneling

1 Measure up from the floor and snap a chalk line to represent the top of the paneling. This line will be ¾" lower than the overall height of the wainscot. Use a pencil to mark the stud locations about 1" above the chalk line. Measure the length of the wall to plan the layout of the sheets. The last piece should be at least 3" wide, so you may have to trim the first sheet to make the last piece wider.

2 Check the wall corner with a level to make sure it's plumb. If it's not plumb, scribe the first sheet to follow the angle or contours of the wall. Cut the first sheet to length so its bottom edge will be ½" above the floor, using a circular saw. Unless you've scribed the sheet, cut from the back side to prevent splintering on the face. Using a caulk gun, apply construction adhesive to the back side.

3 Apply the sheet to the wall so its top edge is flush with the chalk line and its side edge is set into the corner. Press the sheet firmly to bond it to the wall. Drive 6d finish nails at the stud locations, spacing them every 16" or so. Use only as many nails as needed to hold the sheet flat and to keep it in place.

4 Install the remaining sheets in the wall section. If you are paneling an adjacent wall, check the paneled wall for plumb, and trim the first sheet, if necessary. Install the sheet butted against the end sheet on the paneled wall.

5 Prepare the 1 × 6 rail material by sanding smooth the front face and bottom edge. If desired, round over the bottom, outside corner slightly with sandpaper. Install the rail with its top edge flush with the chalk line, fastening it to each stud with two 10d finish nails driven through pilot holes. Butt together rail pieces at inside corners, and miter them at outside corners, following the same techniques used for cutting and fitting baseboard (see "Installing Base Molding," page 90).

6 Mill the 1 × 3 top cap material, using a router and roundover bit. Work on test pieces to find the desired amount of roundover, then rout your workpieces on both front corners. Sand the cap smooth. OPTION: Create a waterfall edge by rounding over only the top edge of the cap (top inset), or chamfer the front edges with a chamfer bit (bottom inset).

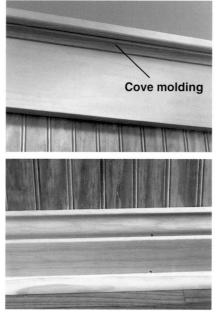

Cove molding

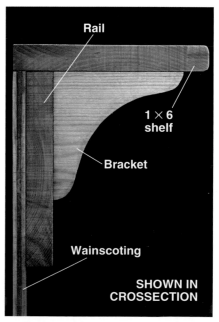

Rail

1 × 6 shelf

Bracket

Wainscoting

SHOWN IN CROSSECTION

7 Install the cap with wood glue and finish nails. Glue along the top edge of the rail and drive a 10d finish nail, angled at 45°, through the cap and into each stud (drill pilot holes for the nails). Miter the rail at corners.

8 Add cove molding to the joint between the cap and rail, fastening it to the rail with 2d finish nails. Install the baseboard along the bottom of the wainscot. Set all nails with a nail set.

Variation: Top your wainscot with a shelf rather than a cap. Use 1 × 6 or wider boards, and mill them as shown in step 6. To support the shelf, add wooden brackets fastened to the wall studs.

Installing Wall Frame Moldings

Adding wall frame moldings is a traditional decorative technique used to highlight special features of a room, divide large walls into smaller sections, or simply to add interest to plain surfaces. You can paint the molding the same color as the walls or use a contrasting color. For even greater contrast, paint or wallcover the areas within the frames.

Decorative wood moldings with curved contours work best for wall frames. Chair rail, picture rail, base shoe, cove, quarter-round, and other suitable molding types are readily available at home centers and lumberyards in several wood species.

To determine the sizes and locations of the frames, cut strips of paper to the width of the molding and tape them to the wall. You may want the frames to match the dimensions of architectural details in the room, such as windows or a fireplace.

Install the molding with small finish nails driven at each wall stud location and at the ends of the pieces. Use nails long enough to penetrate the studs by ¾". If there aren't studs where you need them, secure the molding with dabs of construction adhesive.

Everything You Need

Tools: level, framing square, miter box and backsaw, drill and bits, nail set.

Materials: paper strips, tape, wood finishing materials, construction adhesive, paintable latex caulk or wood putty.

How to Install Wall Frame Moldings

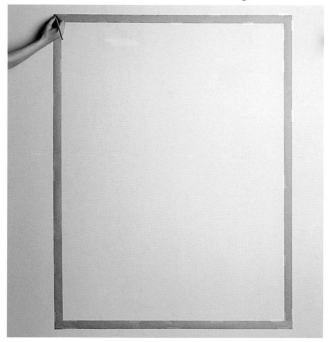

1 Cut paper strips to the width of the molding, and tape them to the wall. Use a framing square and level to make sure the frame is level and the strips are square to one another. Mark the outer corners of the frame with light pencil lines.

2 Cut the molding pieces to length, using a miter box and a backsaw (or power miter saw) to cut the ends at 45°. The top and bottom pieces should be the same length, as should the side pieces. Test fit the pieces, and make any necessary adjustments.

3 Paint or stain the moldings as desired. Position the top molding piece on the placement marks and tack it in place with two finish nails. If necessary, drill pilot holes for the nails to prevent splitting.

4 Tack the side moldings in place, using the framing square to make sure they are square to the top piece. Tack up the bottom piece. Adjust the frame, if necessary, so that all of the joints fit tightly, then completely fasten the pieces.

5 Drive the nails slightly below the surface, using a nail set. Fill the nail holes (and corner joints, if necessary) with wood putty. Touch up the patched areas with paint or stain.

Installing Wainscot Frames

Frame-and-panel wainscot adds depth, character, and a sense of Old-World charm to any room. Classic wainscot was built with grooved or rabbeted rails and stiles that captured a floating hardwood panel. In the project shown here, the classic appearance is mimicked, but the difficulties of machining precise parts and commanding craftsman-level joinery are eliminated. Paint-grade materials (mostly MDF) are used in the project shown; however you can also build the project with solid hardwoods and finish-grade plywood if you prefer a clear-coat finish.

Installing wainscot frames that look like frame-and-panel wainscot can be done piece by piece, but it is often easier to assemble the main frame parts in your shop. Not only does working in the shop allow you to join the frame parts to-

gether (we use pocket screws driven in the backs of the rails and stiles), it generally results in a more professional look.

Once the main frames are assembled, they can be attached to the wall at stud locations. If you prefer to site-build the wainscot piece by piece, you may need to replace the wallcovering material with plywood to create nailing surfaces for the individual pieces.

We primed all of the wainscot parts prior to installing them and then painted the wainscot (including the wall sections within the wainscot panel frames) a contrasting color from the wall above the wainscot cap.

Everything You Need

Tools: laser level, pencil, tape measure, circular saw or table saw, straightedge guide, power miter saw, drill with bits, carpenter's square, pocket hole jig with screws, pry bar, hammer, pneumatic finish nail gun with compressor, caulking gun.

Materials: ¾"-thick MDF sheet stock, 1¹⁄₁₆" cove molding, ½ x ¾" base shoe, ⁹⁄₁₆ x 1⅛" cap molding (10 ft. per panel), panel adhesive, paint and primer.

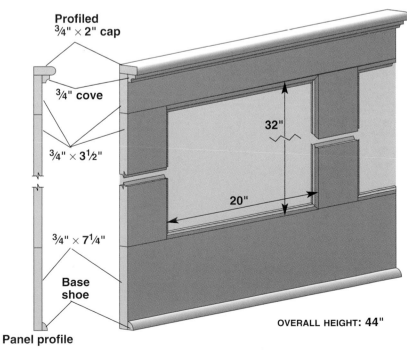

Profiled ¾" × 2" cap

¾" cove

¾" × 3½"

¾" × 7¼"

Base shoe

Panel profile

32"

20"

OVERALL HEIGHT: 44"

How to Install Wainscot Frames

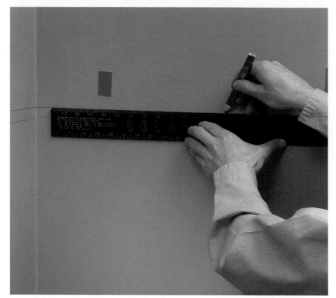

1 Use a laser level and a pencil to mark the height of the wainscot installation directly onto all walls in the project area. Also mark the height of the top rail (¾" below the overall height), since the cap rail will be installed after the rest of the wainscot is installed. Mark stud locations, using an electronic stud finder.

2 Plot out the wainscot layout on paper and then test the layout by drawing lines on the wall to make sure you're happy with the design. Try to use a panel width that can be divided evenly into all project wall lengths. In some cases, you may need to make the panel widths slightly different from wall to wall, but make sure to maintain a consistent width within each wall's run.

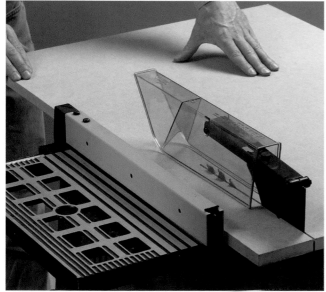

3 Based on your plan, rip a sheet of MDF into strips to make all of the wainscot parts except the trim moldings. In our case, that included the cap rail (2" wide), the top rail and stiles (3½" wide), and the base rail (7¼" wide). Note: These are standard lumber dimensions. You can use 1 × 4 and 1 × 4 dimensional lumber for the rails and stiles (use 1 × 2 or rip stock for the cap rail).

4 Cut top rails, base rails, and stiles (but not cap rails) to length and dry-assemble the parts into ladder frames based on your layout. Plan the layouts so wall sections longer than 8 ft. are cut with scarf joints in the rails meeting at a stud location. Dry-assemble the pieces on a flat work surface.

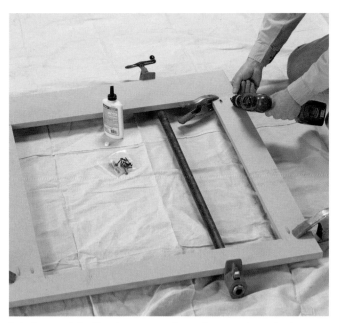

5 Assemble the frames using glue and pocket screws or biscuits. Clamp the parts together first and check with a carpenter's square to make sure the stiles are perpendicular to both rails.

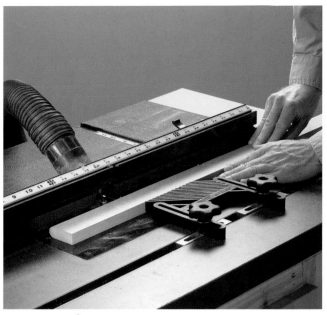

6 Mount a ¾" roundover bit in your router or router table and shape a bullnose profile on the front edge of your cap rail stock.

7 Prime all parts on both sides, including the milled moldings and uncut cap rail stock.

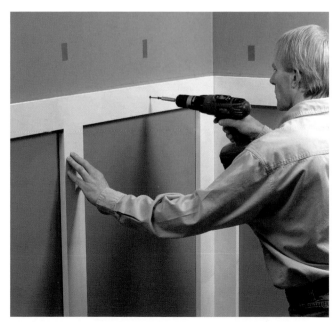

8 Position the frames against the wall and shim underneath the bottom rails as necessary to bring them flush with the top rail marks on the wall (¾" below the overall height lines). Attach the wainscot sections by driving 3" drywall screws, countersunk, through the top rail and the bottom rail at each stud location. If you are using scarf joints, be sure to install the open half first.

(continued next page)

9 Cut the cap rail to length and attach it to the top rail with panel adhesive and finish nails. Drive a 3" drywall screw through the cap rail and into the wall toenails style at each location. Be sure to carefully drill pilot holes and countersink holes for each screw. Miter-cut the cap rails at the corners.

10 Install cove molding in the crotch where the cap rail and top rails meet, using glue and a brad nailer. Then, nail base shoe to conceal any gaps between the bottoms, trials and the floor. Miter all corners.

11 Cut mitered frames to fit around the perimeter of each panel frame created by the rails and stiles. Use cap molding.

12 Mask the wall above the cap rail and then prime and paint the wainscot frames. Generally, a lighter, contrasting color than the wall color above is most effective visually.

Variation: Natural Wood Finish

1 Snap a level line at the top rail height. Because the rails and stiles are the same thickness, the backer panel should run all the way from the floor to just shy of the top of the top rail. Cut the backers so the grain will run vertically when installed. Attach them to the walls with panel adhesive, notching to fit around obstructions such as this window opening.

2 Install the baseboard and top rail directly over the backer panels, using a finish nailer or by hand-nailing with 6d finish nails. The top edge of the top rail pieces should be slightly higher then the backer panels. Use your reference line as a guide for the top rail, but double-check with a level.

3 Attach the cap rail pieces with a finish nailer. The caps should butt flush against the wall, concealing the top edges of the backer panels. Also butt the cap rails against the window and door casings.

4 Cut the stile to fit between the top rail and the baseboard and install them. It's okay to vary the spacing slightly form wall to wall, but try to keep them evenly spaced on each wall. Where the wainscot meets door or window casing, butt the edges of the stiles against the casing. This can mean notching around window aprons or horns as well as door plinth blocks.

5 Add decorative touches, such as the corbels we cut for this installation. The corbels provide some support for the cap rail but their function is primarily decorative. We glued and nailed one corbel at each end of each cap rail piece and above each stile, and then added an intermediate one between each pair of stiles.

Installing a Metal Tile Ceiling

Today's metal ceilings offer the distinctive elegance of 19th-century tin tile in a durable, washable ceiling finish. Available at home centers and specialty distributors, metal ceiling systems include field panels (in 2 × 2-, 2 × 4-, and 2 × 8-ft. sizes), border panels that can be cut to fit your layout, and cornice molding for finishing the edges. The panels come in a variety of materials and finishes ready for installation, or they can be painted.

To simplify installation, the panels have round catches, called nailing buttons, that fit into one another to align the panels where they overlap. The buttons are also the nailing points for attaching the panels. Use 1" decorative conehead nails where nail heads will be exposed, and ½" wire nails where heads are hidden.

Install your metal ceiling over a smooth layer of ⅜" or ½" plywood, which can be fastened directly to the ceiling joists with drywall screws, or installed over an existing finish. The plywood pro-

vides a flat nailing surface for the panels. As an alternative, some manufacturers offer a track system for clip-on installation.

Begin your installation by carefully measuring the ceiling and snapping chalk lines to establish the panel layout. For most tile patterns, it looks best to cover the center of the space with full tiles only, then fill in along the perimeter with border panels, which are not patterned. Make sure your layout is square.

Everything You Need

Tools: chalk line, level, tin snips, drill with ⅛" metal bit, compass, metal file.

Materials: ⅜" or ½" plywood, 2" drywall screws, field panels, border panels with molding edge, cornice molding, masking tape, ½" wire nails, 1" conehead nails, wood block.

How to Install a Metal Tile Ceiling

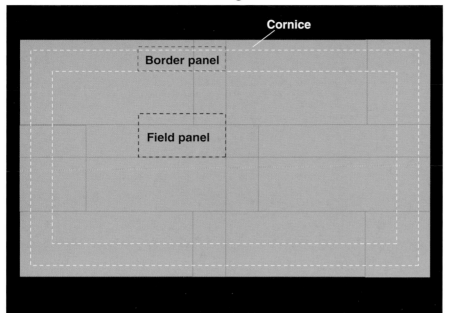

1 Measure to find the center of the ceiling, then snap perpendicular chalk lines intersecting the center. On the walls, mark a level reference line representing the bottom edges of the cornice molding. Where possible, plan to install the panels so they overlap toward the room's entrance, to help conceal the seams.

2 Align the first field panel with the chalk lines at the ceiling's center, and attach it with ½" wire nails along the edges where another panel will overlap it. Drive the nails beside the nailing buttons—saving the buttons for nailing the overlapping panel.

3 Continue to install field panels, working along the length of the area first, then overlapping the next row. Make sure the nailing buttons are aligned. Underlap panels by sliding the new panel into position beneath the installed panel, then fasten through both panels at the nailing buttons, using 1" conehead nails. Where field panels meet at corners, drill ⅛" pilot holes for the conehead nails.

4 Cut the border panels to width so they will underlap the cornice by at least 1". Use sharp tin snips, and cut from the edge without edge molding. Install the panels so the nailing buttons on the molding align with those on the field panels. Fasten through the buttons with conehead nails, and along the cut edge with wire nails. At corners, miter-cut the panels, and drive conehead nails every 6" along the seam.

(continued next page)

 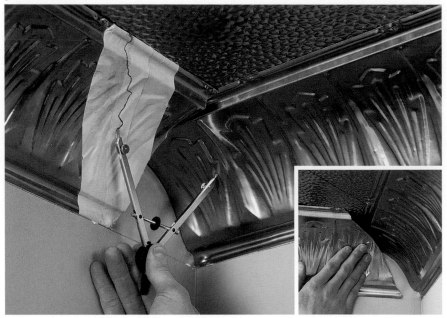

5 Install each cornice piece with its bottom edge on the level line. Drive 1" conehead nails through the nailing buttons and into the wall studs. Don't nail the ends until the succeeding piece is in place. Fasten the top edges to the ceiling.

6 At inside corners, install one cornice piece tightly into the corner, then scribe the mating piece to fit, using masking tape and a compass. Cut along the scribed line with tin snips, and make minor adjustments with a metal file. You may have to cut the mating piece several times, so start with plenty of length. If you have several corners, use this technique to cut templates for the corner pieces.

7 At outside corners, cut the ends of two scrap pieces at a 33° angle. Fit the pieces together at the corner, then trim and mark each piece in turn, making minor adjustments until they fit well. Use the scrap pieces as templates for marking the work-pieces. Fasten near the corner only when both mating pieces are in place.

8 Using a hammer and a piece of wood, carefully tap any loose joints to tighten them. If the cornice will be left unpainted, file the joints for a perfect fit. If you're painting the ceiling, seal the seams with paintable silicone caulk, then apply two coats of paint using a roller with a ¼" nap. Allow the first coat to dry for 24 hours before applying the second coat.

Installing Ceiling Tile

Everything You Need

Tools: 4-ft. level, stepladder, chalk line, utility knife, straightedge, hammer or drill, handsaw, stapler.

Materials: 1 × 2 furring strips, 8d nails or 2" screws, string, ceiling tiles, staples, trim molding.

Easy-to-install ceiling tile can lend character to a plain ceiling or help turn an unfinished basement or attic into beautiful living space. Made of pressed mineral and fiberboard, ceiling tiles are available in a variety of styles. They also provide moderate noise reduction.

Ceiling tiles typically can be attached directly to a drywall or plaster ceiling with adhesive. If your ceiling is damaged or uneven, or if you have an unfinished joist ceiling, install 1 × 2 furring strips as a base for the tiles, as shown in this project. Some systems include metal tracks for clip-on installation.

Unless your ceiling measures in even feet, you won't be able to install the 12" tiles without some cutting. To prevent an unattractive installation with small, irregular tiles along two sides, include a course of border tiles along the perimeter of the installation. Plan so that tiles at opposite ends of the room are cut to the same width and are at least ½ the width of a full tile.

Most ceiling tile comes prefinished, but it can be painted to match any decor. For best results, apply two coats of paint using a roller with a ¼" nap, and wait 24 hours between coats.

Create an area rug effect by covering only a portion of the ceiling with tiles. This technique helps to define living areas in open floor plans by breaking up bland expanses of white ceiling.

Add a faux patina by randomly dabbing the tiles with metallic green or blue paint, using a natural sea sponge.

How to Install Ceiling Tile

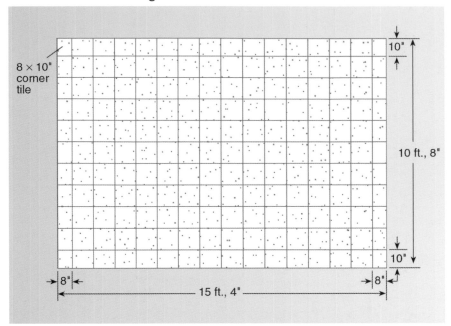

8 × 10" corner tile

10"

10 ft., 8"

10"

8"

15 ft., 4"

8"

1 Measure the ceiling and devise a layout. If the length (or width) doesn't measure in even feet, use this formula to determine the width of the border tiles: add 12 to the number of inches remaining and divide by 2. The result is the width of the border tile. (For example, if the room length is 15 ft., 4", add 12 to the 4, then divide 16 by 2, which results in an 8" border tile.)

2 Install the first furring strip flush with the wall and perpendicular to the joists, fastening with two 8d nails or 2" screws at each joist. Measure out from the wall a distance equal to the border tile width minus 3/4", and snap a chalk line. Install the second furring strip with its wall-side edge on the chalk line.

3 Install the remaining strips 12" on-center from the second strip. Measure from the second strip and mark the joist nearest the wall every 12". Repeat along the joist on the opposite side of the room, then snap chalk lines between the marks. Install the furring strips along the lines. Install the last furring strip flush against the opposite side wall. Stagger the butted end joints of strips between rows so they aren't all on the same joist.

4 Check the strips with a 4-ft. level. Insert wood shims between the strips and joists as necessary to bring the strips into a level plane.

174

5 Set up taut, perpendicular string lines along two adjacent walls to help guide the tile installation. Inset the strings from the wall by a distance that equals that wall's border tile width plus ½". Use a framing square to make sure the strings are square.

6 Cut the corner border tile to size with a utility knife and straightedge. Cutting the border tiles ¼" short will ease fitting them. The resulting gap between the tile and wall will be covered by trim. Cut only on the edges without the stapling flange.

7 Position the corner tile with the flange edges aligned with the two string lines and fasten it to the furring strips with four ½" staples. Cut and install two border tiles along each wall, making sure the tiles fit snugly together.

8 Fill in between the border tiles with full-size tiles. Continue working diagonally in this manner, toward the opposite corner. For the border tiles along the far wall, trim off the flange edges and staple through the faces of the tiles, close to the wall.

9 Install the final row of tiles, saving the far corner tile and its neighbor for last. Cut the last tile to size, then remove the tongue and nailing flange along the side edges. Finish the job by installing trim around the perimeter.

Paneling a Ceiling

Tongue-and-groove paneling offers a warm, attractive finish that's especially suited to vaulted ceilings. Pine is the most common material for tongue-and-groove paneling, but you can choose from many different wood species and panel styles. Panels typically are $\frac{3}{8}$" to $\frac{3}{4}$" thick and are often attached directly to ceiling joists or rafters. Some building codes require the installation of drywall as a fire stop behind ceiling paneling that's thinner than $\frac{1}{4}$".

When purchasing your paneling, get enough material to cover about 15% more square footage than the actual ceiling size, to allow for waste. Since the tongue portions of the panels slip into the grooves of adjacent pieces, square footage for paneling is based on the *reveal*—the exposed face of the panel after it is installed.

Tongue-and-groove boards can be attached with flooring nails or finish nails. Flooring nails hold better because they have spiraled shanks, but they tend to have larger heads than finish nails. Whenever possible, drive the nails through the base of the tongue and into the framing. This is called *blind-nailing,* because the groove of the succeeding board covers the nail heads. Add facenails only at joints and in locations where more support is needed, such as along the first and last boards. To ensure clean cuts, use a compound miter saw. These saws are especially useful for ceilings with non-90° angles.

Layout is crucial to the success of a paneling project. Before you start, determine how many boards you'll need, using the reveal measurement. If the final board will be less than 2" wide, trim the first, or *starter*, board by cutting the long edge that abuts the wall. If the ceiling peak is not parallel to the side (starting) wall, rip the starter piece at an angle to match the wall. The leading edge of the starter piece, and every piece thereafter, must be parallel to the peak.

Everything You Need

Tools: chalk line, compound miter saw, circular saw, drill, nail set, pneumatic finish nail gun (optional).

Materials: tongue-and-groove paneling, 1$\frac{3}{4}$" spiral flooring nails, trim molding.

How to Panel a Ceiling

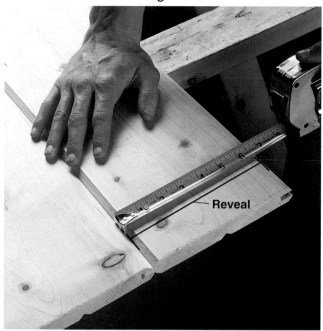

1 To plan your layout, first measure the reveal of the boards. Fit two pieces together and measure from the bottom edge of the upper board to the bottom edge of the lower board. Calculate the number of boards needed to cover one side of the ceiling by dividing the reveal dimension into the overall distance between the top of the wall and the peak.

2 Use the calculation from step 1 to make a control line for the first row of panels—the starter boards. At both ends of the ceiling, measure down from the peak an equal distance, and make a mark to represent the top (tongue) edges of the starter boards. Snap a chalk line through the marks.

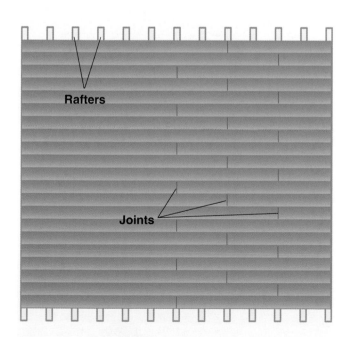

3 If the boards aren't long enough to span the entire ceiling, plan the locations of the joints. Staggering the joints in a three-step pattern will make them less conspicuous. Note that each joint must fall over the middle of a rafter. For best appearance, select boards of similar coloring and grain for each row.

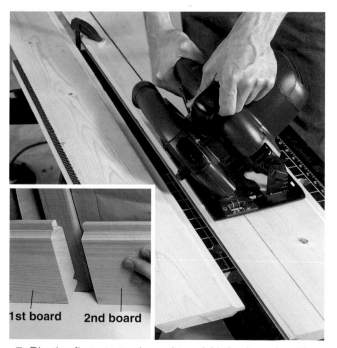

4 Rip the first starter board to width by bevel-cutting the bottom (grooved) edge. If the starter row will have joints, cut the board to length using a 30° bevel cut on the joint end only. Two beveled ends joined together form a *scarf* joint (inset), which is less noticeable than a butt joint. If the board spans the ceiling, square-cut both ends.

(continued next page)

5 Position the first starter board so the tongue is on the control line. Leave a ⅛" gap between the square board end and the end wall. Fasten the board by nailing through its face about 1" from the grooved edge and into the rafters. Then, blind-nail through the base of the tongue into each rafter, angling the nail backward at 45°. Drive the nail heads beneath the wood surface, using a nail set.

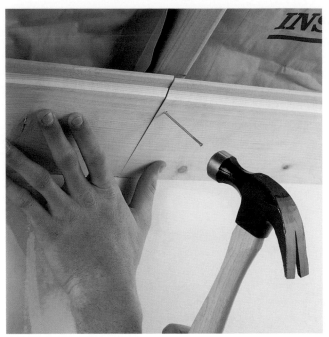

6 Cut and install any remaining boards in the starter row one at a time, making sure the scarf joints fit together tightly. At each scarf joint, drive two nails through the face of the top board, angling the nail to capture the end of the board behind it. If necessary, predrill the nail holes to prevent splitting.

7 Cut the first board for the next row, then fit its grooved edge over the tongue of the board in the starter row. Use a hammer and a scrap piece of paneling to drive downward on the tongue edge, seating the grooved edge over the tongue of the starter board. Fasten the second row with blind-nails only.

8 As you install successive rows, measure down from the peak to make sure the rows remain parallel to the peak. Correct any misalignment by adjusting the tongue-and-groove joint slightly with each row. You can also snap additional control lines to help align the rows.

9 Rip the boards for the last row to width, beveling the top edges so they fit flush against the ridge board. Facenail the boards in place. Install paneling on the other side of the ceiling, then cut and install the final row of panels to form a closed joint under the ridge board (inset).

10 Install trim molding along walls, at joints around obstacles, and along inside and outside corners, if desired. (Select-grade 1 × 2 works well as trim along walls.) Where necessary, bevel the back edges of the trim or miter-cut the ends to accommodate the slope of the ceiling.

Tips for Paneling an Attic Ceiling

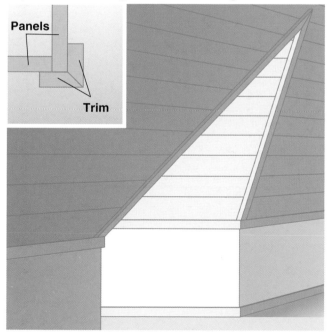

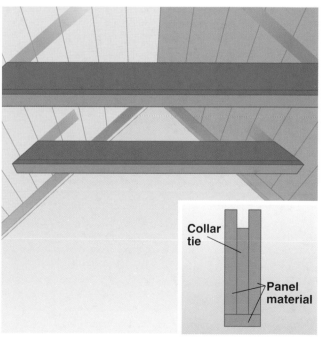

Use mitered trim to cover joints where panels meet at outside corners. Dormers and other roof elements create opposing ceiling angles that can be difficult to panel around. It may be easier to butt the panels together and hide the butt joints with custom-cut trim. The trim also makes a nice transition between angles.

Wrap collar ties or exposed beams with custom-cut panels. Install the paneling on the ceiling first. Then, rip-cut panels to the desired width. You may want to include a tongue-and-groove joint as part of the trim detail. Angle-cut the ends of the trim so it fits tight to the ceiling panels.

Hanger wire   Screw eye   Main

Wall angle   Tee   Panel

Installing a Suspended Ceiling

Suspended ceilings are traditionally popular ceiling finishes for basements and utility areas, particularly because they hang below pipes and other mechanicals while providing easy access to them. However, the commercial appearance and grainy texture of basic ceiling tiles make them an unlikely choice for formal areas such as living rooms. Basic tiles are not your only option.

Suspended ceiling tile manufacturers have a wide array of ceiling tiles to choose from that go above and beyond traditional institutional tiles. Popular styles mimic historical tin tiles and add depth to the ceiling while minimizing sound and vibration noise.

A suspended ceiling is a grid framework made of lightweight metal brackets hung on wires attached to ceiling or floor joists. The frame consists of T-shaped main beams (mains), cross-tees (tees), and L-shaped wall angles. The grid supports ceiling panels, which rest on the flanges of the framing pieces. Panels are available in 2 × 2-ft. or 2 × 4-ft. sizes, in a variety of styles. Special options include insulated panels, acoustical panels that absorb

sound, and light-diffuser screens for use with fluorescent lights. Generally, metal-frame ceiling systems are more durable than ones made of plastic.

To begin your ceiling project, devise the panel layout based on the size of the room, placing equally sized trimmed panels on opposite sides to create a balanced look. Your ceiling must also be level. For small rooms, a 4-ft. or 6-ft. level will work, but a water level is more effective for larger jobs. You can make a water level with two water-level ends (available at hardware stores and home centers) attached to a standard garden hose.

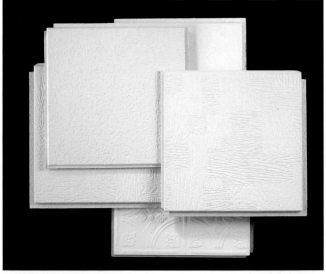

Acoustical ceiling tiles are available in a wide variety of styles. Some mimic the tin or plaster ceilings of the past.

Everything You Need

Tools: water level, chalk line, drill, aviation snips, string, lock-type clamps, screw-eye driver, pliers, straightedge, utility knife.

Materials: suspended ceiling kit (frame), screw eyes, hanger wires, ceiling panels, 1½" drywall screws or masonry nails.

Tips for Installing a Suspended Ceiling

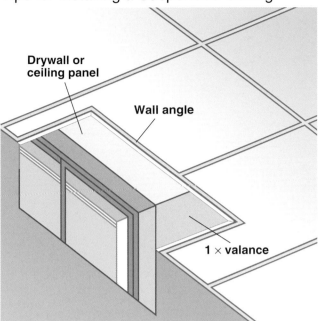

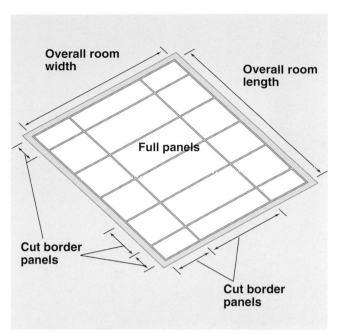

Build a valance around basement awning windows so they can be opened fully. Attach 1 × lumber of an appropriate width to joists or blocking. Install drywall (or a suspended-ceiling panel trimmed to fit) to the joists inside the valance.

Draw your ceiling layout on paper, based on the exact dimensions of the room. Plan so that trimmed border panels on opposite sides of the room are of equal width and length (avoid panels smaller than ½-size). If you include lighting fixtures in your plan, make sure they follow the grid layout.

How to Install a Suspended Ceiling

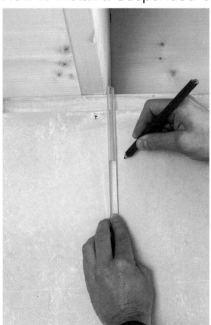

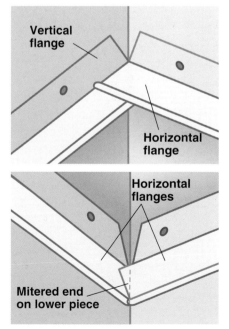

1 Make a mark on one wall that represents the ceiling height plus the height of the wall angle. Use a water level to transfer that height to both ends of each wall. Snap a chalk line to connect the marks. This line represents the top of the ceiling's wall angle.

2 Attach wall angle pieces to the studs on all walls, positioning the top of the wall angle flush with the chalk line. Use 1½" drywall screws (or short masonry nails driven into mortar joints on concrete block walls). Cut angle pieces using aviation snips.

Tip: Trim wall angle pieces to fit around corners. At inside corners (top), back-cut the vertical flanges slightly, then overlap the horizontal flanges. At outside corners (bottom), miter-cut one horizontal flange, and overlap the flanges.

(continued next page)

3 Mark the location of each main on the wall angles at the ends of the room. The mains must be parallel to each other and perpendicular to the ceiling joists. Set up a guide string for each main, using a thin string and lock-type clamps (inset). Clamp the strings to the opposing wall angles, stretching them very taut so there's no sagging.

4 Install screw eyes for hanging the mains, using a drill and screw-eye driver. Drill pilot holes and drive the eyes into the joists every 4 ft., locating them directly above the guide strings. Attach hanger wire to the screw eyes by threading one end through the eye and twisting the wire on itself at least three times. Trim excess wire, leaving a few inches of wire hanging below the level of the guide string.

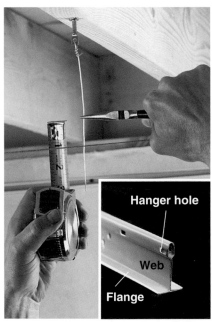

Hanger hole

Web

Flange

5 Measure the distance from the bottom of a main's flange to the hanger hole in the web (inset). Use this measurement to prebend each hanger wire. Measure up from the guide string and make a 90° bend in the wire, using pliers.

6 Following your ceiling plan, mark the placement of the first tee on opposite wall angles at one end of the room. Set up a guide string for the tee, using a string and clamps, as before. This string must be perpendicular to the guide strings for the mains.

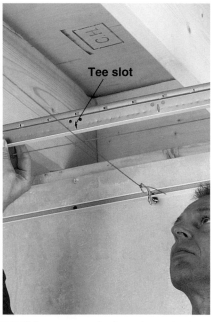

Tee slot

7 Trim one end of each main so that a tee slot in the main's web is aligned with the tee guide string, and the end of the main bears fully on a wall angle. Set the main in place to check the alignment of the tee slot with the string.

8 Cut the other end of each main to fit, so that it rests on the opposing wall angle. If a single main cannot span the room, splice two mains together, end-to-end (the ends should be fashioned with male-female connectors). Make sure the tee slots remain aligned when splicing.

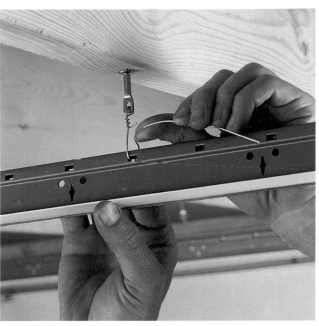

9 Install the mains by setting the ends on the wall angle and threading the hanger wires through the hanger holes in the webs. The wires should be as close to vertical as possible. Wrap each wire around itself three times, making sure the main's flange is level with the main guide string. Also install a hanger near each main splice.

10 Attach tees to the mains, slipping their tabbed ends into the tee slots on the mains. Align the first row of tees with the tee guide string; install the remaining rows at 4-ft. intervals. If you're using 2 × 2-ft. panels, install 2-ft. cross-tees between the midpoints of the 4-ft. tees. Cut and install the border tees, setting the tee ends on the wall angles. Remove all guide strings and clamps.

11 Place full ceiling panels into the grid first, then install the border panels. Lift the panels in at an angle, and position them so they rest on the frame's flanges. Reach through adjacent openings to adjust the panels, if necessary. To trim the border panels to size, cut them faceup, using a straightedge and utility knife (inset).

Installing Ceiling Beams

Installing ceiling beams adds depth and visual appeal to vaulted or high ceilings, or even regular 8-ft. ceilings that are a bit on the bland side. The beams of this project are purely decorative, but meant to suggest the heavy-duty structural members of timber-frame construction. Choose a higher-grade lumber for a cleaner look, or a lower grade for a more rustic approach. The species of wood you use to build the beams may match your existing trimwork, although clear-coated hardwood beams will be more expensive than paint-grade counterparts.

Whenever possible, install ceiling beams with fasteners driven into blocking or joists. Installation of ceiling beams is not recommended without solid backing. Standard wallboard construction is not built to hold the weight of this project with hollow wall fasteners and construction adhesive alone. Use hollow wall fasteners only when absolutely necessary.

Exposed beams lend a feeling of strength and structure to a room, even if they're really just hollow shells like the beams seen here. Because they can be attached directly to the ceiling surface, installing decorative beams is a relatively easy trim carpentry project (as long as you're comfortable working at heights).

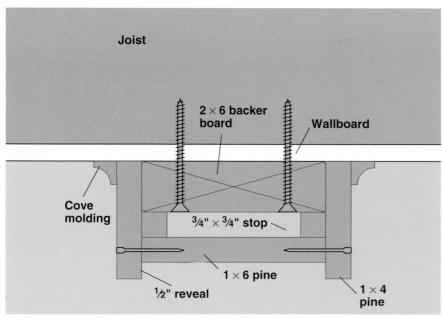

A crossection view of the exposed beams shown being installed here reveals that they are hollow inside and actually quite simple in structure. You can install beams in any direction, but perpendicular to the ceiling joists (as shown above) is the easier orientation to work with.

Everything You Need

Tools: Pencil, tape measure, circular saw with straight-edge guide, power miter saw, drill with bits, pneumatic finish-nail gun and compressor, caulk gun, combination square.

Materials: painter's tape, chalk line, 1 × 6 and 1 × 4 boards, 2 × 6 framing lumber, cove moldings, 3" Wallboard screws, construction adhesive, hollow wall fasteners, 1¼" pneumatic finish nails, wood glue.

Installing Ceiling Beams

1 Plan the approximate location of each ceiling beam and locate the ceiling joists in the desired areas with a stud finder. Mark the joists on the ceiling with tape.

2 Mark the end of each joist at the point where the ceiling meets the wall. If you will be installing the beams parallel to the joists, as shown here, measure out from the center of each joist one-half the width of the backer board you'll be installing ($2\frac{3}{4}$" for a 2×6) and make a reference mark. Make reference marks at the same relative spots where the opposite wall meets the ceiling. For installations parallel to the joists, offsetting the marks results in visible reference lines for the edges of the backer boards.

3 Use a chalk line to snap straight reference lines across the ceiling. Have a helper hold the line on the corresponding reference mark. If you are installing the beams perpendicular to the joists, you may want to avoid snapping a chalk line, since marking chalk (especially red chalk) is hard to remove and can even telegraph through paint. An option that won't mark up the ceiling is to string a grid of unchalked lines across the ceiling to mark the positions of the beams and the locations of the joists. Then, mark an X at every point where the lines intersect and remove the lines before installing the backer boards for the beams.

(continued next page)

Reference line

4 Measure, cut, and install 2 × 6 backer boards according to your reference lines. Use construction adhesive to adhere the blocking to the ceiling and drive 3" wallboard screws through the blocking and into the joists. TIP: If you're working alone, drive a few screws into the backers (preferably at known joist locations) before you position it. Then, you can hold the board in place with one hand and drive the screws with the other hand. A better plan, of course, is to recruit a helper.

Option: In areas where a ceiling joist is not available and blocking is difficult to install, use hollow wall fasteners (such as the toggle bolt shown here) to install the backers. At the end of each backer you can drive 3" screws toenail style into the top plate of the wall to provide additional support.

5 Set the blade of a combination square to 1¼" and mark the back face of the 1 × 4 beam sides with a pencil. Slide the square along the edge of the piece and hold the tip of the pencil against the end of the blade. Mark enough stock for each beam side.

6 Use a table saw (best tool) or a circular saw and a straightedge guide to cut ¾" × ¾" strips off of pine for the stop molding. Cut enough stock to apply to each beam side piece.

7 Align the stop-molding strips with the reference marks on the beam sides. Nail and glue the ¾" strips to the back faces of the beam sides with 1¼" finish nails and wood glue.

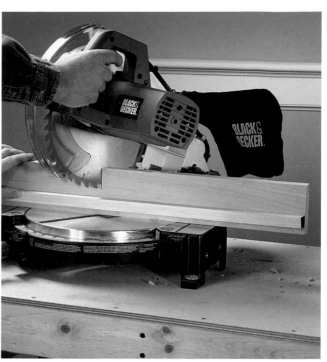

8 Cut the side pieces to length with a power miter saw, using scarf joints to join each piece that is more then 8 ft. long. Butt the ends of the beams into the opposing walls, making sure the joints are tight. Nail the sides in place using 1½" finish nails driven every 12" into the blocking.

9 Install the bottom pieces of the beams with wood glue and 1½" nails driven into the ¾" strips on the inside of the beams. Make sure the ends butt into the walls snugly, and use scarf joints where joining pieces together (offset the scarf joints from seams in the beam sides).

10 Install cove molding along the seam between the beams and the ceiling with 1¼" finish nails. Drive the nails into the sides of the beams. Apply the finish of your choice to the beams, filling the nail holes appropriately.

Ceiling medallions are classic trim accessories, and most sold today are designed to be installed in conjunction with a ceiling light fixture. Some medallions come as solid discs (carved wood, cast plaster, or more commonly, urethane) and others are two-piece assemblies that can be slipped between the light and the ceiling and snapped together.

Installing Ceiling Medallions Above a Light Fixture

A ceiling medallion is an elegant style accent that can highlight a light fixture or establish the visual focal point of a room all on its own. Most medallions available today are made of polyurethane and are available at home centers off the shelf in various styles and sizes. Specialty restoration dealers carry extensive lines of medallions as well.

In the project shown, a medallion is installed over a light fixture. Depending on the style of medallion you choose, a hole may need to be cut in the center to allow access to the electrical mechanicals in the ceiling. If you are installing the medallion over a light fixture, turn off the power at the main service panel before you begin.

Everything You Need

Tools: screwdriver, adjustable wrench, pencil, drill with bits and circle cutter, daulk gun

Materials: medallion, 150-grit sandpaper, polyurethane adhesive, threaded nipple, wallboard screws, paintable latex caulk.

How to Install a Ceiling Medallion

1 Remove the cover plate of the light fixture. Disconnect the fixture wires, taking note of the color of the wires of each connection. If necessary, unscrew the supporting nipple in the center of the electrical box and set the fixture aside.

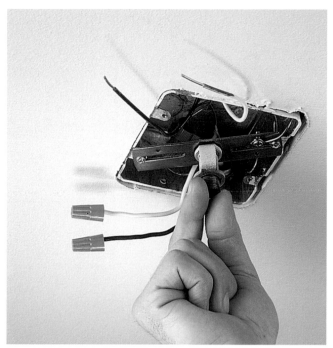

2 Compensate for the added thickness of the medallion by adding a longer nipple to the center of the electrical box. If a nipple is not used, purchase longer screws to reattach the cover plate to the mounting strap once the medallion is installed.

3 Cut a hole in the center of the medallion using a circle cutter and a drill. The hole should be smaller than the cover plate, but large enough to access the screw holes on the mounting strap. Lightly sand the back of the medallion with 150-grit sandpaper.

4 Position the medallion on the ceiling centered over the electrical box. Trace the outline with a pencil. Apply adhesive to the back of the medallion, staying 1" away from the outer edge. Align the medallion with the pencil line and press it to the ceiling.

5 Drill countersunk pilot holes in inconspicuous areas of the medallion and drive wallboard screws through the holes to hold it in place until the adhesive dries. Fill the holes with paintable latex caulk, smoothing the holes with a wet finger. Paint the medallion as desired, and reattach the light when the paint is completely dry.

Exterior Trim

How to Wrap Posts & Beams

Whether they support a porch roof or a deck, posts and beams can look spindly and plain. Rather than spending the money for large timbers, it is a common practice among builders to wrap the posts and beams with finish-grade lumber to give them a more proportional look. The finish-grade pine cladding shown here gives 4 × 4 posts and doubled 2 × 8 beams the look of more substantial stock.

Everything You Need

Tools: basic hand tools.

Materials: finish lumber, siding nails, plywood strips.

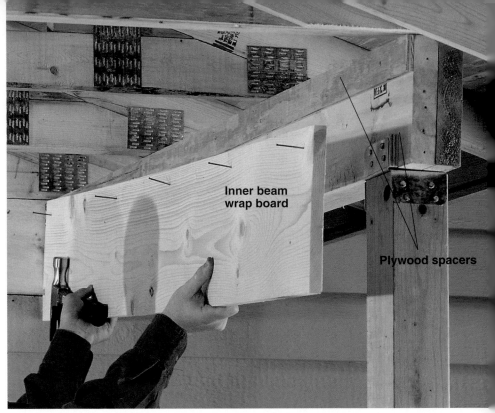

Inner beam wrap board

Plywood spacers

1 Cut cladding boards for the inner sides of the beams to the same length as the beams, using finish lumber wide enough to cover the beams and any metal saddles or joiners. We used 1 × 10, but sanded ¾" plywood can be used instead. Attach the inner-side boards to the beams with 8d siding nails—in the project shown here, we added ½" plywood strips at the top and bottom of the beam to compensate for the ½" spacers in the metal post saddles.

Side board

Bottom board

2 Cut strips of wood to cover the bottoms of the beams. Position each strip next to a board cut the same size as the inner beam wrap. The difference in length between the side board and the bottom board should equal the distance of the beam overhang at the post. Preassemble the bottom board and side board by driving 8d finish nails at the butt joint, making sure to keep the joint square. Attach the assembly to the beam so the free end of the bottom board forms a butt joint with the inner beam wrap board.

3 Cut boards to create an end cap for each beam— we cut a piece of 1 × 10 to fit over the ends of the beam and the beam wrap, and attached it to a piece of 1 × 4 cut to cover the gap beneath the beam overhang. Nail end caps over the end of each beam.

4 Cut boards for wrapping the posts so they span from the post bottoms to the beam bottoms. For a 4 × 4 post, two 1 × 4s and two 1 × 6s per post can be used. Nail a 1 × 6 to the front of the post, overhanging ¾" on the outside edge. Nail a 1 × 4 to the outer face of the post, butted against the 1 × 6.

5 Preassemble the other two wrap boards, nailing through the face of the 1 × 6 and into the edge of the 1 × 4. Set the assembly around the post, nailing the 1 × 6 to the post and nailing through the other 1 × 6 and into the edge of the 1 × 4 (there will be a slight gap between the second 1 × 4 and the post).

6 Cut pieces of finish lumber to fit around the bases of the posts (called "post collars"). We used 1 × 6 to create the bottom post collars, and 1 × 4 to create the top collars where the posts meet the beams. Nail the collars together with 4d finish nails. Cut pieces so the front collar board covers the end grain of the side boards. Cove molding around the tops of the collars gives a more finished look and sheds water.

Furring strip

7 Roof ledgers often are visible after the porch ceiling is installed, so cover the ledger with finish lumber. If the ledger protrudes past the siding, cut a furring strip to cover the gap between the inside face of the ledger cover and the siding. Cut the ledger cover and furring strips to fit, and install with 8d nails. If the ledger extends past the outer face of the beam, the easiest solution is to paint it to match the siding.

How to Finish the Cornice & Gable

The gable and the cornice are prominent features on many houses. The gable is the area just below the peak, which is usually covered with trim and siding material. The cornice, sometimes called the "cornice return" or the "fascia return," is usually fitted with trim that squares off the corner where it meets the soffit. The project shown here involves putting the finishing touches on a new porch, but these areas commonly require repair as well.

Everything You Need

Tools: basic hand tools, miter box, straightedge guide.

Materials: plywood, framing lumber, finish-grade lumber, cove molding, nails, caulk.

The cornice and gable are finished to match the siding and trim on your house. Use plywood or finish-grade lumber to make the cornice, and use siding that matches your house for the gable trim. Caulk seams at the peak of the gable, and between the fascia boards and the cornice (inset).

How to Install a Cornice

1 At each end of the front porch, measure the area from the end of the gable fascia to a spot about 6" inside the porch beam. Lay out a triangular piece of plywood or finish-grade lumber to fit the area, using a carpenter's square to create right angles. Cut out the cornice pieces, using a circular saw and straight-edge.

2 Test-fit the cornice pieces over the ends of the porch gable, then install with 8d finish nails driven into the ends of the beams, and 4d nails driven up through the ends of the cornice pieces and into the underside of the gable fascia. Use a nail set to embed the heads of the nails below the surface of the wood, being careful not to split the cornice pieces.

How to Install Gable Trim

Gable fascia

Frieze board

1 Measure the dimensions of the area covered by the gable sheathing on the house. If you have installed fascia and frieze boards, measure from the bottom of the frieze boards. Add 2" of depth to the area to make sure that siding will cover the edge of the ceiling once the ceiling and soffits are installed. Snap a horizontal chalk line near the bottom of the gable sheathing to use as a reference line for installing the siding.

2 Mark a cutting line that matches the slope of the roof onto the end of one piece of siding. Use a framing square or a speed square to mark the slope line. OPTION: Position a scrap board on the horizontal chalk line on the gable sheathing, and mark the points where the edges of the board intersect with the frieze board: connect the points to establish the slope line. Cut the siding or scrap board on the slope line and use it as a template to mark siding for cutting. Cut the bottom siding board to length.

3 Use 4d siding nails to install the bottom siding board so it is flush with the bottom edges of the frieze boards—the bottom edge of the siding board should be 2" lower than the bottom of the gable sheathing. Cut the next siding board so it overlaps the first board from above, creating the same amount of exposed siding as in the rest of the house. Be careful to keep the siding level. Continue cutting and installing siding pieces until you reach the peak of the gable.

193

How to Install Soffits & Ceilings

Soffits are panels that close off the area between rafter ends and the side of a house. They can be nailed directly to the rafters, or attached to nailers on the house or porch beams so they are horizontal. A porch ceiling can be made from plywood or tongue-and-groove boards to give the porch a finished appearance.

Plowed groove

Everything You Need

Tools: basic hand tools, straightedge guide, torpedo level, caulk gun, miter box.

Materials: plywood, plowed fascia board, nails, nailer.

Option: Attach soffit directly to rafters. Attach a fascia board with a plowed groove (inset) to the rafter ends. Measure from the back of the fascia plow groove to the beam, following the bottom of the rafter tail, to establish the required width for the soffit panel. Measure the length from the house to the cornice or gable, then cut a piece of ⅜"-thick plywood to these dimensions. Insert one edge of the plywood panel into the plowed groove, and press the soffit panel up against the rafter tail. Nail the panel in place with 4d galvanized common nails, then caulk the edges before painting the panel.

How to Install Horizontal Soffit Panels

1 Install a fascia board with a plowed groove. Use a torpedo level to transfer the top height of the groove to the beam, near one end. Mark the groove height at the other end of the beam, then connect with a chalk line. Install a 2 × 2 nailer just above the chalk line.

2 Measure from the back of the plowed groove to the beam, just below the nailer, to find the required width of the soffit panel. Measure the length, then cut a piece of ⅜"-thick plywood to fit. Insert one edge of the soffit panel into the plow, then nail the other edge to the nailer with 4d nails.

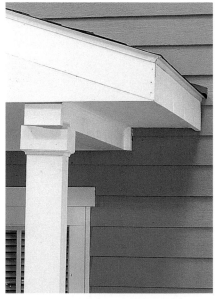

TIP: Paint soffits to match the rest of the porch trim. Add quarter-round molding at the joint between the soffit and the beam, or fill the gaps with tinted exterior-grade caulk.

Tips for Applying Finishing Trim Touches

A few final touches add personality and a completed look to your home's exterior. There are a wide range of decorative trim types that can be purchased or built, then installed to dress up the porch or help it blend with the style of your house. Look through millwork catalogs to find ideas for trimming out your new porch. Also visit salvage yards to find authentic millwork, like gingerbread types, that will blend in with the rest of your house.

Avoid getting carried away with decorative trim. A few elegant touches will go a long way.

Use gable ornamentation to soften the hard lines of the gable peak. Fan-style trim (above) and many other trim types that fit into a peak are made to fit a range of different peak angles. Make sure to measure your peak angle carefully before purchasing or ordering gable ornamentation.

Install decorative trim to enhance the appeal of your porch. The scalloped fascia boards above were cut from plain 1 × 6 pine, using a jig saw, to add a touch of flair to a plain gable.

Put stock moldings, sold at any building center, to creative use on a porch. The simple cove molding above is installed at the joint between a post collar and the post, to create more graceful lines.

Creating Custom Moldings

Creating your own custom moldings can be a great cost-saver on a large trim project. But more than that, it allows you to choose the exact profiles and dimensions and wood species you want for your molding.

Creating Custom Moldings

Creating your own custom trim moldings can be a simple and rewarding process if you own the right tools and start out with proper materials. Nothing looks better than a room with one-of-a-kind trim, and your pride in knowing that you didn't just install the trim, but actually created it yourself will stay with you forever. Beyond the satisfaction of knowing that you did it yourself, you may be asking why anyone would make their own trim work.

The most common reason to create your own trim is to match the existing moldings of your home. The moldings of older homes are more unique and in some cases were milled by hand, making it difficult to match the profiles with any of today's stock materials. If the trim from a remodeling project is not salvageable, you may find a need for just a few lineal feet of matching material. Short runs of specialized trim components from professional mill shops are expensive and not cost effective.

Another reason to create your own moldings is to match an existing species of wood in your home. Stock moldings are generally available in a few commonly used materials, leaving out species such as walnut, cherry, ash, or hickory.

If the hardwood floor of your formal dining room is hickory, finding matching casings for the windows and doors will be nearly impossible. Unless you do it yourself.

No matter the reason, creating your own moldings requires patience and proper materials. Using machinery to create trim that is uniform from the first foot to the last can be challenging. Router settings must be precise, and bits must be sharp. Whenever possible, machine each piece of trim you need plus a few extra to make up for bad cuts and blemishes in the material.

Material preparation is the most important part of creating uniform custom moldings. "Blank" stock that will be turned into moldings needs to be machined squarely and at a uniform thickness with a planer, jointer, and a table saw. Inaccurate thicknesses and material that differs in width will show up at every joint of the installation. If you do not have access to this machinery, consider asking a small cabinet shop in your area to provide the service for you. Finish-sand each piece of material prior to molding it. This will avoid excess chatter marks and unnecessary sanding, which could remove the profile you mold.

Types of Routers

Routers are available in three specific horsepower ranges to perform a variety of shaping and routing operations. Each size has its own pros and cons, depending upon the type of work you will be doing. Added to the size options are two specific styles: fixed-base and plunge style. Choosing between a fixed-base or a plunge router can be difficult. Some manufacturers sell router kits that have one motor unit that fits into multiple bases.

3 hp.: The largest-capacity routers available for home use are 3 hp. These heavy-duty, workhorse routers are not only the most powerful, but the bulkiest and most difficult to use for hand-held operations. They are most commonly used to turn large-diameter bits (1" or greater) while mounted in a router table.

1½–2 hp.: The most common size of router for general use is the 1½ – 2-hp model. These medium-duty routers work well for hand-held operations and when mounted in a table. Medium-duty routers can be used for small chamfers as well as larger-diameter bits. However, larger bits require multiple passes for large material removal.

1 hp.: The smallest router class is 1 hp or less. These routers are commonly referred to as "laminate" or "trim" routers. Their smaller size limits them to very light trimming of thin materials such as laminates, but also makes them easier to handle for smaller roundovers or chamfers in intricate trim work.

Fixed Base: The typical fixed-base router has a low center of gravity, with large handles and a broad, round base. Many woodworkers prefer the feel of a fixed-base router, especially when edge forming, due to the stability of the tool and the ease of control. Although the stability may be

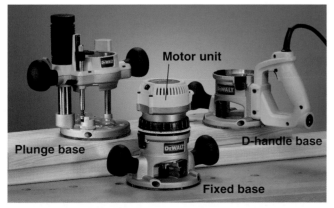

Many manufacturers sell router kits that include an interchangeable motor unit and alternate bases: plunge type and fixed.

Heavy-, medium-, and light-duty routers are available for a wide variety of shaping and routing applications. Most often, heavy-duty models are mounted in a router table, while the smaller trim router is intended for handheld use only. Medium-duty models (1½ to 2 hp) are good for general purpose use.

greater, it is difficult to repeat a specific depth with a fixed-base router because there are no positive stops. This means that each operation must be completed to each workpiece before moving on to the next step. While that may not sound bad, if you are creating a large run of moldings, you will need to handle each piece every time, for every operation. This can be time consuming and requires a lot of space.

Plunge: Plunge routers can accomplish any task that a fixed-base router can, but with less ease and stability. The higher motor and handles make the tool more prone to tipping when the base isn't fully supported; however, this issue only applies for handheld use. Plunge routers excel at making inside cuts such as mortises or the fluted grooves for Neo-classical-style casings. Some plunge routers have multiple depth stops that can be preset for running multiple passes quickly. This greatly reduces the time needed for changing the bit depth, and makes it possible to repeat earlier passes on new workpieces with precision.

Plunge-style routers move up and down on spring-loaded tubes, making them the ideal choice for stopped cuts such as flutes. Multiposition depth stops make quick work of multiple passes on moldings.

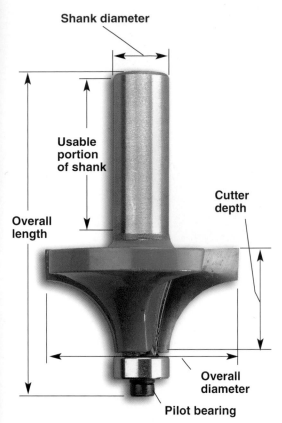

Shank diameter

Usable portion of shank

Overall length

Cutter depth

Overall diameter

Pilot bearing

When purchasing router bits, you will see specifications including the diameter, shank size, and height or cutter depth. For some roundover bits, the radius of the rounded section also may be given.

Bits without bearings are designed for grooving a workpiece rather than forming an edge. Look for bits with a clean finish and a high-quality cutter. Carbide bits stay sharp longer than high-speed steel bits. Painted coatings reduce friction and provide greater visibility.

Router Bits

Router bits are offered in many different styles and shapes and are made from either high-speed steel, solid carbide, or carbide-tipped steel. Carbide-tipped bits are by far the most common because they offer a good combination of durability and price. HSS bits are economy bits used with softer woods for short durations and then discarded. Solid carbide bits are expensive and limited to a few bit styles.

Knowing a little about the basic design elements of router bits will help you select the proper bits and give you points to compare when shopping.

Bit Anatomy

All router bits have a shank, which is chucked into the router collet; a body; and cutters (although some bits have only one). The flutes are the cutaway spaces in front of the cutters. Flutes are sometimes called gullets or chip pockets because they provide a space for catching and ejecting the waste chips removed by the cutters. Bits that are piloted, or bearing-guided, have a ball-bearing pilot attached to the shank that controls the bit's cutting depth, although some pilots come in the form of a small, solid pin on the end of the bit or a smooth section of the shank that serves as the pilot.

The photo at left shows the basic elements of a router bit and some of the terms commonly used for bit specification. Note that the "usable length" of the shank includes only the completely cylindrical portion. The area where the shank cuts away into the flute (or where it flares out as it meets the bit body) should not be placed into the collet and therefore doesn't count as usable length. This dimension typically is not provided by the manufacturer, so you'll have to measure it yourself when choosing a bit.

Overall diameter is an important consideration for several reasons. First, the bit must be smaller than the center hole in your router's subbase. If it's too big, you'll have to find or make an alternative subbase. Second, large-diameter bits are safer and more effective at slower speeds—as a general rule, bits over $1\frac{1}{4}$" in diameter should run at less than 18,000 rpm. You need a variable-speed router to use these bits properly. Bits over $1\frac{3}{4}$" in diameter are often tricky to use and typically should be used only on a router table.

Router bits are commonly available with $\frac{1}{4}$" and $\frac{1}{2}$" shank diameters. As a general rule, $\frac{1}{2}$" shanks are stiffer and stronger, making them more resistant to vibration, deflection, and breakage. Larger-diameter bits often cost the same as their $\frac{1}{4}$" counterparts.

A bit's cutting edges can reveal a lot about its quality, and they directly affect performance and longevity. Better bits are made with micrograin carbide, which wears slower and cuts cleaner than coarse-grade carbide. Check the grind of each cutter by running a fingernail along the front and back edges. They should be smooth and flat.

Many bits have painted or coated bodies. This smooth coating reduces friction and resin buildup, speeds waste ejection, and prevents corrosion. The coatings also improve the visibility of the cutter during use.

Although there is no official method for classifying the hundreds of different types of router bits, it is simple to group them by the type of work that they do, which in turn dictates certain design characteristics—for example, most grooving bits have plunge-cut capabilities, while edge-forming bits are usually piloted.

Grooving Bits

The primary grooving tool, and perhaps the most versatile, is the straight bit. This has both side and bottom cutters, for cutting dadoes, rabbets, and for trimming a workpiece. There is a great selection of decorative grooving bits to choose from, used for everything from cutting flutes to free-hand carving. Some of the most popular are core-box, V-groove, veining, and point-cutting bits. These bits plunge vertically into the workpiece and then cut a decorative profile horizontally.

Edge-forming Bits

Edge-forming bits cut decorative profiles into the edges of stock and into the faces of narrow trim material. Edge forming is probably the most common type of routing and involves the greatest variety of bit types. Most edge-forming bits are piloted, with an attached bearing that rolls along the workpiece, so that the bit cuts at a uniform depth. Bargain bits with solid nonbearing pilots have a tendency to burn or scar the workpiece and should be avoided. Most edge-forming bits have bearings at the end of the bit, and in some cases the bearing can be changed to alter the bit's cutting depth.

The decorative profiles on edge-forming bits allow you to cut everything from a simple roundover or chamfer to traditional details such as ogee, cavetto, cove, and bead. You can use any combination of edge-forming bits to mill your custom molding.

Some guided bits come with a variety of bearings of different sizes to change cutting depth.

Grooving Bits

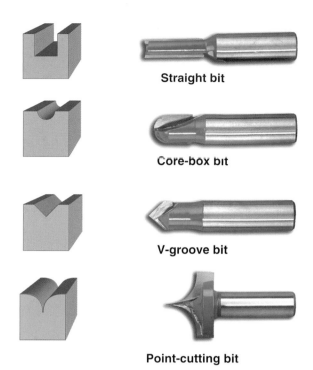

Straight bit

Core-box bit

V-groove bit

Point-cutting bit

Edge-forming Bits

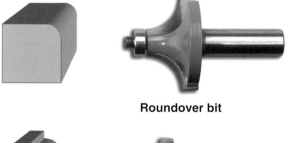

Roundover bit

Ogee bit with bead

Multi-form bit

Multibeading bit

Router Tables

Router tables add a considerable amount of versatility to routing. With the tool secured below the table and the bit exposed above, you can use both hands to run the workpiece past the bit, often without hold-downs or special clamping. The fence provides the means for controlling the cut, just like a table saw fence. Together with the flat, stable surface of the tabletop, the fence allows for safe, accurate cuts with quick setups. Using a bearing-guided bit you can rout without the fence, using the table for support. A basic shop-made version can be inexpensive and easy to build, and may be all you need. Or you can buy one of the many commercial tables available.

As a general rule, router bits with a diameter over $1\frac{3}{4}$" are much safer to use in a router table. Big bits can be hard to control with handheld routers,

A shop-made router table is built from parts available at woodworking stores and catalogs. A variable speed control dial with on/off switch as well as a fence with integrated dust collection are just a few of the available options.

Roller stands provide quick, convenient workpiece support behind or alongside the saw. Most roller stands adjust up and down to suit different saw heights.

A commercial benchtop table with frame-style open base, flip-up blade guard, two-piece fence, vacuum port, and base-mounted switch. Always clamp the base to the supporting workbench for safest use.

especially on edge-forming operations. When using large bits with the router table, cover as much of the bit as possible with the fence and cut incrementally with light passes. Make sure to adjust the speed of the router when possible, according to the bit manufacturer's specifications. Many large bits are designed for use in a table only.

Commercial tables are available as clamp-on tabletop, benchtop, and floor models. In terms of quality, the overall field runs wide, as does the price range.

When shopping, look closely at the main components—the tabletop, the fence, and the base—and compare the usability features such as fence adjustments and overall versatility. There are many great tables to choose from with quality safety features.

Shop-made router tables can be every bit as advanced as commercial units by purchasing specific components through a woodworking store or supply catalog. Often, shop-made units are a better option because they allow you to adjust the table size to suit the type of routing you most frequently do. Purchasing the individual components of your router table also allows you to customize each piece with the options you want, rather than a complete package.

Understand proper feed directions and techniques before you begin using a table router. Unlike handheld operations where the material is clamped down, with a router table the workpiece moves freely, creating the possibility off kickbacks and other dangerous situations. Read all manufacturer's warnings and techniques before you begin.

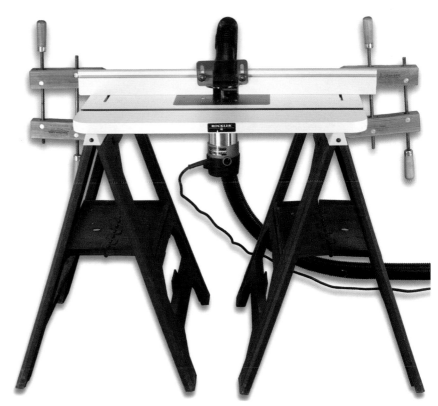

The most simple table design may be all you need. This clamp-on tabletop is good for small shop spaces and performs just like any other table.

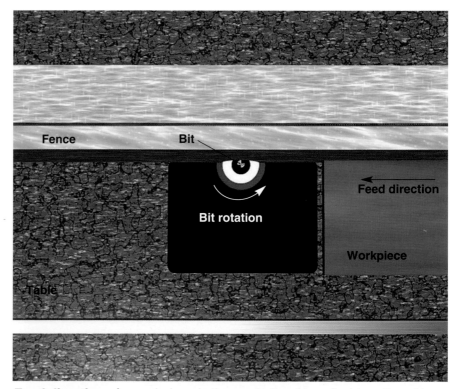

Feed direction of a workpiece is the opposite of handheld routing. Always push the workpiece against the spin of the bit to avoid unwanted kickback or ejection of the piece, and keep your hands clear of the bit.

Common Lumber Defects

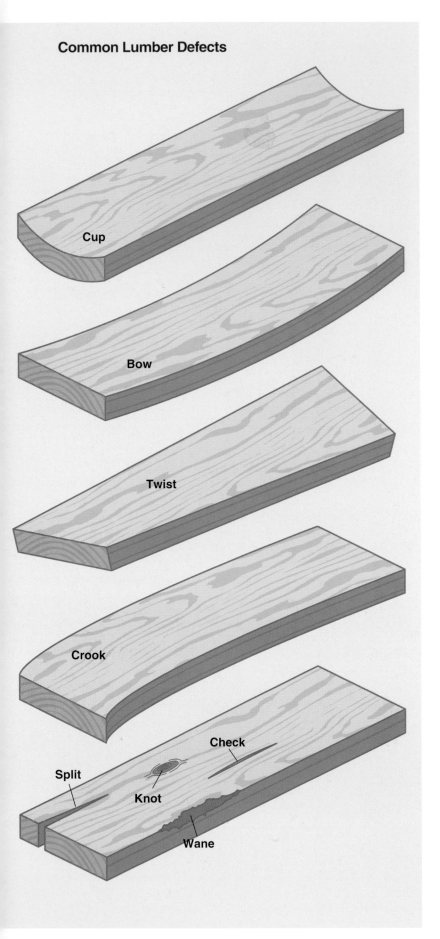

Cup

Bow

Twist

Crook

Split

Knot

Check

Wane

Material Preparation

Before you can begin routing and molding to create wood trim, you need to prepare the material to uniform dimensions so that each piece of molding turns out the same. In a perfect world you could purchase lumber, bring it home, and start routing. But this rarely works out in practice.

There are a variety of naturally occurring defects in dimensional lumber, including cupping, bowing, twisting, crooking, and splitting. Some of these defects can be corrected easily; others make the lumber unusable.

To begin the milling process, one straight edge and one flat face must be created so the piece can be cut safely with a table saw. Not all the lumber you have will require jointing or planing before it can be ripped down the width. To determine whether you need to joint or plane a board, hold it on edge and sight along the length. If the edge rises or dips, it isn't flat enough for ripping. Likewise, if the board is twisted or cupped across its face, you'll need to flatten it on a jointer. Do not attempt to flatten excessively warped boards. In fact, you are better off not using it for anything other than firewood. More than likely it contains an internal stress that will make it warp again even after it is flattened or cut into smaller pieces.

If you do not have access to the equipment used to flatten and straighten material, contact a local cabinet shop or lumberyard. Often material can be purchased with one straight edge and flat face, or surfaced on all four sides. Smaller shops may be willing to perform additional operations such as ripping the pieces to a uniform width or thicknessing the material to a specific dimension.

After all of your stock has been flattened and properly thicknessed, take a few moments with a light-grit sandpaper and go over each workpiece. It isn't necessary to finish-sand the edges of the material, but lightly going over the entire piece may save you some sanding time after the piece has been machined into molding.

How to Prepare Rough Stock Material

1 Begin preparing the material by passing the edge of the board several times over a jointer set for a light cut—1/32" is a good depth setting. Continue passing the material over the cutter head until the jointer shaves the entire edge of the board. Once you have a flat edge, flatten one face of the board on the jointer.

2 With one flat face and edge run the board through a surface planer with the flat face down, to smooth the other face of the board and bring the board to the desired thickness. Alternate the board faces with each pass, removing equal amounts of material from both sides. This will help avoid further warping.

3 Rip the pieces down to the desired width using a table saw. Lightly sand each piece with a high-grit sandpaper to remove any burrs from cutting.

OPTION: If a board has two waney edges, make one edge flat by attaching a straight board and ripping one waney edge off. Once one edge of the workpiece is flat, remove the straight board and rip the work-piece as usual with the flat edge against the rip fence.

Carbide-tipped router bits keep their edge longer than high-speed steel bits, but they are brittle and easily damaged. Storing bits in a drilled board will keep them from clattering around in a drawer and banging together, increasing their life expectancy.

Bit Maintenance

Keeping router bits clean and sharp is just as important as using quality bits. Sharpening your own carbide is just too difficult to be practical, and it's a good way to distort the cutting edges or destroy the balance of the bit. Some people like to touch up carbide bits between professional regrindings, but proper storage and thoughtful care of your bits will get you nearly as far. The brittle edges of carbide bits can chip fairly easily when knocked against metal tools or other carbide edges. A simple storage system of a board with holes the same diameter as the bit shanks (see photo above) is a simple device for keeping your bits safe when not in use. Place the bit shanks into the holes and place the board where the bits won't be bumped around. This type of storage also makes it easy to see the profile of each bit when selecting one.

Clean your bits between each use to avoid buildup of pitch, resins, and dust. If the bit has a bearing, check to make sure it is functioning smoothly. Use a commercial bit cleaner for each cleaning. Spray the bit with the cleaner, wait a few minutes, and brush the bit with a nylon brush. Wipe down the bit with a soft rag and in-spect the shank to make sure it is clean and smooth, with no scratches or burrs. Never use a metal tool to clean a bit. You'll scratch the body of the bit or chip the carbide edges.

Clean bits regularly with bit cleaner and a nylon brush to maintain peak bit efficiency.

Identifying a Dull Bit

Dull router bits send clear signals to let you know when it's time to sharpen them. Usually, the first indication is that it's harder than normal to feed the router or workpiece, and there will be a noticeable increase in the motor's noise.

Several clues to dullness may be found in the cut. A dull bit can burn the wood or leave a bumpy or otherwise flawed cut. Waste removed by a dull bit often looks more like sawdust than sliced shavings. On softwood, dull bits will tear the fibers from the wood rather than slice them.

Because bits often get used more in one capacity than another, it's typical for them to wear unevenly along the length of their cutters. One sign of this kind of wear is a line or step that appears on a workpiece when the bit is set deeper than usual. You can check for this by making a test cut with the bit set at full depth.

Burns and torn fibers are good signs that your router bits is dull and needs to be sharpened or replaced

Also take a look at the bit itself: shiny, burnished areas along a cutting edge indicate dullness. Chipped carbide is an obvious cry for help. Regrinding can eliminate shallow chips, but a severely chipped bit should be thrown out.

When to Sharpen Bits

For serious router users, a good sharpening service is a valuable resource. A well-made carbide-tipped bit can be sharpened four or more times in its life. Depending on your usage, however, you may never have to sharpen most of your bits. If you do, be aware that even a proper grinding can change the size or geometry of a bit. When the size or angle of the cutting path is critical, such as with flush-trimming bits and those used for joinery, you're taking a risk by having them sharpened. Edge-forming bits and straight bits used for basic material removal generally can be sharpened without creating problems.

A dull bit will often have shiny, burnished areas. Bits, like the straight bit above, that do not have curvilinear profiles are easier to sharpen and there is less risk of ruining the cutting line.

Featherboards, Hold-downs & Push Sticks

Push sticks, featherboards, and hold-downs help you feed the work safely past a bit or blade and are especially useful for small and narrow stock that might endanger your fingers. A push stick can have almost any design and can be made with scrap wood. For narrow work, a solid stick with a notched end will suffice. For routing larger stock, attach a handle to a scrap block (make sure the block has square corners) to make a push sled that doubles as a backer board to prevent tearout. Trim the block or move the handle to a new block when the old one has seen too many cuts. Use featherboards—either shop-made or commercial—anytime a second pair of "hands" can help you keep the work in line.

Push sticks and push pads can be purchased in many shapes and sizes. Or, you can make your own from scrap wood. Push sticks should have a comfortable handle and a notch along the bottom for holding workpieces securely.

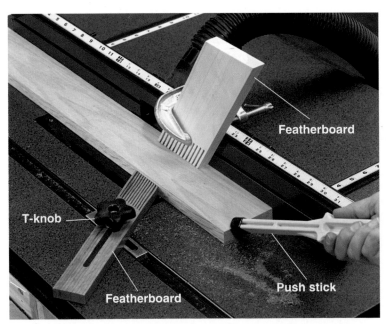

Featherboards and push sticks improve workshop safety. Featherboards can be clamped onto the fence, or you can use T-bolts and knobs in the miter slot. Push sticks can be purchased or made from scrap lumber.

A push sled with a notch safely holds small stock for table routing. A handle grip keeps fingers away from the blade.

How to Make A Featherboard

1 Select a straight piece of 1 × 4 that is free of knots and cracks. Mark a stop line 8" from the end of the board. Mark a series of parallel lines ¼" apart from the end of the board to the stop line.

2 Mark the end of the board at a 20° angle and clamp the workpiece firmly with the end line overhanging the work surface. Cut off the end of the board using a jig saw.

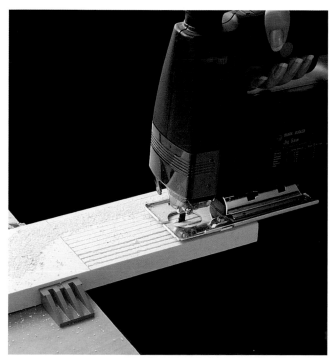

3 Make a series of parallel cuts from the end of the board to the stop line, carefully following the cutting lines. Let the blade come to a complete stop before removing it.

Tip: To use a fingerboard, set the workpiece 4" in front of the saw blade. Clamp the fingerboard slightly over the edges of the workpiece so they apply light pressure, forcing the workpiece against the rip fence and the table. The "fingers" should flex slightly as the workpiece travels forward.

Loading & Setting Bit Depth

Always unplug the router before loading or removing a bit. To load a bit, loosen the collet and make sure it's clean inside. Make sure the bit shank is clean, insert the shank into the collet until it bottoms out, then pull it back out about 1/8". At least 3/4 of the shank should be inside the collet. Any portion of the shaft that is cut away (at the tops of the flutes) or flared (where the shaft meets the cutter body) should not be inside the collet. Tighten the collet snugly by hand, then tighten it using the collet wrenches (or one wrench if the router has a shaft lock). For two-wrench systems on fixed-base routers, it's easier (and safer for your knuckles) to lay the motor sideways and use the bench to hold one of the wrenches in place while you crank the other by hand. Or, you can use a one-handed scissors method. Tighten the collet firmly, but do not overtighten.

The exact procedure for setting the bit depth is specific to the type and model of router, but the basic steps are similar.

Setting fixed-base bit depth: For all fixed-base routers, the bit depth equals the amount of cutter that is exposed below the surface of the sub-base. An easy and accurate way to set the depth is by using a depth gauge tool. With the router upside down on your workbench, raise the bit until it touches the gauge's flange, then tighten the base clamping mechanism to lock the motor in place.

Another method is to set the depth by sight. Place the router on the workpiece so the bit clears the piece's edge. Lower the bit to the desired depth, then lock the motor in place. A third method is to use the router's "zero-out" feature (if it has one), following the same procedure used for zeroing-out a plunge router (see below).

Setting plunge bit depth: To adjust a plunge router, start with the tool upright on top of the workpiece. Plunge the motor down until the bit just touches the work surface, then engage the plunge lock to keep the motor in place. If the tool has a turret stop, rotate it so the lowest setting is in line with the depth stop rod. Drop the stop rod until it contacts the turret stop, and lock it in place. Next, zero-out the depth setting by moving the depth cursor to "zero" on the scale. Using the cursor as a gauge, raise the stop rod to the desired depth, then lock it in place. Release the plunge lock, and you're ready to rout.

To make the cut incrementally, rotate the turret stop to the highest setting before starting the router. After each pass, retract the bit from the cut and rotate the turret to the next-lowest setting until you reach full depth.

Tips for Loading Bits

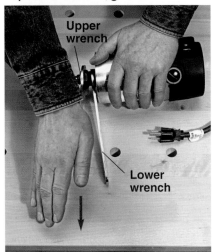

Tighten a two-wrench collet by bracing the lower wrench against a workbench and pushing down on the upper wrench. Using an open hand will prevent you from hurting your knuckles.

Two-wrench collets can also be tightened by gripping both wrenches like scissors and squeezing. Hold the motor body steady with the other hand.

Tighten a single-wrench collet by depressing the shaft lock with one hand and tightening the collet with the other.

Tips for Adjusting Cutting Depth

A router bit depth gauge gives a quick and accurate depth check.

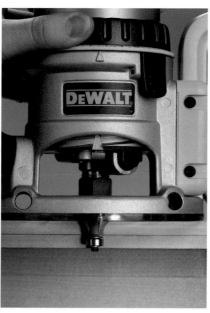

If you don't have a depth gauge, draw a line to mark the bottom of the cut and align the bottom of the cutter blade with the line.

TIP: Setting Depth for Profile Cuts. An easy way to see what you'll be cutting away with a decorative edge-forming bit is to use a scrap cut from the workpiece material. Place the scrap on the router base so its edge touches the bit's pilot bearing. The cutter's profile will show what the cut will look like.

Begin setting a plunge router by zeroing the cursor. With the bit touching the wood, the turret stop at the lowest setting, and the depth stop touching the turret, set the cursor to zero.

To set the desired cutting depth, use the cursor as a gauge to raise the stop rod to the desired depth.

A molding head mounted in a table saw is a powerful tool for making larger quantities of profiled moldings. One great advantage to this setup versus a router table is that you can cut complex profiles in a single pass.

Creating Thin Moldings

Creating your own thin trim moldings is a simple process with the right tools. There are three different methods for creating your own thin trim moldings that utilize different types of cutter heads. The first method requires a table saw with a molding head. The second option uses a router with an edge-forming bit. The third option requires a shaper. A shaper is a machine dedicated to machining profiles into various types of stock. Shapers are generally expensive machines used only in production cabinet and millwork shops. For DIYers, it makes the most sense to concentrate on the first two methods.

Using a table saw with a molding head is a fairly straightforward operation that produces excellent results with the proper setup. Molding heads consist of a center hub that accepts interchangeable cutters called knives. Knives come in many profiles for both conventional and unusual types of moldings. Molding heads are available from a variety of stores either in kits with multiple knife profiles, or as individual knife sets for a specific profile.

Exercise extreme caution when using a molding head. Kickback guards and splitters must be removed from the table saw, so safety is of even greater concern. Molding heads only have two to four knives that can be easily overwhelmed with too much material removal. Overloading a molding head leads to kickback.

With a multitude of router bit profiles to choose from, it's hard to beat a good midsize router for producing smaller moldings. In the example shown, router bits with bearing guides are mounted in a router table. This setup was chosen for speed, accuracy, and safety. Because the bits in this example have guide bearings, use of a router table is not necessary, but defects from the edge of your workpiece will be more visible when using a handheld router.

Always mill more stock than necessary to complete the job by 10%. Custom-milled moldings are difficult to recreate, and the extra material and time will pay off later if the piece is needed. Purchase material that is as close to the best grade available as possible. This will minimize scrap due to knots and other imperfections.

If you own a jointer and a table saw you may want to purchase rough-sawn material and mill it yourself to save money. If you do not own these tools, you will have to purchase material that has already been planed to the proper thickness and has one straight edge, otherwise known as "straight-line ripped." It is important that the material you purchase be milled to precise dimensions.

If you're making narrow moldings, shape the profile along the edge of wider stock, then rip the molding free with a standard blade. This keeps your hands a safer distance from the knives and makes it easier to control the cuts.

For those instances where you must shape the edge of narrow workpieces, make a shroud around the knives to hold workpieces as you feed them through the blade. Here's how (see photo and illustration below): Attach a sacrificial rip fence, then fasten another scrap with a flat edge to the wood fence to form a top hold-down. Position the top support on the wood fence so its height off the saw table matches the width of the workpieces you'll be milling. The top support thickness should match the workpiece thickness. Fasten a side support to the top support to act like a solid-surface featherboard alongside the cut. Make the top and side supports shorter than the length of the workpieces so the workpiece ends will protrude out from the shroud on both ends. This helps you maintain a better degree of control over the workpieces while feeding them into the knives.

To mill profiles with this blade shroud, set the knives to make shallow passes of ⅛" at a time. Feed workpieces into the shroud with a scrap of workpiece stock that fits into the shroud opening. Push the workpiece all the way through before shutting off the saw and removing the pushing scrap. If you're milling lots of strips with this setup, feed them end to end so the next workpiece serves as a push stick for the previous one.

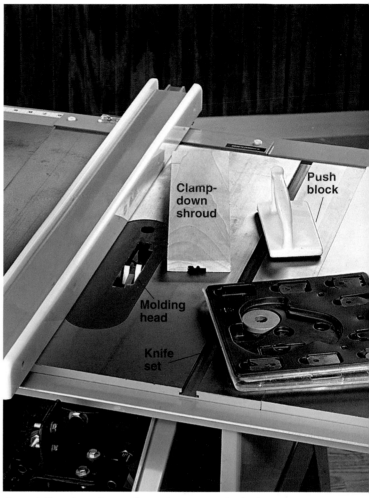

A molding head consists of a center hub that accepts sets of interchangeable molding cutters called knives.

How to Make a Fence Shroud for a Molding Head

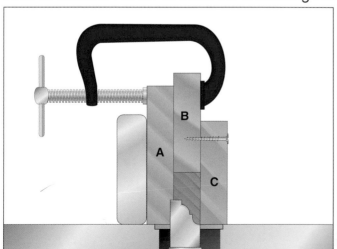

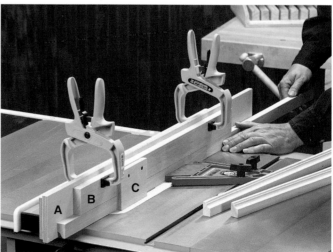

To cut molding profiles onto narrow strips, create a shroud of scrap pieces attached to the rip fence like this. The scrap closest to the rip fence (A) keeps the molding knives away from the metal rip fence. A second scrap over the knives (B) acts as a hold-down, and its thickness should match the workpiece thickness. A third scrap in front (C) keeps workpieces from drifting away from the rip fence during shaping. Feed strips one after the next so they act as push sticks.

213

Routing a Chair Rail

Creating your own custom chair rail is a great opportunity for the novice woodworker or carpenter to become better acquainted with table routing and the capabilities of a midsized router. Because chair rails vary in dimension and style so dramatically from one house to the next, your options when designing one are endless. Chair rails basically fall between widths of 1½" to 5" wide and range in depth from ½" to 1½".

To make the chair rail shown, four passes are required with the router. Two passes are done with an edge-forming bit, and two using the router fence as a guide. The end result is a symmetrical chair rail that is neither boring nor overly elaborate.

When choosing router bits for your chair rail, take into account the style of the door and window casings in the room. Chair rails that have a greater depth than the outer edge of the casings require returns to avoid ugly joints. These returns can be difficult to cut and may complicate your installation.

Most stock chair rail profiles are rather ornate and curvilinear. If your tastes run more toward the beefy and geometric, making your own molding is a good way to get the trim you want.

Everything You Need

Tools: midsized router, edge-forming bits, grooving bits, router table.

Materials: prepared stock.

How to Make Chair Rail Molding

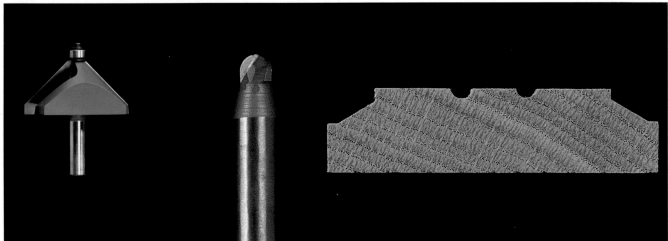

1 Prepare your material to the dimensions shown in the illustration. Think through the process of creating your molding step by step, taking note of the placement of each bit pass and type of bit. Some larger bits are designed for use in a router table only. Do not attempt to use these bits with a handheld router.

2 Load the grooving bit in the router and set up the router in a table. Set the fence of the router table so that the grooves will fall ¼" from the center. Adjust the height of the grooving bit so that the width of the groove will be about ⅛" wide.

3 With the bit in the proper position, run the prepared stock through the bit. Make a pass on each edge of the workpieces, creating symmetrical lines off the center. Run the stock at a uniform rate, keeping it flat on the table.

4 Remove the grooving bit and replace it with the edge-forming bit. Remove the fence assembly from the table and install a starting pin or fulcrum point. Test the height of the bit by running scrap material, adjusting the height of the bit as desired.

5 With the bit at the desired height, run the prepared stock, making a pass on both edges. For nonsymmetrical work, change the bit after making a pass on one edge only, and replace it with a different style of edge-forming bit with similar dimensions.

Creating Custom Base Molding

Along with a table saw and molding head, you can make your own custom base moldings with a router table and edge-profiling bit. Many base moldings available at home centers consist of a single profile molded into the top edge of the piece. The middle section and bottom edge of base trim are commonly left square for the possible addition of other moldings such as base shoe or stop molding. That doesn't mean your molding should be as simple as a single pass; however, more intricate moldings require multiple router passes, which can complicate machining of larger runs.

Maintaining constant material dimensions is a priority when milling your own custom moldings. Standard stock base molding profiles begin at approximately 2¾" tall and range in thickness from ⅜" to 1". As a general rule, base trim dimensions should expand together. Avoid creating taller moldings that have thickness less than ½". Taller base trim appears more balanced with larger molding profiles, and thinner stock will limit your depth of cut, reducing your router bit options.

The following options of base trim have been chosen to reflect two different scenarios. In the first option, a basic profile that closely matches a stock solid wood molding is created. This option is the most basic of the two and is meant for use when you want to use a species of wood that is not available with a basic profile. This option requires only the bit and a router.

The second option is an example of a more elaborate base trim that requires multiple passes from different types of bits and router setups. This more creative option is meant for use when you want to design a whole new trim profile. Keep in mind that this option is only a guide for methods and is a good place to begin your own design. Feel free to change the router bits used, the size of the prepared material, and the locations of the profiles on the trim piece to suit your liking. However, it is a good idea to leave the bottom ¾" of the trim square to provide a solid nailing surface for base shoe or quarter round.

A router table fitted with an edge-profiling bit is an invaluable tool for creating your own cutom base moldings. You can also use a table saw with a molding head to profile the edges.

Create different profiles with the same bit by adjusting the bit depth or running the bearing along a template mounted beneath the workpiece. A template will provide better support for the bearing, especially when the workpiece is thin.

Everything You Need:

Tools: midsized router, edge-forming bit, clamps.

Materials: prepared stock.

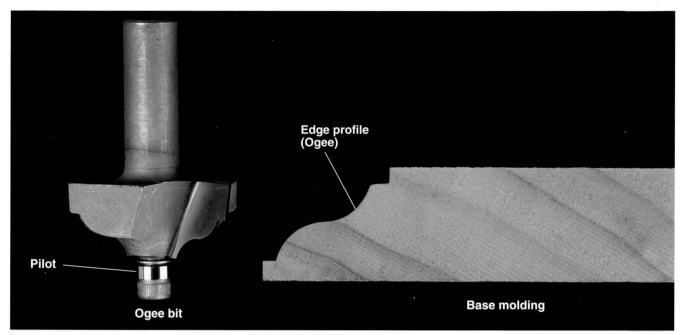

Edge profile (Ogee)

Pilot

Ogee bit

Base molding

Edge profiling is the essential skill you need for creating most custom base moldings. Although you can use a table saw with a molding head, a router fitted with an edge-profiling bit will give you many times more profile options. The classic Ogee shape shown here is one of the most common edge profiles, and lends itself well to creating base moldings (see pages 218–219). The vast majority of edge-profiling bits are piloted (they have either a spinning or fixed guide at the bottom) so you can use them freehand. But for more control, it's usually better to mount the bit in a router table so you can take advantage of the fence.

How To Hand-Rout Edge Profiles

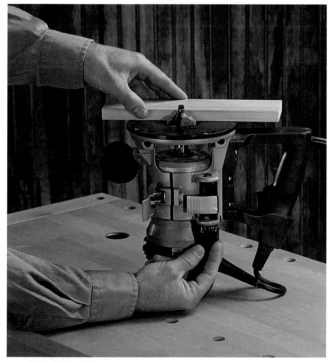

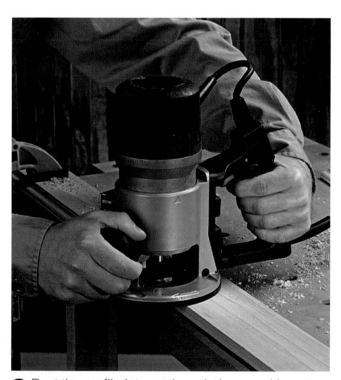

1 Select a piloted edge-profiling bit and mount it into your router. Adjust the height of the bit to ensure the bearing will guide properly along the edge of the material, and the profile routed will mimic the desired style. Test the depth by routing a few scrap pieces first.

2 Rout the profile into each workpiece, making at least 10% more molding than you need for your project. Clamp the workpiece to the edge of your worksurface in multiple locations, relocating the clamps as you go. Lightly sand the routed profile with fine-grit sandpaper.

Custom base molding is relatively easy to make. It can be simple and made from common lumber like the base molding seen here (you'll save a lot of money making it yourself) or it can have a unique profile and be made from any wood you choose, even an exotic wood.

Single Profile Base Molding

Base moldings and other moldings with profiled edges are perfect projects for making in your home workshop. You can produce them very efficiently by employing the following method. Start by choosing an edge-profiling bit that you like for the top profile, such as the Ogee bit and the roundover bit shown below. Then, select wood stock that is a little more than twice the width of your planned molding height (for exam-

ple, to make 5½"-tall molding, select 12" wide stock). Then, rout the edge profiles into both edges of the stock on a router table. Now all you need to do is rip the stock down the middle and you'll have two identical strips of molding.

Everything You Need

Tools: router table with mid-size router, edge-profiling bit, table saw.

Materials: prepared stock.

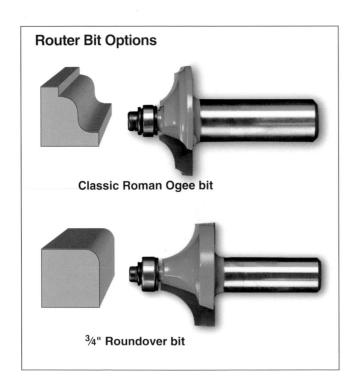

Router Bit Options

Classic Roman Ogee bit

¾" Roundover bit

TIP: If you own a jointer, you may choose to joint both edges of the workpiece smooth before routing the subsequent profiles. For best results, alternate between the router, table saw, and jointer for smoother, cleaner edges.

How to Make Base Molding With a Router

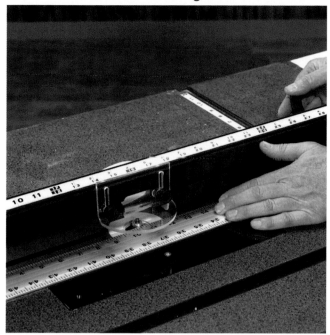

1 Prepare ¾" thick material to the maximum board width possible with two straight edges. Set the fence on the router table so that it is flush with the front edge of the bearing guide. Use a straightedge to help align the fence. If your stock is rough, set the fence slightly in front of the bearing guide so the fence guides the cut.

2 Use scrap material to fine-tune the height of the router bit. Adjust the height until you achieve the desired profile. Check the workpiece for troublesome tear-out areas and determine optimum test feed rates when running scrap material.

3 Rout the edges of your prepared material one side at a time, maintaining an even feed rate and applying adequate downward and lateral pressure to the workpiece. Profile both edges.

4 Set the table saw fence to rip the profiled molding stock in half, and then rip-cut the stock to release two sections of molding that have a profile on one edge and are square-cut on the other edge. Sand the square edge of the molding to remove rough saw blade marks.

Base molding is relatively easy to make from common lumber, like the edge-profiled oak base molding seen here (you'll save a lot of money making it yourself). Or, it can have a unique profile and be made from any wood you choose, even an exotic wood.

Multiple Profile Base Molding

Base moldings and other moldings with profiled edges are perfect projects for making in your home workshop. You can produce them very efficiently by employing the following method. Start by choosing an edge-profiling bit that you like for the top profile, such as the Ogee bit and the roundover bit shown below. Then, select wood stock that a little more than twice the width of your planned molding heigh (for example, to make 5½"-tall molding select 12" wide stock). Then, rout the edge profiles into both edges of the stock on a router table. Now all you need to do is rip the stock down the middle and you'll have two identical strips of molding.

Everything You Need

Tools: router table with heavy-duty router, bits (multibeading, core-box).

Materials: prepared stock.

Router Bit Options

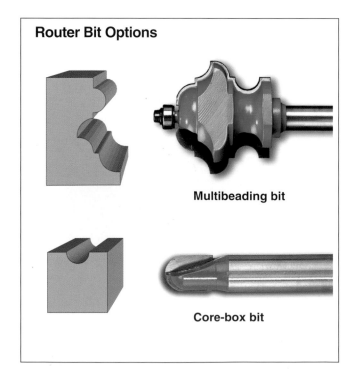

Multibeading bit

Core-box bit

How to Cut Multiple-Profile Moldings

1 Load the edge-forming bit (a multibeading bit is used here) into your router. Using a straightedge guide, adjust the router table fence so the piloted bearing is flush or slightly behind the fence.

2 With the fence properly positioned, raise the bit the desired height and run a test scrap to make sure the cutter is properly placed. Rout the edge profile on the prepared stock for your entire project. Push the material against the cutter direction, working from right to left.

3 Unplug the router and remove the bit. Replace it with a core-box bit and adjust the height so that the bit will cut a groove approximately 1/8" deep. Check the height of the bit with a depth gauge. Slide the fence away from the bit the desired distance.

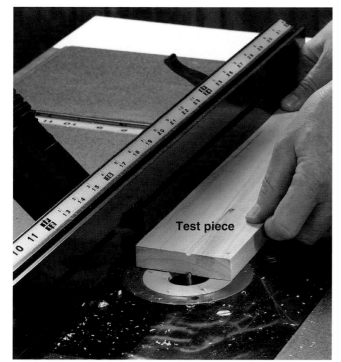

Test piece

4 Test the location of the groove by running a test scrap and adjusting the fence. After the fence is adjusted properly, rout all of the workpieces, using the fence as a guide. Keep your hands clear of the bit and use hold-downs and push sticks if necessary.

Test piece

5 Adjust the depth of the fence again to locate the second groove location. Use a test scrap to properly place the groove. Rout all the workpieces with the second line. Lightly sand the pieces with fine-grit sandpaper.

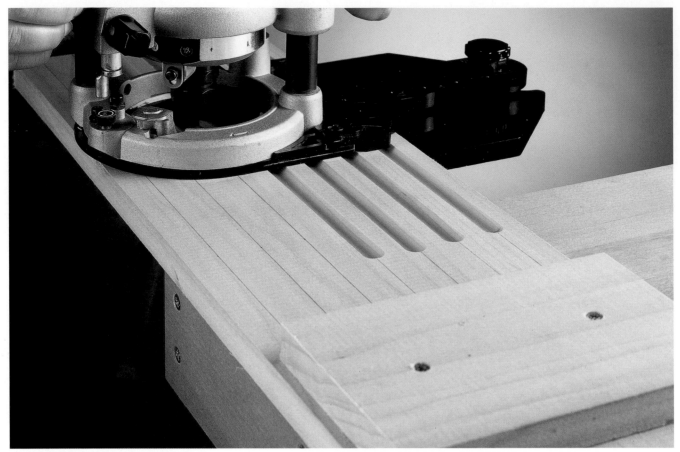

Case molding is sold prefabricated in many styles, but unless you want to spend a fortune you're limited to a couple of very plain profiles. But with a router and a grooving bit or two, you can fabricate your own distinctive casings from just about any species of wood (or manmade wood product) you wish.

Building Custom-grooved Casing

Window and door casings are often the most visible design component of a room and define its overall personality unlike any other type of trim. Casings cover the gap between drywall and a window or door frame and are generally smaller and thicker than base moldings. Casings can be used alone around each side of a doorway or used in conjunction with other architectural elements, such as decorative headers, rosettes, and plinth blocks.

Making your own casings is a challenging task that allows you the opportunity to create a unique style for any room. Whether you are mimicking an existing molding style or going out on your own completely, keep in mind the style of the other trim elements of the room when you choose dimensions and router bits. Single-piece casings are available in two distinct styles: beveled and symmetrical. Most symmetrical casings are approximately ¾" thick, ranging in width from 2¾" to 4". The thickness is generally

larger than beveled casings to allow for deeper grooving and decorative detail. Beveled casings are thicker at the outer edge and "bevel" back to the opening. Standard sizes range from ⁷⁄₁₆" to 1" at the thickest depth and 2¾" to 5" wide.

The examples of casings provided show an overview of how to create a symmetrical, decorative grooved casing as well as a step-by-step explanation of how to create your own beveled casing. Feel free to use a different bit combination along with the methods described to create a different molding.

Everything You Need

Tools: midsized router or mid-size plunge router, commercial edge guide, grooving bit, clamps.

Materials: prepared stock, scrap wood.

Creating Custom Casings

Flutes and other decorative grooving: Decorative grooves are controlled cuts made with a nonpiloted bit. Because they typically run parallel to a board's long edges, they're easiest to make with a handheld router and edge guide or on the router table. Stopped grooves, however, require precise plunging to initiate the cut

Beaded profile with a beading bit

and quick retraction of the bit at the end, so are best made with a handheld plunge router. Classic surface treatments, like fluting and beading, take some time to set up, but the general techniques are simple and straightforward.

V-groove profile with a V-groove bit

Start by laying out the cuts across the face of the stock. Work outward from the center if the design is symmetrical. Mark the centerpoint and outer edges of each cut to ensure even spacing and help with adjusting the fence. For router table work, also mark one end of the stock as a reference for setting the fence. With the layout complete and the bit loaded, set the edge guide or table fence so the bit is centered over

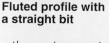

Fluted profile with a straight bit

the outermost groove. With a symmetrical design, you can rout the corresponding grooves on both sides before changing the fence setting.

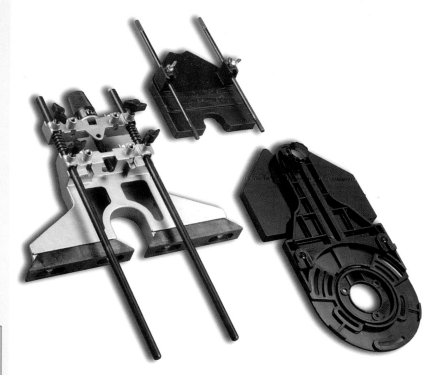

Edge guides that let you follow an edge while routing (decreasing setup time) are available for most router models either from the manufacturer or through an aftermarket source. Some guides have graduated depth gauges that simplify making decorative grooves at uniform distances.

When making stopped grooves, as with this classical flute design, use stop blocks to keep the ends of the grooves even.

Sophisticated casing profiles can be achieved by shaping the face of a board with an assortment of different profiling router bits. The casing seen here was created with chamfer bits (two sizes), a handrail bit and a vertical ogee bit.

Creating Custom Profiled Casing

Routing a profile across a 3"-wide piece of stock is a task usually left for a shaper with custom knives. But if you use a heavy-duty ½"-collet router and an assortment of profiling bits, you can replicate just about any complex casing profile that a shaper can produce.

Everything You Need

Tools: router table with heavy-duty router, router bits (chamfer, vertical ogee, handrail).

Materials: prepared stock, ¾" × 3".

Bits You'll Need

Vertical ogee   Chamfer

Chamfer   Handrail bit

How to Create Profiled Casing

¹⁄₁₆"
flat
top

1 Load a chamfer bit into your router and place the router in the router table. Adjust the height of the bit and the fence so that the workpiece is guided by the fence and and so that all but ¹⁄₁₆" of the edge is machined. Run the molding through the bit at an even rate to avoid burning the material.

2 Unplug the router and remove the chamfer bit. Load the vertical ogee bit into the router and place the router in the table. Adjust the height of the bit so that the bottom edge of the cutter lines up with the chamfered edge from the first pass, maintaining a casing thickness of approximately 1/4".

3 Run the molding through the vertical ogee bit using elevated featherboards to keep the workpiece tight against the fence. If necessary, make multiple shallow passes to avoid overloading the router and to extend the life of the bit.

4 Remove the vertical ogee bit and replace it with the handrail bit. Use a straightedge to align the fence with the bit bearing. Raise the bit to its full height and run a piece of scrap material to check the cut, using multiple shallow passes if necessary. Note: Multiple shallow passes require moving the fence further in front of the bearing.

5 Run the material through the handrail bit at a slow, steady rate. Use featherboards and push sticks as necessary. After the final pass, lightly sand each work piece with fine-grit sandpaper.

A cove-cutting jig lets you align cutting guides so you can shape your own custom cove molding on a table saw. The adjustable parallelogram jig can be shop-built, or you can order one from a woodworking supply catalog.

Cutting Cove Molding

Cove molding with smaller profiles is readily available at any home center, but you won't find moldings with radii larger than about ¾". For larger profiles, you can use your table saw as a makeshift shaper and mill your own cove molding. It's easy to do with a simple parallelogram jig and a fine-toothed plywood blade. The technique involves passing the wood over the blade at an angle and shaving the cove profile in multiple shallow passes, raising the blade ¹⁄₁₆" with each pass. By varying the angle of approach on the blade, you can change the shape of the cove. Profiles ranging from steep and tight curves to gentle and wide arches are possible, depending on the angle you choose.

If you plan on shaping a large amount of cove molding, consider purchasing a special cove cutting head for your table saw (see next page).

Cove cutting heads are thicker than a standard blade and produce cleaner results with fewer passes of the material.

As with all operations on a table saw, use caution when cutting coves. Attempting to remove too much material at one time may result in kickback of your material, or cause damage to the arbor of your table saw. Always use appropriate safety gear, including push pads and a push stick. As you push the material through the blade, maintain constant downward pressure on the workpiece. Try to sustain a uniform feed rate of the material, slowing your rate if the blade becomes bogged down.

Commercial parallelogram jigs are available through woodworking supply stores if you would rather not build your own. With a commercial jig, you do not need additional straightedge material; instead, the jig also serves as a straightedge.

You can build an adjustable parallelogram jig from straight strips of 2"-wide scrap. Make the long sides 4 ft. and the short ends 1 ft. Attach the parts with short carriage bolts, washers, and wing nuts so you can adjust the jig shape by hand. The jig will establish the angle you'll need to cut a cove with a specific curvature and width. If you choose to use your own jig with straight-edge guides, it is a good idea to do a test run through the "tunnel" with the blade completely lowered beneath the tabletop and the saw turned off. This will ensure that the workpiece fits snugly between the straightedges. It also ensures that the workpiece will not bind up halfway through a cut due to warping of the piece.

You can also cut partial coves using this procedure by burying a portion of the blade in the fence. Once you've established the fence angle using the parallelogram jig, adjust the bevel gauge to this angle. Hold the fence against the bevel gauge and clamp the fence down. Raise the blade into the fence until the width of the blade that's exposed matches the width of your partial cove layout line.

Everything You Need

Tools: table saw with blade, clamps, T-bevel

Materials: straight ¾" dimensional lumber, carriage bolts, washers, wing nuts, prepared material (for cove molding).

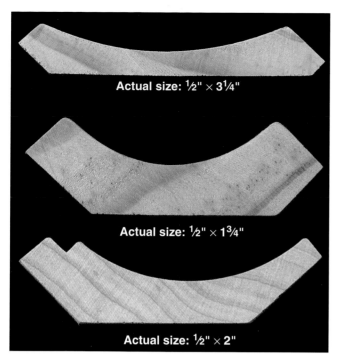

Actual size: 1/2" × 3 1/4"

Actual size: 1/2" × 1 3/4"

Actual size: 1/2" × 2"

Cove moldings can be milled with a table saw in a variety of different shapes depending on the position of the blade and the angle of the jig. By varying the angle of approach on the blade, you can change the shape of the cove. Profiles range from steep and tight curves to gentle, wide arches, depending on the angle you choose. Partial coves are also an option.

Parallel cutting guides on your table saw table let you guide your workpiece across your saw blade at an angle, producing a cove cut. The guides are positioned using a parallelogram jig like the one on page 226. To "spring" the coved molding (so they look like the ones in the photo, left) you'll need to make beveled rip cuts on a table saw.

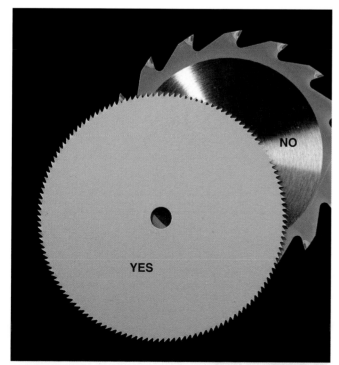

NO

YES

TIP: For smoother cuts, install a fine-toothed plywood-cutting blade with hardened steel teeth. This blade will produce a smoother end result than a carbide-tipped general-purpose blade; however, both blade types will work.

Cove cutting heads are mounted on a 10" table saw. Thicker than a standard blade, they produce cleaner results with fewer passes of the material. Photo courtesy Woodhaven.

How to Cut Coves with a Table Saw

1 Mark your workpiece to the cove shape you want to cut, and raise the blade to match the deepest part of the cut.

2 Open the parallelogram jig so the inner opening matches the width of the cove profile. Pivot the jig on the saw table so its inside opening touches the front and back blade teeth.

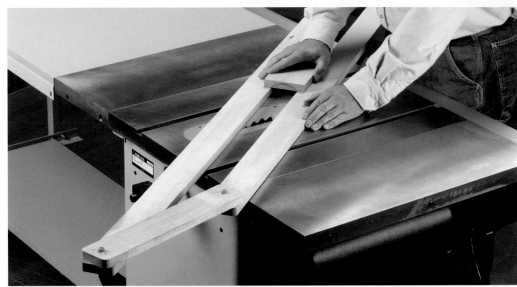

3 Without shifting the jig's position, use a bevel gauge to record the jig angle on the saw. Lock the gauge and remove the jig.

4 Clamp a straight-edge to the saw table at the jig angle. Position the inside edge of the straight-edge so the cove lines up with the blade. Set the workpiece in place, and clamp a second straightedge behind it, parallel with the first straightedge.

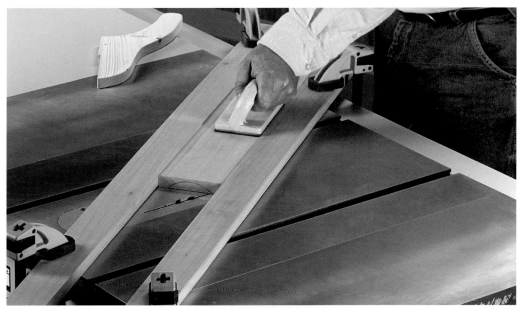

5 Cut the cove to shape in a series of shallow passes, starting with the blade teeth about 1/16" above the saw table. Increase the cutting height no more than 1/16" with each pass.

OPTION: You can cut partial coves by shifting the straightedges so the blade cuts partway into one straightedge. Cut the partial cove the same way as a full cove in many passes of increasing depth.

Troubleshooting Poor Router Cuts

Problems with router cuts can be due to several factors, including operator error, poorly milled material, improper setups, and using the wrong bit or router for the job. Some problems, namely burning and tearout, are common pitfalls that are linked to the router's design, and avoiding them requires constant vigilance. Listed here are some of the most common cutting flaws and suggestions for correcting them.

Burning
• Make sure bits are sharp (see marks of a dull bit, below).
• Don't hesitate during the cut. Pay special attention to points where you naturally tend to slow down, especially at the beginning or end of a cut and when routing around corners. Also try starting with a sweeping motion.
• Make light passes. Cutting too deeply in a single pass forces a slower feed rate, which commonly leads to burning.

Dips and bumps in the workpiece (like this knot) will transfer to the router cut when using a handheld router with a bearing guide. Use a router table fence as a guide rather than the bit bearing to eliminate dips in the cut.

A worn or nicked blade will result in burned areas or a flawed cut.

Burning and torn, rather than cut, fibers indicate a worn bit.

- Remove burn marks by making an additional light pass with the router, if you can afford to remove the extra material. The alternative is sanding, which is difficult at best and often impossible on end grain.

Tearout

- Maintain a constant feed rate with light passes.
- When routing the perimeter of a board, or adjacent perpendicular sides, make the cross-grain cuts first. This allows you to clean up the tearout when you make the long-grain cuts.
- Prevent top-side tearout (usually a fuzz) from making a rough ride for the router by using a template or straightedge and a template guide.

This lifts the router subbase off the surface of the workpiece for a smoother ride and cleaner cut.
- Clean the bit or use a sharper bit.

Problems with bearing-guided bits

- When a cut is flawed due to a rough workpiece edge, either clean up the edge and re-rout, or switch to a setup with a straightedge guide and a pattern bit or template guide. A base-mounted edge guide can help bridge minor dips in the workpiece edge.
- If the uncut edge of a workpiece is burnished or scored, check the travel of the bearing, and replace it if necessary. Don't use edging bits with solid pilots.

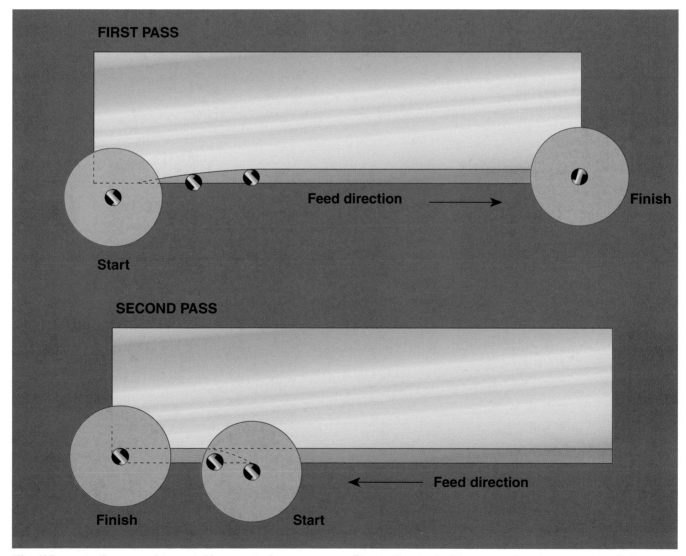

FIRST PASS

Feed direction →

Finish

Start

SECOND PASS

Finish   **Start**

← Feed direction

Tip: When starting an edge cut, it's easy to leave a burn mark if you push the router straight in until the base contacts the edge guide or bearing, then move it sideways to make the cut. There's just enough hesitation to burn the wood. Instead, start with a curved, sweeping motion so that the bit reaches its full cutting position a few inches from the end of the workpiece.

Run to the end of the cut using the same feed direction. Complete the cut by returning to the beginning and making a second pass, again sweeping into the workpiece but with an opposite feed direction, to finish off the first few inches. Typically, this final pass is a climb cut, so be careful. Make sure the router base is supported by the board at the beginning of the motion.

231

Glossary

Apron — A piece of horizontal window trim applied against the wall below the stool.

Astragal — An interior molding attached to one of a pair of doors or sash in order to prevent swinging through.

Back cut — A relief cut in the back of a piece of trim that removes material that could interfere with the fit of a joint.

Base — Molding applied around the perimeter of a room at the point of intersection of the wall and finish floor, also called baseboard.

Bead — A rounded profile.

Bevel — An angled cut through the width or thickness of a board or other piece of stock.

Biscuit joiner — A tool that cuts an oval-shaped slot in wood for the insertion of a small spline of wood known as a biscuit.

Blocking — A piece of lumber used between framing members for additional support for the installation of finish materials.

Cap — Upper piece of an entrance, wainscot, partition, or pilaster.

Casing — Molding applied to the perimeter of door or window jambs, also classified as "side" or "head" casing.

Ceiling medallion — An ornamental round ceiling accent sometimes used as a trim collar for ceiling fans or hanging lights.

Chair rail — A molding used to define the lower section of a wall, and to protect the wall from scratches from furniture. When used with paneling or wainscoting, the rail serves as an ornamental cap.

Chamfer — The edge of a board beveled at a 45-degree angle.

Collet — A collar used to hold a router bit shank in place when tightened.

Column — A supporting or decorative circular or rectangular pillar used in building.

Coped joint — A joint between two pieces of molding where one piece is cut to match the profile of another.

Corbel — A decorative bracket.

Corner blocks — Square blocks used in place of mitering the side and head casings.

Cornice — Interior trim used at the meeting of the ceiling and walls.

Cove molding — Molding with a concave profile used primarily where two pieces meet at a right angle.

Crosscut — To cut a board across its length.

Crown molding — A sprung molding used where two surfaces meet at an angle.

Dentil block — A small rectangle block spaced closely together in a series or in sequence with molding.

Easy reader — A tape measure with a fractional readout along the gradation scale to make measurements easier to read.

Flush — Arranging two or more items so that their surfaces create a level plane.

Flute — A long, parallel, rounded, decorative groove on the shaft of a column or pilaster.

Frieze — A decorative, horizontal band along the upper part of a wall in a room.

Header — A piece of lumber used as a support beam over a doorway or window opening.

Jamb — Top and two sides of a door or window frame that contact the door or sash; head jamb and side jambs.

Level — A line or plane that is parallel to the surface of still water.

Load-bearing wall — Any wall (interior or exterior), that bears some of the structural weight of a house. All exterior walls are load-bearing.

MDF — Medium density fiberboard, a wood product sheet good made of tiny wood fibers compressed together with a bonding agent.

Miter cut — A 45° bevel cut in the end of a piece of molding or a framing member.

Molding — Ornamental strip used to decorate a surface, as well as conceal the joints of adjoining surfaces.

Molding block (inside, outside) — A component of miterless moldings that eliminates the need for difficult angled cuts.

Ogee — An "S"-shaped or reverse-curve profile.

Pediment — The top piece of a formal entryway, including the ornamental caps or heads above windows and interior doors.

Picture molding — A molding along the perimeter of walls, near the ceiling line, used to support hooks for picture hanging.

Pilaster — Vertical column, often ornamental, that projects slightly from the wall. Most are purely decorative. May be rectangle or half round; often has a base (plinth block), shaft (middle section), and capital. Used most often as simulated columns in entryways and other door openings as well as fireplace mantels.

Plinth block — Square block at the base of a column or door casing; plinth blocks are thicker and wider than the adjoining pieces.

Plumb — Standing perfectly vertical. A plumb line is exactly perpendicular to a level surface.

Plywood — A sheet good made up of multiple thin layers of wood known as plies.

Pneumatic — Powered by air.

Prehung door — A door unit that is sold prehung in its jambs for easier installation.

Rail — The horizontal member of a door or frame-and-panel molding.

Return — A piece of molding that finishes off the end of a run by turning into the wall.

Reveal — A term used to describe the small setback of a window or door casing on the edge of the jamb.

Rip — To cut a piece of wood parallel to the grain.

Rosette — A square block with a circular decorative design in the center, usually used as a corner block as part of the casing around windows and doors.

Scarf joint — A joint made by beveling the ends of two pieces of lumber or molding and nailing them together so that they appear to be seamless.

Shoe molding — A thin trim piece similar to quarter round trim applied at the bottom of baseboard where it meets the floor.

Sill — The bottom horizontal member of a window opening.

Sprung — A term used to describe a type of molding that projects from the wall rather than lying flat on the surface.

Stile — The vertical member of a door or frame-and-panel molding.

Tongue-and-groove paneling — A type of lumber with a machined tongue on one side and a groove on the other, so that when pushed together, the groove of one board fits snugly over the tongue of the adjacent board.

Veneer — A thin layer of wood used on the outer layer of plywood.

Wainscoting — A lower interior wall surface (usually 3 to 4 ft. above the floor) that contrasts with the wall surface above it. An interior wall composed of two different interior wall surfaces, one above the other.

Wane — An irregular edge defect in dimensional lumber.

Wallboard — Also known as drywall; flat panels available in various sizes made of gypsum covered with durable paper. Used for most interior wall and ceiling surfaces.

Resources

Andersen Windows, Inc.
800-426-4261
www.andersenwindows.com
page 124

Armstrong Ceilings
800-426-4261
www.armstrongceilings.com
page 173 (all)

Balmer Architectural Mouldings
271 Yorkland Blvd.
Toronto, ON
M2J 1S5
www.balmer.com
store.balmer.com
800-665-3454
pages 10, 146, 188 (top)

Brian Greer's Tin-Ceilings, Walls & Unique
  Metal Work
519-743-9710
www.tinceiling.com
page 170

Delta Machinery
800-223-7278
www.deltamachinery.com
page 71

Digital Vision, LTD.
800-462-4379
www.digitalvision.com
page 12 (top)

Fypon, LTD.
800-446-9373
www.fypon.com
pages 7 (bottom right), 11 (all), 17 (bottom left),
147 (bottom left and right)

Madawaska Doors, Inc.
800-263-2358
www.madawaska-doors.com
page 148

Marvin Windows and Doors
888-537-8268
www.marvin.com
page 126, (top left)

Pittsburgh Corning Corporation
800-624-2120
www.pittsburghcorning.com
page 13 (bottom)

Van Millwork
(508) 966-4141 |
vanmillwork.com
page 4 photo by Shelley Harrison Photography

Weather Shield Windows and Doors
715-748-2100
www.weathershield.com
page 9 (all)

Woodhaven
800-344-6657
www.woodhaven.com
pages 226, 227 (bottom right)

Woodport Interior Doors ©by Heritage
  Products, USA
715-526-2146
www.woodport.com
page 13 (top right)

Photographers

© Karen Melvin for Eric Odor and Sala
Architects.: page 8; page 176.

©Andrea Rugg : p. 13 (top left) for Rehkamp
Larson Architects, Inc.; p. 18 for David Heide
Design

©Brian Vanden Brink pages 6, 7
(bottom left).

©Jessie Walker: page 7 (top).

Reference Charts

Converting Measurements

To Convert:	To:	Multiply by:
Inches	Millimeters	25.4
Inches	Centimeters	2.54
Feet	Meters	0.305
Yards	Meters	0.914
Square inches	Square centimeters	6.45
Square feet	Square meters	0.093
Square yards	Square meters	0.836
Cubic inches	Cubic centimeters	16.4
Cubic feet	Cubic meters	0.0283
Cubic yards	Cubic meters	0.765
Ounces	Milliliters	30.0
Pints (U.S.)	Liters	0.473 (Imp. 0.568)
Quarts (U.S.)	Liters	0.946 (Imp. 1.136)
Gallons (U.S.)	Liters	3.785 (Imp. 4.546)
Ounces	Grams	28.4
Pounds	Kilograms	0.454

To Convert:	To:	Multiply by:
Millimeters	Inches	0.039
Centimeters	Inches	0.394
Meters	Feet	3.28
Meters	Yards	1.09
Square centimeters	Square inches	0.155
Square meters	Square feet	10.8
Square meters	Square yards	1.2
Cubic centimeters	Cubic inches	0.061
Cubic meters	Cubic feet	35.3
Cubic meters	Cubic yards	1.31
Milliliters	Ounces	.033
Liters	Pints (U.S.)	2.114 (Imp. 1.76)
Liters	Quarts (U.S.)	1.057 (Imp. 0.88)
Liters	Gallons (U.S.)	0.264 (Imp. 0.22)
Grams	Ounces	0.035
Kilograms	Pounds	2.2

Lumber Dimensions

Nominal - U.S.	Actual - U.S.	METRIC
1 × 2	3/4 × 1 1/2"	19 × 38 mm
1 × 3	3/4 × 2 1/2"	19 × 64 mm
1 × 4	3/4 × 3 1/2"	19 × 89 mm
1 × 5	3/4 × 4 1/2"	19 × 114 mm
1 × 6	3/4 × 5 1/2"	19 × 140 mm
1 × 7	3/4 × 6 1/4"	19 × 159 mm
1 × 8	3/4 × 7 1/4"	19 × 184 mm
1 × 10	3/4 × 9 1/4"	19 × 235 mm
1 × 12	3/4 × 11 1/4"	19 × 286 mm
1 1/4 × 4	1 × 3 1/2"	25 × 89 mm
1 1/4 × 6	1 × 5 1/2"	25 × 140 mm
1 1/4 × 8	1 × 7 1/4"	25 × 184 mm
1 1/4 × 10	1 × 9 1/4"	25 × 235 mm
1 1/4 × 12	1 × 11 1/4"	25 × 286 mm
1 1/2 × 4	1 1/4 × 3 1/2"	32 × 89 mm
1 1/2 × 6	1 1/4 × 5 1/2"	32 × 140 mm
1 1/2 × 8	1 1/4 × 7 1/4"	32 × 184 mm
1 1/2 × 10	1 1/4 × 9 1/4"	32 × 235 mm
1 1/2 × 12	1 1/4 × 11 1/4"	32 × 286 mm
2 × 4	1 1/2 × 3 1/2"	38 × 89 mm
2 × 6	1 1/2 × 5 1/2"	38 × 140 mm
2 × 8	1 1/2 × 7 1/4"	38 × 184 mm
2 × 10	1 1/2 × 9 1/4"	38 × 235 mm
2 × 12	1 1/2 × 11 1/4"	38 × 286 mm
3 × 6	2 1/2 × 5 1/2"	64 × 140 mm
4 × 4	3 1/2 × 3 1/2"	89 × 89 mm
4 × 6	3 1/2 × 5 1/2"	89 × 140 mm

Liquid Measurement Equivalents

1 Pint	= 16 Fluid Ounces	= 2 Cups
1 Quart	= 32 Fluid Ounces	= 2 Pints
1 Gallon	= 128 Fluid Ounces	= 4 Quarts

Converting Temperatures

Convert degrees Fahrenheit (F) to degrees Celsius (C) by following this simple formula: Subtract 32 from the Fahrenheit temperature reading. Then, multiply that number by 5/9. For example, 77°F - 32 = 45. 45 × 5/9 = 25°C.

To convert degrees Celsius to degrees Fahrenheit, multiply the Celsius temperature reading by 9/5. Then, add 32. For example, 25°C × 9/5 = 45. 45 + 32 = 77°F.

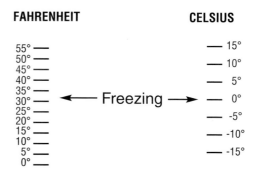

FAHRENHEIT		CELSIUS
55°		15°
50°		10°
45°		5°
40°		
35°		
30°	← Freezing →	0°
25°		
20°		-5°
15°		-10°
10°		
5°		-15°
0°		

Index

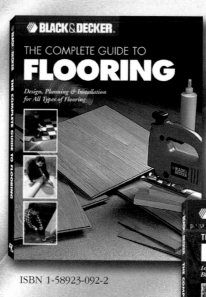
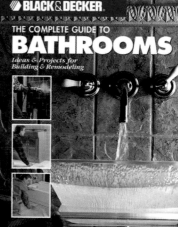
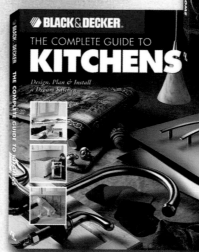

Also from

CREATIVE PUBLISHING INTERNATIONAL

IdeaWise Activity Spaces
IdeaWise Basements & Attics
IdeaWise Bathrooms
IdeaWise Decks &Patios
IdeaWise Garages
IdeaWise Kitchens
IdeaWise Porches & Sunrooms
IdeaWise Storage
IdeaWise Yards & Gardens

ISBN 1-58923-157-0

ISBN 1-58923-158-9

ISBN 1-58923-203-8

CREATIVE PUBLISHING INTERNATIONAL
18705 LAKE DRIVE EAST
CHANHASSEN, MN 55317
WWW.CREATIVEPUB.COM